Vivien

Working the Spaces of Power

Working the Spaces of Power

Activism, Neoliberalism and Gendered Labour

Janet Newman

BLOOMSBURY ACADEMIC

First published in 2012 by

Bloomsbury Academic
an imprint of Bloomsbury Publishing Plc
50 Bedford Square, London WC1B 3DP, UK
and
175 Fifth Avenue, New York, NY 10010, USA

Copyright © Janet Newman 2012

This work is published subject to a Creative Commons Attribution Non-Commercial Licence. You may share this work for non-commercial purposes only, provided you give attribution to the copyright holder and the publisher. For permission to publish commercial versions please contact Bloomsbury Academic.

CIP records for this book are available from the British Library and the Library of Congress

ISBN 978-1-84966-489-9 (hardback)
ISBN 978-1-84966-490-5 (paperback)
ISBN 978-1-78093-277-4 (ebook)

This book is produced using paper that is made from wood grown in managed, sustainable forests. It is natural, renewable and recyclable. The logging and manufacturing processes conform to the environmental regulations of the country of origin.

Printed and bound in Great Britain by the MPG Books Group, Bodmin, Cornwall

Cover design: Sharon Cluett
Cover image: © Alice Kettle

www.bloomsburyacademic.com

Contents

Participants

The book draws on interviews with over fifty women who have taken activist commitments into their working lives. In the notes below I indicate some of the kinds of politics and work they talked about in our conversations. Their engagements with power span six decades, from the 1960s to the present, and the notes also suggest the generational cohort to which each participant is linked. These are not exact and refer to the period of their political formation rather than age. Generation 1 (G1) came to politics in the 1940s and 1950s; generation 2 (G2) in the 1960s and early 1970s; generation 3 (G3) in the late 1970s, 1980s and early 1990s; and generation 4 (G4) in the 1990s and beyond.

The notes against each name do not extend beyond the date when we met (interviews were conducted 2009–2011) and by no means do justice to the richness and complexity of the participants' individual working lives.

Beverley Anderson (G1) Jamaican Foreign Service; local government councillor; teacher, Inner London Education Authority; head teacher, Oxfordshire; presenter of 'Black on Black' TV programme; Council of Educational Technology; Board of the Arts Council; Chief Executive of Booker Trust.

Marian Barnes (G3) Local government researcher; universities of Leeds, Birmingham and Brighton; Mental Health Act Commissioner; Professor of Social Policy; researcher and author.

Bec Bayliss (G4) Women's refuge manager; social worker; Sandwell Rape Crisis Centre; South Birmingham Women's Forum; Women's Aid schools project.

Sue Beardsmore (G2) Further education teacher; youth arts projects; London Borough of Hackney councillor; Leeds Voluntary Action project; organization development consultant.

Hannah Berry (G4) Anti-capitalist activism; women's community and voluntary sector; Gender Audit Project; PhD student, Manchester.

Esther Boyd (G2) Architect, Birmingham City Council; Lane Neighbourhood Advice Centre; Moseley and District Housing Association; Chair, Moseley Forum; Chair, SUSMO (Sustainable Mosley); Trustee, Quaker Properties; Business in the Community; Habitat Humanity.

Avtar Brah (G2) Equalities work at Greater London Council (Women's Support Unit); Asian Women's Network and Resource Centre; founder member of

Southall Black Sisters; Open University course production; Board, *Feminist Review* journal; Emeritus Professor of Sociology at Birkbeck, University of London; author.

Sue Brownill (G3) Community planner and activist with Docklands Forum; academic at Oxford Brookes University; author; member of local voluntary and housing groups.

Adi Cooper (G2) Health worker; social worker; PhD; Association of Directors of Adult Social Services; Strategic Director of Adult Social Services and Housing, London Borough of Sutton.

Davina Cooper (G3) Local government councillor; Warwick School of Law; University of Keele; University of Kent; Arts and Humanities Research Council Centre for Law, Gender and Sexuality; Professor of Law and Social Theory; author.

Deena Dajani (G4) Activist and research associate, OECUMENE, Open University.

Sukhwant Dhaliwal (G3/4): Newham Monitoring Project; domestic violence refuge work; Southall Black Sisters; Women Against Fundamentalism; Delhi University Gender Studies Group; Race Equality Foundation; Working Lives Research Institute; Goldsmiths College PhD.

Catherine Durose (G4) De Montfort University; academic researcher and author.

Naomi Eisenstadt, CB (G2) Nursery worker/manager; Save the Children Fund; National Council for Voluntary Organisations; Chief Executive, Family Service Unit; Director, Social Exclusion Task Force in Cabinet Office; government advisor on children's services; Director, Sure Start.

Jan Etienne (G3) Labour Party politician; diversity consultant; Women's Rights Officer, London Borough of Hackney; Race Relations Adviser in the London Borough of Haringey; head of the Race Equality Unit, London Borough of Hammersmith & Fulham; former Chair, Ebony Sistren Housing Association and Africa Refugee Housing Association; tutor at Birkbeck, University of London.

Jane Foot (G2) Community work; housing campaigns; anti-privatization; Services to Community Action and Trade Unions; local government policy roles, London Borough of Camden; Local Government Improvement and Development Agency; head of policy and quality, London Borough of Merton; consultant; researcher; author.

Lisa Harker (G3) BBC; Child Poverty Action Group; Chair, Day Care Trust; Institute for Public Policy Research; Civil Service (advising on child poverty targets, formation of National Childcare Strategy).

Carole Harte (G2) Ruskin College; Birmingham Women's Advice and Information Centre; partnership bodies; Sandwell Council for Voluntary Service.

Sue Himmelweit (G2) Women's Budget Group; International Association for Feminist Economics; Greater London Council; National Abortion Campaign; professor of economics, The Open University.

Sonia Khan (G3) Development Trust Association; Hackney Council for Voluntary Service; Creative Industries Manager, Hackney Training and Employment Network; strategic commissioning team, London Borough of Hackney.

Sarah Lamble (G3) Volunteer, rape crisis centre; advocacy work then employment with Elizabeth Fry Society; anti-poverty campaigns; work with women facing jail for welfare fraud; anti-prison work; University of Trent, Canada; Kent Law School; Birkbeck, University of London.

Hilary Land (G2) Academic at School for Policy Studies, Bristol University; Rights of Women Campaign; member of Central Policy Review think-tank; management committee, Women's Budget Group; Fawcett Society; Professor Emeritus; author.

Maria Lehane (G3) Social Services, Home Care and Care Management; further education college lecturer and manager; lecturer and PhD student, Kent University.

Gail Lewis (G2) Greater London Council; Lancaster University; Open University; Professor of Sociology; author.

Ruth Lister, CBE, Baroness Lister of Burtersett (G2) Child Poverty Action Group; universities of Bradford and Loughborough; Social Justice Commission; National Equality Panel; member of the House of Lords.

Julia Lowndes (G3) Birmingham Public Libraries; Neighbourhood Offices manager; Community Safety Partnerships; Domestic Violence Forum; Hate Crime Partnerships; former Chair, Birmingham Against FGM; magistrate.

Marion Macalpine (G2) Equal Opportunity Officer, Greater London Council; Head of Training and Staff Development, Inner London Education Authority;

Women and Work Programme; trainer; consultant; co-director masters programme in leadership and partnership for health and social care managers.

P.G. Macioti (G4) Migrant and sex workers rights activist with the x:talk project; translator; PhD student, OECUMENE, Open University.

Mary MacLeod, OBE (G2) Barnardo's; local government social work; Edinburgh and North London universities; ChildLine; Family and Parenting Institute; trustee, Gingerbread; independent policy advisor on children and families.

Ann McPherson, CBE (G2): member of Our Bodies Ourselves collective; general practitioner; Fellow, Royal College of General Practitioners; author; researcher, Department of Health; Medical Director, DIPex Health Experiences Research Group at Oxford; Chair, Healthcare Professionals for Change.

Alessandra Marino (G4) Activist and research associate, OECUMENE, Open University.

Angela Mason, CBE (G2) Solicitor, London Borough of Camden; Director, Stonewall; Director, Women's and Equality Unit; member of Equal Opportunity Commission; Chair, Fawcett Society; Deputy Leader, Camden Council; advisor to Improvement and Development Agency; Honorary Fellow at the London School of Economics; Commissioner, Equality and Human Rights Commission.

Ursula Murray (G2) Coventry City Council; Canning Town Community Development Project; Tottenham Employment Project; Haringey Women's Employment Project; Head of Services, London Borough of Haringey; PhD; lecturer, Birkbeck, University of London.

Kate Oliver (G3) PhD; transport and peace campaigner; public transport strategy, Greater London Council; policy advisor, Birmingham City Council; school governor; flexi-time schooling campaigner; foster-carer; Director, Birmingham Children's Fund; Trustee, Bristol Refugee Rights.

Susan Pell (G4) Voluntary work in Canada; postdoctoral work on social movement archives, Goldsmiths College.

Kate Raworth (G3) United Nations Development Programme; senior researcher on climate change, Oxfam.

Sue Richards (G2) Civil servant; co-founder, Office for Public Management; director, Strategic Leadership, National School of Government; School of Public Policy, University of Birmingham; Institute for Government; professor and author.

Liz Richardson (G3) Researcher, London School of Economics; University of Manchester; author; Board, National Community Resource Centre; various local volunteering as a resident, e.g. community festival.

Tess Ridge (G3) Greenham Common; social policy academic, University of Bath; Child Poverty Action Group.

Sasha Roseneil (G3) Feminist, anti-militarist, anti-racist, environmentalist and queer activist; Greenham Common; University of Leeds (founding director of the Centre for Interdisciplinary Gender Studies); Professor of Sociology and Social Theory, Birkbeck, University of London.

Dana Rubin (G4) Activist and PhD student, OECUMENE, Open University.

Stella Semino (G3) Activist Monteros movement, Argentina; refugee in France, UK and Denmark; Lambeth Social Services; Migrants Resource Centre, London Borough of Ealing; PhD student, Roskilde University, Denmark.

Steve Shirley (G1) Founder of F-International; served on several cabinet committees; founder and supporter of charities relating to autism; philanthropy through the Steve Shirley Foundation.

Kate Simmons (G3) Campaigner, charity for special education needs; school governor; researcher and academic.

Theresa Stewart (G1) Labour Party councillor, Birmingham City Council; Chair, Birmingham Brook Advisory Service for young people; Regional Hospital Board; Chair, Social Services; Chair, Community Development Programme; Leader of Birmingham City Council.

Helen Sullivan (G3) Birmingham City Council; INLOGOV (Institute for Local Government Studies, University of Birmingham); Cities Research Centre, University of the West of England; Professor of Government and Society, University of Birmingham; Director, Centre for Public Policy, University of Melbourne; author.

Ida Susser (G2) Campaign for Nuclear Disarmament and student activism in the United Kingdom and United States; academic at Hunter College and the Graduate Centre at City University, New York; researcher and activist on community mobilizations involving public assistance, contamination and women's activism regarding AIDS in South Africa, the United States and Puerto Rico; Professor of Anthropology; author.

Marilyn Taylor (G2) Community Development Foundation; School for Advanced Urban Studies; Professor of Social Policy, Brighton; author.

Munira Thobani (G3) Haringey Women's Employment Project; race equality advisor; Head of Equalities, London Borough of Hounslow; Office of Public Management.

Mary Upton (G2) Universities of Bath and Bristol; Open University; Feminist Archive work; adult education teaching; international development researcher.

Kitty Ussher (G3) Local councillor; ministerial special advisor; MP for Burnley; Minister in the Treasury and Department for Work and Pensions; director of Demos.

Heather Wakefield (G3) National Council for Civil Liberties (now Liberty); Commissioner to the Low Pay Commission; Head, Local Government Service Group of Unison.

Camilla Warren (G3) Greater Manchester Campaign for Nuclear Disarmament; Women Working Worldwide; human rights lawyer.

Cecilia Wee (G3) Senior producer, Sounds and Music; Royal College of Art; regional council member, the Arts Council; independent curator.

Jane Wills (G3) Trade unionist; local government worker; academic at Queen Mary, University of London; active in London Citizens campaigns.

Tricia Zipfel (G2) Welfare rights worker, United States; London School of Economics; cooperative housing projects; Priority Estates Programme; Neighbourhood Renewal Unit; consultant and researcher.

Acronyms and Abbreviations

AHRC	Arts and Humanities Research Council
CASCA	Canadian Anthropology Society/Société Canadienne d'Anthropologie
CCT	compulsory competitive tendering
CDF	Community Development Foundation
CDP	Community Development Programme
CND	Campaign for Nuclear Disarmament
CPAG	Child Poverty Action Group
FGM	Female genital mutilation
FPI	Family and Parenting Institute
GAP	Gender Audit Project
GLC	Greater London Council
ILEA	Inner London Education Authority
ILO	International Labour Organization
IPPR	Institute for Public Policy Research
LGBT	Lesbian, gay, bisexual and transgender
LSE	London School of Economics
NHS	National Health Service
NGO	Non-governmental organization
OECUMENE	Citizenship after Orientalism programme, Open University
SCAT	Services to Community Action and Trade Unions
WBG	Women's Budget Group

1

Introduction: Research as Mapmaking

I want to begin with events and encounters that inspired the research on which this book is based. The first was a retirement party where I realized that the room was full of women who had been part of the social movements of the 1960s and 1970s and who had taken their politics into different forms of paid and unpaid work. While talking with them it became evident that their work had helped to shape many of the policy innovations and new governing rationalities of subsequent decades. But in the process the changes they sought became subject to what some critics view as governmental processes of incorporation and depoliticization. Feminist claims that 'the personal is political' had opened up a range of new government policies concerned with how personal lives are lived. Community activism had been transformed – and in part depoliticized – through successive governmental programmes promoting active citizenship, volunteering and civic responsibility. Anti-racist struggles had been partly deflected through discourses of multiculturalism and social cohesion. Women's claims for equality had been incorporated through processes of 'mainstreaming' that have served to bureaucratize and depoliticize feminism. Struggles on the part of disabled people had been accommodated through consumerist logics of choice. Experiments in cooperative living and working had prefigured new organizational forms geared to promoting the commitment of both workers and stakeholders. And so on.

A second inspiration came from a series of encounters with young women involved in contemporary struggles: mobilizing against cuts, involved in transnational environmental movements, participating in anti-globalization protests and the Occupy movement, engaged in lesbian, gay, bi- and transgender politics, and aligned with revolutionary struggles in India, the Arab nations and South America. Such women were passionate about the movements and struggles in which they were engaged, but faced a much less hospitable environment in which to conduct politics, and much tougher employment prospects, than had the groups associated with the 'new social movements' of the 1960s and 1970s. But they were helping constitute new waves of radical protest following the banking crisis and, in Britain, the election of a government committed to austerity and retrenchment. And, like earlier generations, they were also engaged with a more practical politics in which their labour – paid and unpaid, formal and informal – was helping to mitigate the consequences of cuts for particular groups, and to exemplify new ways of living, working and performing politics for the present and future. These new forms and styles of politics were less subject to narratives of incorporation, but were potentially subject to accommodations through the rise of consumerism and expansion of new markets and cultural forms.

These encounters led me to a series of puzzles about the strained relationship between political activism and neoliberal forms of rule, and how this relationship is mediated through gendered labour. I wondered how far the politics that many women carried into their working lives had really been eradicated, how far the energies of social movements had been co-opted and how emerging struggles were being accommodated and contained. Such questions arise in the context of existing narratives that trace the exhaustion of feminism and other social movements in the face of neoliberalism or, conversely, demonstrate their complicity in generating new capitalist logics and neoliberal rationalities (Baggueley 2002; Baker 2008; Eisenstein 2006; Eisenstein 2009; Fraser 2009; Laurie and Bondi 2005; McRobbie 2009; Richardson 2005). Women's work in a series of unpaid or low paid jobs – in voluntary organizations, partnership bodies, community projects, project teams and in a whole series of hybrid organizations – is viewed as integral to the management of the contradictions of capitalism and to dealing with those 'left behind' in the rollout of new neoliberal forms (Katz 2005). Women who moved into more 'strategic' roles in central and local government, non-governmental organizations (NGOs) and policy teams have been seen as agents of 'professionalization' or as the much maligned 'femocrats' and 'governance' feminists who became complicit with governmental power (Watson 1990; Yeatman 1990). But such accounts do not, it seems to me, satisfactorily solve the puzzles I wanted to explore. What actually happens as multiple rationalities are negotiated and aligned – or not – in particular spaces of power? How can this illuminate the tensions faced by activists and campaigners, workers and students at the beginning of their working lives? How far can their activism be sustained in the current climate of cuts and retrenchment? Might future governments and corporations pick up on their success, draw on their energies and rework their claims in ways that strip them of their politics? In short, might the dominance of neoliberal forms of governance erase the successes of activist politics – or is there a more complicated story to be told?

To engage with such questions this book draws on interviews with over fifty women across four generational cohorts. They had prefigured new ways of living and working across the borders of activism and policy; between 'community' or 'civil society' and government; between different sectors and services; between research and policy, and between public and personal lives. Some had begun by working in community projects and brought their experience and skills into government and local government. Others had successfully translated campaigning work into jobs in voluntary and non-profit organizations, getting more or less entangled with new governmental pressures and policy opportunities in the process. Yet others had brought political commitments into professional and public service occupations and the academy. And some had served as local or national politicians. One – my oldest participant – moved between the Civil Service, entrepreneurship, philanthropy and policy advice. And across these (rather unstable) groupings many worked – at some point in their life – as consultants, trainers, researchers or social entrepreneurs. All worked the spaces of power generated through contradictions in the ruling relations of their time, mobilizing new spaces of agency, prefiguring alternative rationalities and opening out spaces for those that followed. Their work did not just 'reflect' the profound social and political transformations of their day but were generative of them.

The chapters that follow map some of the ways in which spaces of power are both mobilized by and negotiated through women's labour. They offer a series of stories – snapshots from working lives – about how many women attempted to 'make a difference', the decisions they took about where and how to pursue radical change, the dilemmas they faced, and how they reflect on the times they lived through. The accounts of those participating in the research (hereafter 'participants') show how they opened up and occupied diverse spaces of power associated with the unsettling of the post-war consensus in British society, the rise of Thatcherism, the development of managerial forms of governance, the emergence of new political projects and state forms under Blair, and the austerity politics of the early twenty-first century. The political struggles that took place in these transformative periods informed the lives and work of women who helped shape, worked within and often struggled against new political projects and shifting governmental practices. The book also, then, says something about the shifting politics and culture of Britain. It is not, however, a history book. It is possible to trace some shifts over time as new struggles arose, as new political tactics developed and as different governmental regimes displaced each other. But as I will show, the picture of change offered is dynamic rather than sequential (see especially Chapter 8). Nor does the book set out to be a history of feminism or address the rise (and, some would argue, fall) of a series of social movements. Rather, the book seeks to engage with contemporary debates on the incorporation or assimilation of activist struggles by the overwhelming force of neoliberalism.

The 'gendered labour' of the subtitle reflects my emphasis on how women have acted to bring about social and political change in their working lives – with work defined broadly to include paid and unpaid, formal and informal labour. I argue that such work was generative of a succession of new political, cultural, social and organizational shifts. As I will show, such shifts were often double-edged, opening up innovations that could be aligned with new governmentalities and neoliberal rationalities. But they also produced new forms of organizing and ways of performing politics that are not easily erased, even in the current climate of cuts and austerity.

This generative labour has at least three dimensions. First, it was about *making visible*: bringing into view perspectives, voices, agendas and issues, and asserting and performing difference. The work of participants was that of overcoming silences (on issues ignored or rendered invisible) and absences (asserting the voices of marginalized and exploited groups). Such work, as I will show, also enacted alternatives to dominant ideologies and practices; it was performative as well as critical. Second, it was about *generating public conversations*. Such conversations were crucial to winning support for policy or legislative reform, but also generated wider processes of political and cultural change. Participants not only promoted public conversations through relational labour (brokering between different power bases and actors) but also by generating new discursive repertoires within which such conversations could be conducted. Third, it was about *creative labour*: making new things and generating the possibilities of alternative ways of living, working and practising politics. Examples of each of these three kinds of 'work', and their interconnections, are threaded through each of the subsequent chapters, and I offer more substantial commentary on each at various points (see especially in Chapters 6, 7 and 8).

My focus on work, then, is not about traditional concerns about gendered patterns of exploitation and inequality. Although some experienced exclusion and discrimination, many also benefited from the expansion of education and employment opportunities for (some) women in the economic shifts that brought access to higher education and to jobs in the expanding public sector of the second half of the twentieth century. But they tended to work on the edges and borders of mainstream institutions and most had fractured and highly varied working lives. Few talked of 'glass ceilings' that impeded their progress: more often the focus was on the ways they had used opportunities created by new governmental projects or shifting organizational forms to redirect their political energies. They spoke of the pleasures of agency – of their pride in and enthusiasm for their work and their capacity to bring about change. But they also frequently spoke of the unsustainability of the places in which they found themselves. Working lives were frequently punctuated by periods of illness, by a shifting balance between 'public' and 'personal' lives as care and other responsibilities came to the fore, and by decisions to change sectors or to develop a new direction.

I am grateful to those participating in the research for their willingness to share the experience and to open their lives up to the researcher's gaze. In the chapters that follow I draw on their accounts to better understand shifting formations of governance, politics and power, and to make maps that others might use to make sense of their lives.

Gendering the analysis

The impact of feminist scholarship beyond the cultural and linguistic turns means that it is somewhat unfashionable to focus on women's experiences as sources of historical knowledge or contemporary political analysis (Downs 2004). Women can no longer be viewed as a distinct category and the assumption that common gender identities can form the basis of political agency has been unravelled (Butler 1999; Butler and Scott 1992; Mohanty 2003). Such arguments inform much of the analysis of this book. Nevertheless, I want to argue that it is women's embodied agency that has informed – and continues to shape – the political and institutional changes with which I am concerned. I focus on women's working lives for at least three reasons.

First, changing material conditions of work are gendered in their effects, such that women have often found themselves bridging the boundaries between paid and unpaid labour, between a focus on public and personal lives, between organizations characterized as belonging to state, market or civil society, or between mainstream and marginal organizational spaces. As such they have often taken on the roles of brokers and transactors, bringing skills and resources generated through political activism, civil society engagements or 'edge-work' projects into the generation of new political, policy and governance rationalities.

Second, I focus on women's lives because of the significance of the women's movement in the formation of contemporary politics and culture. This book is inspired by feminist politics – broadly defined – and the accounts of participants show how a feminist sensibility came to inflect a range of activist struggles: on race and ethnicity, on sexuality, on environmental and antipoverty movements and so on. But the women's movement is not the only struggle with which I am concerned, and it was not necessarily the foundational politics that shaped the lives of participants. The accounts of their political formation (see Chapter 2) confound any depiction of politics as a series of social movements, all distinct from each other and with individuals 'belonging' to one or another. Rather, I use the idea of feminist-inflected 'activism' to suggest how politics was lived and practised across a range of struggles. Of course, not all of the women would welcome the term activist – many viewed themselves as 'less political' than that term suggests, and some deliberately distanced themselves from a particular image of activism. Indeed, one of the younger participants commented:

> I have ever quite felt that I'm an activist. I do go on demos but I find open space technologies and consensus decision-making too woolly and time consuming. And I'm not a vegetarian.

But their labour has nevertheless generated alternative ways of 'doing' politics that have resonated across a series of struggles through the later decades of the twentieth century and that prefigured the ways in which contemporary movements – on global justice, anti-capitalism, climate change and other issues – seek to bring about change.

Third, however, it is feminism and its presumed demise that has generated significant discussions about the capacity of neoliberalism to incorporate or assimilate the energy of those who seek political change – for example, by 'empowering' women as consumers to drive economic development and renewal, or to play their part in the shift from manufacturing towards the development of a more flexible and mobile economy. Women, it is sometimes argued, have become ideal neoliberal subjects – and their role in generating new markets and patterns of consumption can be located in the ways in which feminism freed us from old patriarchal ideologies and paternalistic institutions (Aapola, Gonick and Harris 2005; Baker 2008; Gill and Scharff 2011; Gonick 2006; McRobbie 2009). In the process women have become subject to new forms of exploitation – as flexible and often un-unionized workers, as sex workers, as migrants juggling multiple care roles stretched across the globe, as consumers responding to shifting cultural norms of femininity and family life, as mothers producing the next generation of citizen-workers equipped for the high pressure information economy and, of course, as the neighbours, carers and civic actors taking up the responsibilities shed by retreating welfare states and cash-strapped public services.

I focus on women, then, because of the centrality of 'second wave' feminism to the profound transformations of culture and politics since the 1960s. I began this book in the year that marked the fortieth anniversary of the first Women's Liberation conference in Britain. Looking back there is a certain nostalgia for the heady politics of that period – not only feminism but also a range of other movements, protests and radical gatherings. Reassessments of that period (Baggueley 2002; Rowbotham 2001; Segal 2007) have highlighted the partiality of its politics and the privileged economic and cultural backgrounds of many of those involved. The period is also paradoxical: it was a period of opening up new spaces and possibilities, but also of profound silences and silencings – especially around 'race' and the resonances of colonialism (Brah 1996; Mohanty 2003). However, there is nevertheless a sense that something shifted in chilly, grey, post-war Britain that opened up new forms of agency and prefigured the remaking of politics and culture.

Politics did indeed change. Without the women's movement the 'new' could not have been put into New Labour, despite the subsequent fate of the Labour women MPs entering Parliament in 1997 who quickly became marginalized as power was progressively centralized. The assumption that politics should address issues of childcare, parenting, sexuality and more elusive ideas of well-being – the very stuff of everyday life – would never have become part of the realization that the personal was, indeed, political. Equal opportunities and anti-discrimination legislation might not have become such defining features of what it meant to be a 'modern', western state, marked out from the dangerous 'others' both within and beyond the nation. The relational and cultural dynamics of politics – feelings, attachments, identifications – would not have presented such significant challenges to the rationalities of political participation (Young 1990). And the feminist-inflected post-structural and discursive turns in political theory might never have taken place (see Chapter 6).

These are all, of course, contradictory legacies. They represent the success of feminism and other social movements of the 1970s, while also closing down many of the progressive and radical possibilities they heralded. How can we understand this? As noted above, several propositions have been offered, ranging from the complicity of feminism with new capitalist logics (Fraser 2009), the incorporation of 'femocrats' into state bureaucracy (Sawer 1990; Watson 1990; Yeatman 1990), the disbenefits of mainstreaming (Duggan 2003), all rolled into broader theories of neoliberal adaptation and cultural appropriation (Eisenstein 2006; Eisenstein 2009; McRobbie 2009). Some 'second wave' feminists have resisted the deconstruction of gender identity, arguing that poststructuralism produces a form of 'post modern paralysis' that circumscribes political agency (Hoff 1994). Others have noted the coincidence between the post-structuralist deconstruction of gender as a category of analysis and the erasure of feminist politics (Genz 2006). These are all, of course, critiques from the left and from within feminism itself: there is a whole other agenda of charges of the harm done by feminism, the cultural evils of political correctness, the social harms of poor parenting resulting from female equality, lack of social mobility and even the moral degradation of a feminized, secularized society.

In order to limit the potential of such claims to become hegemonic, I think we need to face – and address – the contradictions in our own history. That feminism is not a singular entity but encompasses multiple and ever-changing struggles is a fairly obvious point, but one that is often missing from accounts of mainstreaming or incorporation, and from debates about whether feminism – as a presumed singular entity – has any continued relevance. Its multiplicity thus troubles depictions of the confluence of feminism and neoliberalism. What feminism is it that is at stake in such claims? The interviews reveal multiple feminisms, but also different orientations to 'feminism' as a political discourse. Most – though not all – of the participants in the project claimed the term; however, their accounts showed the complex articulations between feminism and other struggles, especially around those of 'race', class and sexuality. McRobbie argues that the forces of neoliberalism have offered an impoverished conception of feminism by disarticulating it from other struggles (McRobbie 2009); it is this process of impoverishment that has allowed it to be mainstreamed and assimilated. I am sympathetic to this view; however, the interviews suggest that the politics of those working the spaces of power continue, in practice, to show complex entanglements between different commitments and struggles. Indeed, it is these connections that sustain them and form the basis of their political agency.

I do not want to suggest that the experiences I trace in this volume are necessarily particular to women. However, I decided early on to focus on women's accounts of their engagements within shifting 'spaces of power', partly because these accounts are largely unwritten, but also because the exploration of neoliberal governance from the standpoint of women both generating these shifts and managing the contradictions they produce might add something important to the understanding of governance and processes of social and political change. While gender may be a category ripe for deconstruction, the experience of embodied women is often 'outside', marginal or fragmentary in relation to economic and political power – and this may be a source of innovation, a way of bringing different perspectives and experiences into productive alignment. Such alignments may challenge existing institutions or they may of course offer new resources and capacities that enable entrenched forms of power to renew themselves or find new sources of legitimacy. But it is in trying to exert influence – sometimes from the margins, sometimes in more mainstream places – that new and emergent spaces of power have been generated, occupied and sometimes transformed by embodied women in their working lives.

Personal and political – doing the research

The research on which this book draws was conducted from the standpoint of an older, white, western feminist. I was one of the 'baby boomers' (born in Britain in 1945) involved in the profound political and cultural transformations of the 1960s and beyond. I participated in many of the political movements and counter cultural practices of the period, but my politics was most deeply shaped by my engagement in the early Women's Liberation Movement in Birmingham. I tried to bring some of this orientation into my work in local government and later, as a social/public policy academic, I brought both cultural and feminist perspectives into the analysis of questions of governance, politics and power.

The research is, then, in part a way of making sense of my own life and that of others whom I have met and worked with on the way. But it is also a way of engaging in wider narratives that link feminism to the rollout of neoliberalism. Following the episodes with which I began this chapter I began talking to colleagues about what might be going on and how to engage in a process of research that might illuminate the relationship between activism, work and social and political change. An early conversation with Wendy Larner led to a bid to conduct research in the UK and in New Zealand, where we would focus on the experience of both UK and Maori women and try to foster transnational conversations between activists in the global north and south. The bid was unsuccessful so, despite my interest in transnational connections and relationships, the project was, in the end, confined to women currently living in or visiting Britain.

Access to participants was gained through my own networks and brokered by some significant others. The process was iterative: emerging foci provided the basis for eliciting further interviews that could add depth to particular areas of analysis or extend the profile of those participating. My aim was to ensure that the study took account of three main axes of difference. The first was that of *generation*. This is deliberately a cross-generational study since I wanted to explore how activists responded to and engaged with shifts in politics and culture, and I hoped that the study might promote cross-generational learning. My approach draws on other literatures that have worked with the concept of political generations (Maskovsky 2009; Whittier 1995; Whittier 1997; Woodward and Woodward 2009) or have attempted to distinguish between successive 'waves' of social movement activism (Roth 2000; Walby 2009). But generation is a slippery concept. It flattens the complex relationships between time, place and personal history, and implies that time flows in a linear fashion in which the experiences of one generation are neatly packaged before giving way to those of the next. The list of participants at the beginning of the book where (after consultation) I have depicted each as a member of a particular generational cohort should, then, be treated with caution. As Chapter 2 shows, many participants were ambiguous about their generational belonging, and stubbornly refused to be part of a sequential, and very British, history of social movements. While they often had strong conceptions of the times through which they were living, and connections with others engaged in trying to shape political responses to the events they witnessed, this often had little relationship to the date of their birth, and there were as many resonances across generational cohorts as differences between them.

The second main axis of difference is that of *political identity*. As I show in Chapter 2, some came to activism through social movements, some through involvement in trade unions and political parties, some through an upbringing in a politically active family, some by witnessing key political events, and some through personal experience of inequality and injustice. While the predominant focus is on the transformations of British political culture, many participants had been involved in anti- and post-colonial political struggles in other nations or in global environmental and social justice movements. But I did not attempt to elicit 'representatives' from different social movements or political struggles, and some readers may be disappointed not to see their own experience reflected here (for example, there is little engagement with issues of ageing, care and mental or physical disability). Nor did I want to depict political identities as being formed once and for all through participation in a particular movement or group: indeed, the work of many participants can be viewed as 'bridge building' between different movements, identities and struggles (Meyer 2002; N. Rose 1999; Roth 2003). Their accounts also challenge static notions of identity, showing how different axes of subordination and the struggles they generate are entangled, and how individuals occupy and deploy multiple subject positions.[1]

The third axis of difference was that of *work*. I have already noted that this encompasses work that is paid and unpaid, formal and informal. Most of the participants worked across these categories, for example, combining voluntary work with their formal job or combining campaigning with research roles and often 'going beyond the contract' (financial or relational) to ensure that what mattered to them was delivered at whatever personal cost. Many held multiple roles, stitching them together in different ways across a life-course and managing the tensions between them as best they could. But across this diverse terrain I wanted to ensure that I drew on the accounts of women with different standpoints in relation to governmental, professional, institutional or political power. Some were undoubtedly 'insiders' while others held clear oppositional, 'outsider' identities: some held significant political or governmental posts (though often did not remain in them), while others worked predominantly in 'community' and 'civil society'. But, as I will show, their lives did not conform to such categories: many worked between government and community, or across multiple occupational identities. I show how some participants moved from community based or trade union activism into different forms of governmental work (Chapter 3); from social movement involvement into spaces in which they might influence the making and enactment of policy (Chapter 4); and from political action into managerial, 'entrepreneurial' forms of work (Chapter 5) or into research roles (Chapter 6). And some moved between all of these categories. In order to give a sense of the changing entanglements of work and politics across a life-course I follow the work of a few participants through successive chapters. This is designed to give a more dynamic sense of change across a life-course, and to suggest the different forms of 'border work' at stake as participants moved between different organizational, professional and political cultures, and between 'insider' and 'outsider' identities.

Border work was intrinsic to the research process itself. It worked across a number of disciplinary traditions and bodies of literature, and sought to bring participants of different ages, backgrounds and experiences into some kind of virtual conversation with each other. It also raised questions about the borders between objective knowledge ('this happened then') and more subjective ways of knowing ('how it felt', 'what it meant') that were, in part, co-constructed in the conversations between myself and participants. Further details on the interview process, method of analysis and the ethical issues raised by the research are given in the Appendix.

Research as mapmaking

Given the aims of the project it has been important to recognize that the events and actions had a collective, not just individual, significance. What took place in the interviews was a conversation: episodes and stories frequently triggered my own memories ('Ah, yes, that reminds me of when I worked in xx ...' or 'I was at that event too ...'). And the narrow dialogue between 'interviewer' and 'respondent' was often broadened to include non-present others ('Oh, several people have used that term – do you think what you are saying is the same?'), colleagues of the person I am interviewing ('Then I met xx and she was really influential') and collective subjects ('What we decided to do was ...') and even other pieces of research.

Tracing collective sensibilities, then, was as important as tracing individual experience. One way of doing this was to note where, in the interviews, the language shifted to 'we' and a collective actor was summoned. The collective actor might be a social or political movement ('The left', civil rights movement, environmental activism); a particular project or organization (Southall Black Sisters, a trade union resource centre), or women connected through networks (women working 'in and against the state'; women creating links between research and policymaking; or women working on 'community' programmes). These offered different spatial imaginaries of connectedness. Social or political movements often linked local and transnational struggles; some projects were transported to new sites and others were explicitly mobile.

In thinking about how to analyse such connections I have been inspired by Dorothy Smith's wonderful work on institutional ethnography. This, Smith argues, is a method of enquiry that works from the actualities of people's everyday lives and experience to discover the social as it extends beyond the local and the everyday. She describes the process as 'mapmaking':

> a method of enquiry into the social that proposes to enlarge the scope of what becomes visible from that site, mapping the relations that connect one local site to others. Like a map, it aims to be through and through indexical to the local sites of people's experience, making visible how we are connected into the extended social relations of ruling and economy and their intersections. And though some of the work of enquiry must be technical, as mapmaking is, its product should be ordinarily accessible and usable, just as a well-made map is, to those on the terrain it maps. (D. Smith 2005: 29)

I really like this quote for several reasons. First, it offers a spatial metaphor that I want to play with as I try to make connections between events and projects, between actors and governmentalities, between politics and policy. This implies a series of maps with different scales, legends and features. Second, it emphasizes the value of research to those whose experience it records. This 'making visible' is integral to my project, and one of my purposes in writing this book is to engage in a process of collective sense-making – or mapmaking.

In doing so, however, I think there is a need to recognize that maps, while appearing to be objects that authentically represent what is real, have to be subjected to cultural analysis that troubles the representations offered. This is not a point taken up by Smith, though her methodology explicitly works across the duality between being an embodied, subjective knower and, at the same time, part of an objective, universalizing set of relations.

Smith's work is also helpful in thinking about how to be respectful of the specificity of the lives and stories of each of the participants in the research while also going 'beyond particularity'. Smith suggests that, rather than beginning with the researcher's theoretical categories, an institutional ethnography would 'begin in the actualities of the lives of some of those involved in the institutional process and focus on how those actualities were embedded in social relations, both those of ruling and those of the economy' (D. Smith 2005: 31). Through such work the 'problematic' of the research would become specified. The problematic is not constructed from what is specific to an individual, but from what happens as accounts move from individual experience to explore the social relations in which that experience is embedded. In trying to respect Smith's approach I did not set out with a pre-given set of themes on to which I mapped individual experience. Instead, as the connective and generative work began to fall into clusters, I sought out other participants who might be able to add depth to a particular experience or to illuminate it from a different standpoint. In the chapters that follow I develop the analysis around several such clusters.

The maps I am making, then, do not seek to illuminate the 'facts on the ground' but to delineate continued areas of struggle and contestation. But mapmaking is not only the work of the researcher; it is the work that is and has been done by the participants in this project. They are not just people to whom things happen: they are seeking to bring about institutional, cultural and political change in the name of those others whose local or specific experiences they have encountered or shared. Avtar Brah, one of the participants, notes in her own writing how:

> The 'individual' narrator does not unfold but is produced in the process of narration. Rather, the deeply invested self that speaks the events relies heavily upon the hope that its version will resonate with the meaning constructed by my various 'imagined communities'. My individual narration is meaningful primarily as a collective re-memory. (Brah 1996: 11)

My project is to expand the possibilities of 'collective re-memory' within and across generations. Other texts have recounted women's experiences of some of the political and social shifts I am concerned with here: biography and autobiography have been important ways not only of enabling particular women to have a voice but also of shaping the emergence of collective identifications and political histories. Texts such as McCrindle and Rowbotham's *Dutiful*

Daughters (McCrindle and Rowbotham 1977) and Sarah Maitland's *Very Heaven: Looking Back at the 1960s* (Maitland 1988) provide collective testimonies, while individual biographical accounts from authors such as Lynne Segal (Segal 2007), Sheila Rowbotham (Rowbotham 2001) and others offer powerful combinations of personal and political history. But as Julia Swindells (Swindells 1989) has argued, testimony can easily slide into nostalgia and biography into individualism. In addition biographies and testimonies that look back to the 1960s and 1970s can serve to intensify the mythic status of an iconic moment that separates the women who participated it from others, whether the 'others' are the working class, lesbian or women of colour whom it excluded or the women from successive generations and in other places.

This is partly why I have not followed a strictly biographical approach. I have not, in what follows, attempted to provide a coherent account of the individual lives of those I interviewed. Some may be disappointed to read only fragments of what they shared with me and to find themselves juxtaposed with surprising others in unexpected places. But what is lost in terms of depth of understanding of a particular life-course is, I hope, complemented by what the institutional ethnography approach offers. The juxtapositions offer both resonances and contrasts that seek to illuminate a particular site of activism or work from different perspectives.

The structure of the book

In this book I explore with participants some of the paradoxes that arise as their personal and political commitments encounter dominant ruling relations. Each chapter illuminates the current political moment through an understanding of the changes that have taken place over the previous sixty years. And each speaks to different possible processes of neoliberalization, processes that may engage, redraw and exploit activist projects.

Chapter 2 – 'Talking Politics' – shows something of the range of political struggles and movements that participants were involved in, and how these were entangled in individual lives. It traces processes of political formation, showing something of the significance of transnational encounters and of key political events as well as of family, party and first-hand experience of poverty, racism and discrimination. It traces different forms and sites of political practice, and shows something of the multiple ways in which politics is embodied, lived and performed across time and place.

Chapter 3 – 'Perverse Alignments' – focuses on 'community' as a space in which radical political projects encounter governmental programmes of 'empowerment', 'active citizenship' and 'localization'. It shows the complex – and often perverse – alignments between activism and the succession of projects that have sought to enrol and manage potentially unruly populations through the production of community as a governable space. Processes of community development and empowerment can be viewed as constituting 'non economic' actors as new entrepreneurial subjects, while informal and 'alternative' community projects can create innovations that open the way for new cycles of capital accumulation. But at the same time, as I will show, governmental projects and programmes designed to develop and manage through community can be appropriated and their resources mobilized by activists. 'Community', then, remains an intense focus of ideological and political struggles as welfare states seek to devolve responsibilities for care and welfare to 'local', personal, familial and faith-based actors.

Chapter 4 – 'Close Encounters' – assesses the different spaces of power in which social movements came to shape social policy and influence strategies of governance. Not only did women seek to influence policy and legislative reform, but their work prefigured mainstream developments, from the inscription of equality in institutional practice to the use of 'monitory power' to check the actions of the powerful. The social policy reforms for which women worked were realized, in part, in the 'social investment state' that constituted women as full worker citizens, but which, at the same time, enabled capitalist and state enterprises to access a cheaper, more flexible, less unionized workforce, as well as investing in the capacity of future generations to take their part as productive worker citizens in the global economy. The 'mainstreaming' of activist struggles in policy and governance served to strip them of much of their oppositional strength; however, the 'close encounters' also led to significant changes in the institutions themselves. This contradiction was lived and worked in different ways, and the paradoxes it opened up are particularly telling in a context in which many of the policy achievements are rapidly being undone through programmes of public sector cuts, welfare reform and state retrenchment.

Chapter 5 – 'Modernizing Moments' – continues this theme of contradiction and paradox in exploring women's influence in transforming 'traditional' institutions. It shows women bringing activist commitments into the professions, local government and the Civil Service; the ways in which their work helped generate the shifts towards more collaborative, partnership-based and participative styles of governance; and the development of 'entrepreneurial' spaces in which work and activism could be (uncomfortably) aligned. It shows how their labour was inflected through the valorization of the 'reflexive' self and the use of 'soft' power, both of which are associated with the new governmentalities of advanced neoliberalism; and with the economic shifts that produced more 'precarious' forms of labour.

Chapter 6 – 'Critical Engagements' – focuses on researchers, professionals and academics seeking to transform hierarchical orderings of knowledge and power. It draws on the accounts of participants seeking to democratize knowledge, to bring 'experience-based' ways of knowing into professional work and public service delivery, and to move towards the co-production of research. It traces how academics have been drawn into new forms of 'close encounter' with governments, and the tensions about legitimacy and power that result. Finally, it shows how those working in and beyond the 'cultural turn' open up rather different questions about the relationship between knowledge, power and the performance of politics.

Each of these chapters offers a particular mapping of the paradoxical 'spaces of power' in which multiple neoliberal rationalities and the projects generated by activist movements collide and are aligned – or not –through different forms of gendered labour. The final three chapters look across these mappings to assess broader processes of political and cultural transformation. In Chapter 7 – 'Border Work' – I trace how participants viewed themselves as situated within such transformations, managing the tensions and contradictions associated with political and cultural change. It shows how they spoke of themselves as simultaneously 'inside' and 'outside' (the nation, the polity, the institution, activist politics) and offers different perspectives on the generative labour of border work. Chapter 8 – 'Activism, Neoliberalism and Gendered Labour' – assesses a number of narratives that view neoliberalism as erasing and co-opting activist struggles and interventions. It offers different theoretical framings of neoliberalism and its relationship to feminism and other movements. The chapter reflects on how the work of participants in this book can offer insights into the 'landscapes of antagonism' in which emergent practices and alternative rationalities encounter dominant ruling relations. But its aims are political as well as theoretical; the analysis I offer refuses totalizing narratives that foreclose the possibilities of political agency. Finally, Chapter 9 – 'Postscript: Speaking to the Present' – reviews how the analysis of the book can speak to the current politics of cuts and retrenchment, economic austerity and social conservatism, and explores the possibility of living and enacting alternative forms of politics in these times.

Conclusion

One of my aims in writing this book has been to explore the prospects and possibilities of political agency in neoliberal times. But another has been to make visible the public work of women who sought to bring their commitments and orientations into their working lives and who, in doing so, forged new ways of doing things that sometimes prefigured larger social or governmental shifts. In writing this book I set out to tell what I hope are interesting stories – stories that celebrate the work of some extraordinary women and that also illuminate how and why what Weeks (Weeks 2007) terms 'the world we have made' is as it is. The 'we' of this world is highly contested, and the boundaries of the 'world' we have made are constantly being reimagined; economic retrenchment, the rise of political parties of the right, climate change, global poverty and threats to national security all shift the terrain on which politics is conducted, bringing new claims to voice and challenging the authority and legitimacy of the political gains won by earlier generations. Nevertheless, I want to argue for a better understanding of the processes of social and political change that has taken place over the last sixty years in order to illuminate the constitution of the present and help inform the politics of the future – a theme I return to in Chapter 9.

These are challenging tasks. But my purpose, with Smith, is to 'produce the kind of knowledge that makes visible to activists or others directly involved the order they both participate in and confront' (D. Smith 2005: 32); that is, to focus on mapping connections from the local and specific to encompass what she terms the 'ruling relations'; and making such maps accessible and usable to those on whose experiences they draw. Weeks wrote about his goal of looking to the past to help understand the present and future. At the time of writing – a period of recession and dismay following the financial crisis of 2008 and the uncertainties of mainstream politics following the UK election of 2010 – commentators are returning to notions of paradigm shifts in governance and the rejection of past ways of thinking about society and economy, state and market. I want to claim, in contrast, that we need to offer more nuanced accounts of the reorderings of our social and political worlds. We need, in short, to rethink the tales we tell about the past and the resources on which we draw to imagine and enact other possible futures.

2

Talking Politics

'Politics' is at the heart of this book. But the politics with which I am concerned is not limited to that of political parties and institutions or to a series of distinct social movements. My aim is to show how activist commitments are formed, lived and practised – in different political-cultural moments and in multiple landscapes of antagonism. The emphasis on 'talking politics' is deliberate: I try to use participants' own words to describe how the political self is formed and lived. But I am not just concerned with talk or identity. The accounts also suggest something of the performativity of politics: how commitments and practices bring into being different political worlds. The coverage is necessarily selective, and my use of extracts from the interviews does not do justice to the richness of individual accounts. But each section attempts – in the spirit of the 'institutional ethnography' outlined in Chapter 1 – to bring different participants into a virtual conversation with each other, sometimes across generations and sometimes from different institutional locations.

Finding politics

The chapter begins with participants reflecting on the political self in the making:

> When I went to university at the end of the 1960s it was in the context of the civil rights movement in the US, the anti-war movement in the US, 'Cathy Come Home' etc.[1] in England. I was brought up as a Catholic at the time of the Second Vatican Council and the challenge to the male-dominated hierarchy of the Church and other institutions. We wanted to rethink the norms and protocols underpinning them. The late 1960s also coincided with liberation theology in Latin America, the writings of Paulo Freire and huge military oppression. There were all these radical people who were trying to find a common ground between a Marxist ideology, which as a young student I was hugely interested in, and a Christian ideology. I don't want to overstate this, I was very young and starry-eyed – but these were all part of the ether that was seeping into my bones and forming who I was. (Tricia Zipfel, G2)

> So in a way I fell into feminism with a lot of personal feelings – that you mustn't let them get you. I remember sitting on the stairs in a collective house having a conversation saying 'Wow – do all women feel like this?' I thought it was just me.

Feminism was about finding yourself, finding your place in the world and having a context in which that kind of resentment and anger, alienation, the sense that you were having to fight against them making you someone you didn't want to be, and all of that kind of thing could find a place. It's been really powerful – that energy has continued into wherever I've found myself. So it's the personal and political combined around the biographical. I wasn't a head girl kind of person who got used to success then hit a glass ceiling; it was kind of the opposite. (Jane Foot, G2)

Now, it's human rights and environmental politics that I'm really interested in, But I remember – one of my first politicizing experiences was at a big anti-BNP [British National Party] demonstration in London when I was about sixteen. It was a big demonstration and I remember the police, they blocked the way and just ran their horses through the crowd, tipping people over. And I was scandalized – I didn't think that happened in our country. And they blocked the route so there was a sort of build up of outrage within the crowd. And I thought the papers would be in uproar about the way they'd acted the next day, but instead they blamed the demonstrators and I was absolutely ... now I'm just kind of cynical but at that point I was absolutely scandalized that it could happen. I suppose that was quite a radicalizing thing for me. (Camilla Warren, G3)

I'm really an anarchist, I suppose. I got interested in mainly environmental protests, road camps, stuff around Third World First, now called People and Planet. My parents lived in a Norfolk village; they were kind of left wing, my mother was in CND [Campaign for Nuclear Disarmament]. I thought of myself as a feminist but not with a very nuanced understanding. I was never someone who thought it was a good idea to go into the women's caucus, to sit round with a lot of other women moaning. I was aware of male-domination, but it was doing the gender audit[2] that opened my eyes. I saw that the more you came down to local level, on the ground, the more women there were, and vice versa. I hadn't thought too much about male-dominated decision-making before; I had presumed that men could represent different interests. But at board level – it's a bit of a stereotype – we observed all the men giving information. The only time a woman spoke was to ask a question, but once one woman had spoken then another would come in. The audit showed that there is a real lack of confidence among women to get involved in formal structures. (Hannah Berry, G4)

The first two extracts suggest something of the heady excitement of the 1960s and 1970s, a period in which New Left politics, the civil rights movement, CND and the women's movement flourished, in which many looked to South America and the work of Paulo Freire[3] for inspiration, and in which there was a sense of fundamental and transformative change taking place. The third extract is from someone who came to politics in the context of the adversarial politics of Thatcherism in Britain, while the fourth suggests how some women positioned themselves in relation to the politics of an earlier generation, but also came to define their own.

Despite some patterns, the point I want to draw out from these first extracts here is the multiplicity of political formation and political lives, and the significance of different political-conjunctural moments. Many participants recalled the transformative political climate of the 1960s and early 1970s, the more adversarial politics of the 1980s or the disappointment of the failed promises of Blair as mobilizing forces. Younger generations were often politicized by the rise of anti-globalization and environmental politics. Across these periods women referenced key events – the miners' strike, the Soviet invasion of Czechoslovakia, the South African Springboks rugby tour during the period of apartheid, the fall of the Berlin wall, the election of Barack Obama – as symbolic moments, whether or not they had witnessed them. Myths of the past – of 1968, of Thatcherism and heroic struggles against oppression in Latin America, India, the Middle East, South Africa and Argentina – lived on through cultural images and helped shape contemporary political formations.

But the accounts also show the power of encounters across borders – of nations and movements, between north and south, across divisions of class and race – to open up an awareness of inequality and injustice, and to generate the possibility of politics. Ida Susser (G2) was born in South Africa and speaks of herself as a feminist, a white South African woman in exile, and a political activist supporting women's mobilizations around HIV/AIDS in Africa; Ursula Murray (G2) attended a political conference in Montreal as a student that was *'dominated by Latin America'* and at which she, like Tricia, encountered liberation theology and the work of Freire (*'It was quite Marxist but we didn't realize it at the time'*); Kate Raworth (G3) became involved in participation and empowerment programmes in Zanzibar before going to work for Oxfam; Avtar Brah (G2) brought her engagement in multiple political struggles in the United States in the 1960s and 1970s to her work in London; and Sukhwant Dhaliwal (G3/4) recalls how in her early twenties:

> *I had quite romanticized notions about Latin America basically, and I always wanted to leave the country and I wasn't really sure where I was going to go. I was always torn between wanting to try something in Latin America or something in the South Asian sub-continent, and so I saw an advert for the Nicaraguan Solidarity Campaign for the first Women's Brigade and joined it, and it was one month over a Christmas period with a very mixed ethnic group of women, which was also quite novel for me because I was predominantly in Black politics.* (Sukhwant Dhaliwal)

Although most participants had been influenced by feminism, their political formations were quite complex. Some came from political families:

> *I can't remember a time when politics didn't matter. I was brought up by very political parents, and politics was part of my early life really from my earliest memories.* (Sasha Roseneil, G3)

However as Sasha's account shows, even within families political roots were often highly diverse. Some found politics at work: the first job of Ruth Lister (G2), with the Child Poverty Action group, led her to become involved in campaigns for women's legal and financial independence; Jan Etienne (G3) found politics through trade union involvement, while others became part of radical groupings within the professions. Some came to politics through political parties. Some became politicized in community-based action or by participating in campaigns or demonstrations. But politicization was often not a one off events. Jane Wills (G3) spoke of three different political roots: the first was a nineteenth-century politics, inherited from her parents, of a self-organized Methodist church; the second, a twentieth-century politics based on mass organizing that she encountered in the 1980s while a student; and the third, a twenty-first-century politics confronting the crisis of the left and the search for alternatives. But in recent years the most politicizing issue for her had been the response of the state as she sought support for her autistic son:

In the past I would have defended the state, the NHS, but this experience has led me to look elsewhere for support and care. This, for me, has been more politicizing than anything. (Jane Wills)

Stella Semino (G3), Avtar Brah, Gail Lewis (G2), Sukhwant Dhaliwal and Ida Susser each also spoke of having multiple political roots, but their lives cannot easily be understood through a British chronology of social movements. Stella participated in the Monteros movement in Argentina before fleeing to Europe, where she later became involved in voluntary work in London and taking up forms of environmental politics, latterly in Denmark. Ida Susser was born in South Africa, moved to Britain aged five and subsequently lived in Kanpur in India and New York. Her parents were founders of the anti-apartheid groups in London and Manchester as Ida was getting involved in CND and anti-Vietnam struggles in Britain and the United States. Her political formation, then, was both trans-generational and transnational. Avtar came from Uganda to study in the United States, where she became involved in anti-Vietnam War demonstrations, anti-racist politics and labour union struggles. She lived through the civil rights movement, Black Power, non-violent activism, CND, 'flower power' and the beginnings of second-wave feminism. In her 1996 book she describes how: 'There were rallies, demonstrations, marches, teach-ins, and love-ins. There was energy and optimism that the world could be changed for the better, even if many of us were incredibly naive about the inherent complexity and contradiction' (Brah 1996: 6). But as she became more aware of issues of poverty in the inner cities in California: 'The gentle calls for love and peace of the "flower children" began to sound affected and utopian – the growing up pangs of a privileged post war generation – although the idea of "non violent" forms of struggle continued to touch a deep chord in me' (Brah 1996: 7). This tension was carried into her political work in the UK.

Sukhwant reflected how:

It's really interesting that you have also interviewed Avtar Brah and Gail Lewis, because in a sense I grew up in the shadow of their political negotiations even if I wasn't active myself till the late 1980s/early 1990s. But exposure to all that 1970s/1980s stuff, especially in Southall, possibly gave me a different perspective from some of the other 1990s activist I encountered ... especially on the state. (Sukhwant Dhaliwal)

But the image of the '*1970s/1980s stuff*' is itself problematic. The following is an extract from the interview with Gail Lewis:

I think I was formed in different moments. In part that was because of my own route – I didn't go to university till my mid-twenties, after a crap education followed by a period of factory work. But my family's formation had taken place in the context of Caribbean struggles for independence alongside labourist activities in the Caribbean, and both of these were brought to London with us. So my political formation was in a context that said that class politics would change the world, but it also had to be anti-colonialist. And that was an important grounding for me. Then I went to work, got involved in the Union ... But then the moment when I decided to go to university was after I had been in Sri Lanka for a year, and had experienced the bubbling inter-ethnic conflict there in the 1970s. And it was that experience that brought me to feminism; it was feminism in Sri Lanka, not here, so I never thought that feminism was just a white western project. Then I went to the LSE, took one year out to work in a housing advice centre, then into development studies, then to the GLC in the Livingstone era. (Gail Lewis)

This extract points to multiple moments of political formation, confounding any neat categorization of different generational and national experiences. Gail refers to coming to feminism 'there' – in Sri Lanka – rather than here. Sukhwant spoke of finding feminism in India:

I got a scholarship to go to India to do a Masters in Sociology because I felt like a lot of stuff that was going on within South Asian communities in London was very connected to Indian politics. I went to India to start an academic career, but also because I was really very frustrated with the professionalization of the politics in Britain, and I wanted – whatever I thought in that time, I don't know what it was, what I wanted was a cutting-edge experience ... So I went to India and became active in what was a gender study group then on sexual harassment, but I was also very drawn to class politics and still had some very naïve ideas about being part of an active communist party. But actually when I got to Delhi I found that gender was the issue for me, and got involved in a brilliant, brilliant campus based feminist collective with a gender studies group which today has just repaid me ten-fold. I made the most amazing connections out of that, and I think that sort of transnational solidarity is really important especially if you're working on religious fundamentalism. (Sukhwant Dhaliwal)

We can see in these extracts – from different generations – how political formation is stretched across borders. This is also the case for young scholars moving to the UK to study; for example, for Dana Rubin (G4) her politics were formed in the Arab/Israeli struggles, and P.G. Macioti (G4) was shaped by the politics of migration in Italy. The migrants' rights struggles in which P.G. participated were, at the time, led by the Italian communist party, but she rejected its leadership in favour of more anti-hierarchical, feminist collective groupings of activists. Later, in Berlin, she became involved in anti-racist politics and took part in 'No Borders' activism and, in London, in campaigns on migrants' rights with a particular focus on migrants involved in sex work. I will take up the story of these and other young activist/scholars in Chapter 6. But what I want to note here is how 'place' and 'time' are confounded in the ways in which individuals narrate their lives: Sri Lankan, Indian, Middle Eastern and European struggles are not just 'there' and in the past, but are 'here', in the present, in the ways in which individuals make sense of their political attachments, commitments and identities.

These accounts, together with the opening extracts, also show the complex entanglement of feminism with labour movement politics (Gail, Sukhwant and Jane), anti-racist and human rights struggles (Gail, Avtar and Camilla), HIV/AIDS activism (Ida), the peace movement and anarchist-inflected politics (Sasha, Hannah), with post-colonial struggles (Dana, Sukhwant) and with the politics of migration (P.G.). Each of these intersected with a politics of sexuality; indeed, many participants saw sexuality as the primary axis of their political formation:

> My politics comes out through having a lesbian family, having to go to court three times to create a legal entity. The previous government created a framework of equality politics that actually supported me to do this in a way I would never have dreamed of when I got pregnant with my first child. Never would I have dreamed twenty-seven years ago that I would now have a legal entity, a civil partnership that enabled me to build a lesbian family. It was unimaginable, but for me it still feels quite dissident. There's still an aspect of it where I can't quite believe we've been assimilated into the status quo, even though legally we are. So my politics is played out on that field of struggle; there's still a lot of heterosexism, that happens all the time. Cos you have to come out to people around your family: the kids do and I have to at school, and then when the kids get involved with other people. But it's so different from how it was twenty-five years ago; the gender stuff is amazing and then the sexuality stuff has changed incredibly. (Adi Cooper, G2)

This extract traces the emergence of sexuality as a domain of public and political struggle; a struggle that was mobilized by the early activists in gay and lesbian groups, and by organizations such as Stonewall (see extracts from Angela Mason in later chapters). But it also shows how such struggles are both public (going to court, participating in campaigns) and deeply personal. This personal/political dynamic was interpreted in a rather different way by a younger woman who saw the development of her lesbian identity as a political process. Maria Lehane (G3) described how she felt 'suffocated' until she moved offices and found a group of 'out' lesbian women and began to lead a different kind of life. She saw herself as both inside and outside of the 'lesbian community' and commented:

> You know the old adage, the personal is political; for me it was the politicization of things I thought were private. (Maria Lehane)

We can begin to trace here important intergenerational politics in which the struggles of one generation create institutions and repertoires that sustain those that follow. This was also a key issue raised in the interview with Alessandra Marino (G4), a young woman who stressed the importance of second-wave feminism in her own political formation, and Bec Bayliss (G4), who encountered activists from earlier generations through voluntary work:

The very last course on my BA was on feminist writing, and the person who taught that course was really enthusiastic. She kept talking about '68, the feminist struggles. And for me, coming from a little village in the south of Italy, this was really evoking; it felt like there were still urgent struggles going on, and that made all the difference. I got to politics quite late on, because I was living in this little village, with my parents, with my family, and my life was just normal. You go to university, you come back, and you don't really have the openness to the world. But for me that course on feminist writing, on political struggles, activated a certain sensibility. And after that my life changed; I started to travel more, to get more freedom. (Alessandra Marino)

I was seventeen or eighteen when I first started being introduced to people who were quite political in terms of socialism, communism, even feminism. This was in an organization for people who were homeless, both men and women, but there was also a women's project – it was global enough in its thinking to acknowledge that women had different experiences of being homeless, and the common feature was often abuse, or experiences of violence. And then I thought, 'I've found it, that's what I want to do.' I suppose the bit that was interesting is how it came with passion, energy and motivation. It was something that was meaningful, something that took you home at night and you thought, 'Cor blimey, that's fabulous, beneficial and worthwhile.' So I suppose it's like one big jigsaw piece and it still is really. It's about finding a bit for me, its finding what makes sense in the world, what fits with what I believe and what drives me. (Bec Bayliss)

I want to continue the theme of intergenerational resonances in the next set of extracts from Avtar Brah, one of the founding members of Southall Black Sisters in 1979, and Sukhwant Dhaliwal, who later 'found' this organization at a crucial point in her life. Avtar describes the founding year of Southall Black Sisters as a result of the rise of racist activity and the National Front. Following a big demonstration in 1979 at which Blair Peach was murdered and 340 people arrested, she and others became involved in practical and political work:

In the aftermath of that we were very involved in trying to free them [those who had been arrested], and at the same time we were aware of issues to do with women that couldn't be subsumed into that wider Black politics. So we thought that – it started out as a very practical thing, holding sessions giving advice to women on immigration, housing, we had lawyers coming in to help us. So we were doing this kind of practical work anyway. This was also a time when there were various industrial struggles around women's work and we used to go and support them. Southall Black Sisters emerged out of that – how to look at feminist issues in the context of the politics of the time. We called ourselves a feminist project, and we called ourselves Black but that was in the context of the Black politics of the time – which was African, Caribbean and Asian women working together (though fewer African/Caribbean women are involved now). And as you know we were involved in lots of landmark legal decisions – for example on violence against women. (Avtar Brah)

Her account vividly points to the entanglement of different struggles – class-based, anti-racist, gender – undermining any idea of coherent communities of identity. Indeed, Avtar spoke about the necessity of any focus on gender being formed in relation to issues of race and class, prefiguring the theories of 'intersectionality' (see Chapter 6).

Sukhwant Dhaliwal recalled 'finding' this organization some thirty years later when, aged fourteen or fifteen, she became distressed at the mobilization of religious fundamentalism in the Khalistan movement in India:

There was a politics that I could already see, but I didn't really find a word for it until my introduction to Southall Black Sisters which really encapsulated my general feelings. (Sukhwant Dhaliwal)

It is, then, not just narrow, western feminism that shaped personal and political commitments. Indeed, Alessandra Marino told of how she had not been involved in any particular social or political movements but had travelled widely – predominantly in India and North Africa – as a *'commitment to dismantle a certain western perspective that I knew I had'*. But the work of aligning different movements, working across multiple commitments, managing conflict within and between struggles, tended to be gendered labour.

Enacting politics

I think of it [politics] always as a practice not as an object; it's a practice through which a collective identity can emerge and people can mobilize around a particular issue. (Susan Pell, G4)

Susan and others were sceptical of the idea of social movements, movements that assume a common identity and interests. Instead, politics was something that emerged out of social practice, from trying out different ways of taking action. For many participants this began with small-scale local projects:

I started off as a volunteer in a Neighbourhood Centre in Islington set up by Quakers, and just became excited about what was going on … The activities [running playgroups, working in community projects] were not just meeting needs – at the time I think I was a bit naive, we thought this as part of the revolution. The revolution had to start from your street and your community and work up, and I believed that very strongly. I never felt hugely comfortable engaging in formal politics, it's never been quite my thing, just feels like a lot of talk very often. For me politics is about doing things. (Tricia Zipfel)

*I lived in a really small town [in Canada] and two people who were very close
to me were sexually assaulted, and the only people that they could talk to were
women that were much older and it kind of felt like they were talking to their
mums. And so I started volunteering at the local rape crisis shelter in an effort to
try and provide more peer support for young women. The range of women that
were involved was pretty amazing. A lot of them were survivors of violence, and the
oldest woman in the group she must have been in her seventies and she really took
me under her wing. I mean I did environmental work before that and I had done
work against cuts in education but it was kind of doing the work at the Rape Crisis
Centre where I think I first kind of got a critique of the criminal justice system,
and the kind of failure around women and violence issues.* (Sarah Lamble, G3)

Such 'practical politics' took different forms at different points of a working
life. For many it centred on work on 'local' issues and was 'project' based, but
I do not want to suggest that this represents a subordinate form of politics
outside the public domain of strategic action. To give a sense of what I mean
by politics as practice I want to return to the accounts of Adi Cooper and
Jane Foot, both G2. Adi spoke about applying *'all the familiar work around
networking and groups'* she had developed through her involvement in the
women's movement to the politics of lesbian parenting:

*I started looking at adoption 10/11 years ago, and then went through it myself,
and that experience led me to try to support other women through that process.
And my politics came into all that work: all that kind of familiar work around
networking and groups, and supporting and advising, and being at the end of
a phone, and meeting up so that your children know other children who've got
lesbian parents.* (Adi Cooper)

Jane Foot honed her political skills in community-based projects and drew
on them in later work in governmental projects, policy work, research and
consultancy. When asked what she had taken from her political commitments
into her working life, Jane spoke about herself as a *'community entrepreneur'*:

*I think what I bring is lateral thinking: I am a very good lateral thinker, I like
making connections. I think quite a lot of women do that but [laughs] I also
think that being a socialist feminist – endlessly having to knit things together,
to see how things are connected and to make the connections and to see where
to make the connections and how to exploit the connections and work with
the contradictions. I am not sure whether you learn those things from being an
activist or whether you become an activist because you have got that kind of
brain.* (Jane Foot)

Both of these extracts demonstrate the significance of relational politics in
the work of almost all of the participants. Relational politics signifies work
through networks, but also the generative labour associated with pulling
together new networks, constituting new political entities, performing new
worlds. And such labour rests, in Jane's case, on what she sees as a political
mentality: one of making conceptual connections as well as knitting together
disparate entities. Jane gives an excellent description of the work carried out

by many participants and suggests something of its gendered characteristics – although she acknowledges that this was as much to do with the kinds of activism she had been involved in as with her gender.

Such political skills, and the networks on which women drew, were honed and expanded in the more adversarial politics of the 1980s when many participants worked in and around law centres, trades union resource centres, women's employment projects, tenant participation projects, anti-racist projects, women's refuges, AIDS activism and so on. Jane worked in a Trades Council bookshop and printing service established as part of the Community Development Programme (CDP) in Coventry; and she was active in the women's movement and the National Abortion Campaign of the period. She joined Big Flame, was involved in the Tower Hill rent strike, worked on Hackney Play Bus and in a law centre engaged in supporting tenants' campaigns. She worked for five years at SCAT (Services to Community Action and Trade Unions) doing national campaigns against the sale of council housing, set up a National Housing Liaison Committee and later became part of the Housing Research Group at City University. The breadth, variety and complexity of this experience are striking. But it was not unique; other women of a similar age and political orientation recounted equally complex political lives. Ursula Murray, also G2, began her working life in Coventry City Council, where she encountered the government-funded Community Development Programme. She later moved to London to work on Canning Town CDP:

> This was my education. University had been a dead loss – this [CDP] taught me how to think. My role was to analyse the local economy. It was a fantastically exciting time – different projects were coming together, we were writing joint reports and building rich networks. It lasted five years, all on short-term contracts. (Ursula Murray)

She became pregnant and was made redundant as the funding ended and then, with another woman who had joined the project (also pregnant and unemployed), set up an employment project in north London, working closely with trade unions, and then the Haringey Women's Employment project, which had a focus on Black and working class women's issues:

> We job shared and shared babies. We wanted to bring a woman's focus into work on employment issues. We got money from lots of sources, did action research, published pamphlets and so on. (Ursula Murray)

They subsequently secured major European Union (EU) and Greater London Council (GLC) funding to set up a women's training and education centre, taking over a defunct secondary school and running manual trades courses and computer courses for women:[4]

> I don't think if we had understood what setting up such a big project with lots of staff would be like that we would have done it. Our approach was you come

at it, create something and it will work. We were very innovative but were full
of tensions. By 1986 there was a feeling of exhaustion. Some people had gone
off to work for the GLC, but there was also – there was a feeling that change
had been possible in the era of political funding and sponsorship, now our
work was all about income generation. So I went to work for Haringey Council.
(Ursula Murray)

I will return to these narratives in Chapter 5, showing how such projects were taken 'inside' local government and suggesting something of their transformative effect.

While Jane and Ursula's politics were formed in the proliferating left groups of the late 1970s and early 1980s, others came to politics through different routes. Esther Boyd (G2) had lived in the same inner-city area for some thirty years and spoke about how her work was informed by a Quaker concept of 'service'. She trained as an architect but met considerable discrimination at work:

It was really interesting. I thought that once I had started proper work I wouldn't
need to do all this other stuff because I'd be getting my fulfilment through the
job. But I found out, I'm afraid very quickly, that a woman in a man's world is
not listened to, and I got absolutely mad about that. I was already chair [of a
housing association] but at work I didn't get that sort of fulfilment. I got involved
in the Union, became steward and then chief steward. But in the end the only way
I could achieve the things that mattered to me was outside work. (Esther Boyd)

Esther had an extensive career break to care for her three children during which she helped develop and run a range of local initiatives (twenty-one in a twenty-year period) including housing associations, charities, Quaker bodies and a number of neighbourhood organizations. She had set up a group to coordinate responses to the devastation produced when a local area was hit by a tornado in 2005; became secretary to the local community forum (part of the City Council's devolved structure of participation); was chair of a community action group promoting sustainability and supporting households in cutting carbon dioxide emissions, and led a protracted campaign against a planning proposal by Tesco supermarket. She had an extensive email circulation list through which she kept local people informed and wrote a regular blog on local sustainability issues. The list of projects in which she was involved is extensive, but all were informed by a strong and long-term commitment to the 'local community'.

While Esther's work was informed by a Quaker notion of 'service', the next set of extracts are taken from the interview with Kate Oliver (G3), who describes herself as an activist with non-conformist leanings. The account begins with campaigning work on local transport issues, then moves to her work as a GLC transport planner with a particular focus on women's transport needs. While her children were young she piloted and promoted flexitime schooling while working as a job-sharing local authority strategic planner. She became school governor of the school her children attended, then ran a campaign to keep the school open when it was threatened with closure:

> We saved not just our school but all of the ones in our neighbourhood because I didn't want to set up a campaign where we were picking one local school off against another, and that worked really successfully. It was very time consuming but very rewarding, and it was the time when with local management of schools had just come in so I did spend hours and hours and hours … at one point I was doing about thirty hours a week writing policies, setting up the whole thing. (Kate Oliver)

After a move to the Midlands she set up a local Town Forum in which to debate local political issues and produced an alternative transport strategy that challenged both the official strategy and the planning culture of the local authority. She took up the fostering of a child at the same school as her children after his foster placement broke down and went on to foster five young asylum-seekers. She says that this opened the door to the next stage of her life, because it introduced her to refugee and human rights campaigning. At work she became involved in setting up the Birmingham Early Years Partnership, a policy-oriented New Labour partnership body, and recounts how her range of experiences in her personal and work life gave her both a *'strategic policy and a children's services background'* that enabled her to move into the voluntary sector as Director of the Birmingham Children's Fund.

> In a way the unpaid, voluntary community campaigning politics stuff has actually been the thing that's taken me on to the next project in my working life. I can't possibly grace it with the term career because quite a lot of the time … well, when I had the children of course it dipped for a bit before it started to pick up again. It's all been very kind of ad hoc really and I've had lots of support.
>
> The other thing that I think is key to all of this that my non-conformist Christian grandparents harboured Jewish refugees during the war, and the household that I grew up in was always a very kind of busy, open door one. And I think I've replicated that, that sense that you share what you've got, and that includes your intimate space. (Kate Oliver)

The 'ad hoc' and evolving nature of working lives is a theme replicated in many other accounts. Kate, from a younger generation than Esther, was able to bring the experience gained in informal politics into the making of employment opportunities, especially in the partnership bodies and children's policies that proliferated under the Blair governments. But for both Esther and Kate formal and informal politics, 'lay' roles and activist roles, all centred on issues of quality of life, sustainability and social justice. What is striking in their accounts is the complex relationships between public and private, personal and political. Both women attempted to 'live' their politics not only through their local community or political engagements but also in their personal lives.

These extracts could be read as confirming arguments that women's informal political activity takes place in spaces that are ambiguously public and private, protected from – and perhaps excluded from – the formal politics of the public sphere (Jupp 2010; Staeheli 1996). There is much about the connections between politics and personal lives here, as indeed there was in the accounts of Jane, Ursula and Sarah. But for Esther the public politics of housing were linked to the personal resources offered by the Quaker community, while her voluntary activities could thrive because of her taking an extensive career break to care for her children. This was possible, she explained, because of adopting an explicitly 'anti-consumerist' lifestyle which enabled the family to live on a relatively low income. For Adi, her 'personal' conduct of lesbian politics was connected to more public activities through which she supported other lesbian parents. For Kate, personal and political were connected in the links made between the care of her own children and her decisions to take on the fostering of young asylum-seekers; in her engagement as a parent in the local school; and in her campaigns to promote flexitime schooling and to prevent school closures. Indeed, the references to the 'open door' house and of 'sharing' an intimate space appear as metaphors for an implicitly gendered orientation to a politics of community.

Yet these accounts confound the idea of women's informal politics as operating somehow outside the public domain or in a liminal space between public and private. Each of the women cited here took on extensive public roles (as governors, chairs, managers, campaigners) and had a mix of unpaid, voluntary and paid work in professional and/or policy-oriented roles. All used their strong community embeddedness to develop spaces of power from which to intervene in the wider public sphere, run campaigns and engage in policy interventions. These different political practices are viewed as mutually constitutive and their power as derived from working across personal and political, inside and outside, activist and governmental spaces. But these were not, as later chapters show, comfortable places to be.

In and out of the party

There is an extensive body of feminist literature on women's roles in political institutions. Some focus on issues of representation (Lovenduski 2002; Mackay 2001) while others prefer the language of 'presence' and 'voice' (Phillips 1995; Young 1990). Some challenge the dominance of political science perspectives, linking the analysis to the feminist ethic of care (Mackay 2010) or to concepts of deliberative democracy and difference (Benhabib 1996; Barnes, Newman and Sullivan 2007). My purpose here is more modest: I seek to show the influence of political parties in the formation of political selves, and to trace some of the tensions and ambivalences associated with taking on formal political roles in party, council and government.

Orientation to party was inflected by issues of generation, gender and class and post-colonial belonging. Women who became adults before the rise of the counter-cultural politics of the 1970s frequently found their route into politics through the Labour Party, although they quickly expanded their political work and sought to change the party from within. Theresa Stewart (G1) was a local councillor and served on a number of council committees, as well as on the board of a local hospital, eventually becoming Leader of Birmingham City Council:

I have been a lifelong Labour Party member – I joined when I was a student. I couldn't imagine not being Labour in 1945 in my school – it was just obvious. I did a lot of work – branch secretary and so on – while I was bringing up my children. Then when my youngest started school I put myself forward for election. I was also very active in CND. We had started a branch in Doncaster and helped to organize a march; then I was also involved in the anti-Vietnam War campaign after I came to Birmingham, in 1966. I was also very involved in the women's movement – in 1974 I was very angry with the Labour Party's election campaign because it didn't involve women at all apart from having an image of Shirley Williams with her shopping basket. So I did a leaflet, organized a meeting and we set up a women's section [within the local constituency party], which thrived for quite a few years. (Theresa Stewart)

Theresa was involved in campaigns on access to contraception for unmarried women and for comprehensive education, and she set up the National Association for the Welfare of Children in Hospital. She was elected Leader on a platform of taking resources back into local communities after a period of heavy investment in prestige projects in the city centre. While Theresa's links with the women's movement in the 1960s and 1970s helped bring feminist perspectives into the Labour Party, for Kitty Ussher (G3) it was the politics of Thatcherism that formed a deep moral commitment to bringing about social change through political office. Kitty served as a local councillor, had a period working for MPs, then served in the Labour government of 2005:

Well, I think I'm probably one of the hated career politicians in that I've always been fascinated by Parliament and the way it works, and felt very clearly that … a very strong sense of ideological drive I guess as a younger woman, and that mainstream politics is the way to achieve change. I reached political awareness in the early Thatcher years, and I saw the type of society that she was trying to create as, you know, kind of morally wrong. I hated the class system of Britain and felt very comfortable and at home in the Labour Party, and saw it as a kind of crusading organisation really. A group of people that were all about change leading to improvement, and so I always had it in the back of my mind that at some stage I'd do active politics, and I've known that since I was about seventeen, so for me it was a vocation really. (Kitty Ussher)

Growing up in a family with strong party allegiances was significant for many other women. Davina Cooper (G3), younger sister to Adi, recounted how:

I decided around the age of nine or ten that I wanted to be a politician as a way of being involved in bringing about change. In part, it was the result of seeing my parents active in a party that was so outside the boundaries of institutional power ... When I was twenty-one, just finishing my first year at law school, I got elected to Haringey Council. This was my most intense period involved with institutional politics; it was heady, and hugely challenging. I was involved in a lot of committee work, chairing the Women's Committee and later the Community Development Panel which funded lots of local organizations. (Davina Cooper)

In contrast Esther Boyd, who grew up with similar expectations, was more ambivalent about party politics:

Both my parents were councillors, and I took it for granted that I would be a Labour councillor, I mean that's what one did. And I did once stand for councillor in a ward which was very solidly Labour. And I hated it, the campaigning, because you weren't supposed to do what was right, but what would gain votes. And I couldn't accept that. Things that I could see were wrong I wasn't allowed to mention because that would turn people against me. You do what gets votes, and the Party rules and so on. I found that having voluntary work which didn't have those political issues was actually – I found that very satisfying. It's political with a small 'p'; it's certainly not party political. The Quakers use the word 'service' a lot. Quakers are about action, they are not about God in the sky or anything, so the root of a lot of it for me is Quakerism. (Esther Boyd)

The 'ways of doing' politics emerging from the confluence of feminism and the peace movement noted above were viewed as incompatible with the 'party machine'. But for some from younger generations, the party and trade unions formed the only possible routes into politics. The next extracts are from the accounts of younger women whose political formations took place in the context of colonial and post-colonial encounters:

I came here [from Tanzania] in 1971 at the age of thirteen, completely the wrong age to be moving children, especially from a very hot country to a very cold country, so that kind of time was very traumatic for me because of language problems, being in a tiny minority in those days, and not speaking English, not really knowing how to live in a cold country, and so my first experience was not very good. When I started working in Eveready Batteries that's when I got interested in trade unions and the women's movement, and I was in the Labour Party so I joined the women's section, and then I became very interested in the Black Sections Movement. So I was kind of active in that in the early 1980s, and then there was the miners' strike, so there was quite a lot of political activity. (Munira Thobani, G3)

My dad came (as a migrant from St Lucia in the Caribbean) and worked for London Transport. My mum worked for the National Health Service. I still have very strong links with St Lucia; I'm involved in a project out there which is very important for me. I went to Grenada in 1983 just before the invasion as a youth project worker. We were invited over to work for the Ministry of Mobilisation, and it was all about women getting stuck in to sort of deal with things. But we were thrown off the island just before the Americans invaded and all these dreadful things happened, and of course a lot of the people who I worked with are now dead. So I've always had a strong belief in doing something in one of the Caribbean islands. Meanwhile [in the UK] I became very active in the Labour Party. I was a local councillor in Brent for a little while, but before that I would say that I was informally active in political activism, community activity, but the formal side as a local councillor, and then standing in 2005 in the General Election. (Jan Etienne)

These extracts suggest the significance of trade unions and political parties as routes into politics – for Munira they were perhaps the only routes that could be found in that place in that period, while for Jan they formed part of a more complex, transnational political trajectory. But they also demonstrate something of the entanglements between anti-racist, feminist and socialist politics during the 1980s and 1990s. This was a period of very different mobilizations, with socialist groups confronting the deeply repressive Thatcher governments, the rise of the National Front, the miners' strike, the murder of Blair Peach and the emergence of new lines of racial antagonism.

Across the participants cited in this section we can trace ways in which early experiences led to a 'taken for granted' expectation of participation in party politics. But there are striking differences. While some were engaged in formal politics as MPs or as councillors, others explicitly rejected it, preferring more informal and direct forms of activism:

We really believed we were involved in challenging the system, and that this had to start from your street. (Tricia Zipfel)

But this distinction between formal and informal politics is too crude. Theresa Stewart, for example, connected a pragmatic politics of party work with an involvement in women's politics. And Kitty Ussher spoke with pride of her achievements for her Burnley constituency as well as her excitement about working in the 'Westminster village'. She resigned as an MP so I asked her whether she still sees her work as political:

Yes, I'm a Labour Party person. I don't know if I'll go back [into politics]; what I am not clear about is how far I need it and that worries me at times. I want to achieve change on sort of social justice principles, but I can also enjoy doing it on a piece by piece basis. You know, the neighbour knocking on my door asking for help is equally part of the same thing as far as I'm concerned ... I live in a very vibrant part of the world, I live in Brixton which has got a huge ethnic social mix, and I'm really enjoying getting into that community in an unbranded way. (Kitty Ussher)

The informal activism in community and neighbourhood is a theme to which I return in the next chapter. What is particularly interesting in this extract, however, is the reference to an 'unbranded' politics. This seems to say something both about the ways in which political acts might be perceived as independent from and untainted by associations with particular political parties, and about the shift of identity associated with this participant's move out of formal politics – in which she had a relatively significant role – into a more diffuse political environment in which her role was less clearly defined. But for her these different roles were 'all part of the same thing' – working to certain social justice principles.

Transgressive politics

The idea of politics as transgressive is, of course, not new: practices that challenge traditional forms of politics were deeply inscribed in the women's movement, from suffragettes chaining themselves to railings and engaging in hunger strikes while in prison to dramatic interventions in boardrooms and parliamentary debates. Such acts ruptured taken-for-granted meanings and practices of politics and helped enact new worlds in the making.

Among some of the participants to whom I spoke, the Greenham Common protest[5] was a particularly significant marker of the formation of alternative political repertoires: not only did they publicize the struggle in a radical way but such repertoires were also able to mobilize actors untouched by the political machinery of union or party. Tess Ridge (G3) recounted how:

One of my most political periods started through my involvement with Greenham Common, which was near where I lived. I was expecting a child when the first marches came to the Common and when they started to locate the missiles.

I asked if Tess came to become involved through the peace movement:

I came to that through my mother. We have always been quite a political family in terms of a lot of discussions and a lot of involvement in various things, and my mother got involved in CND, and I had got involved with her to some degree. But what Greenham did was situate a very particular manifestation of power so it was right on our doorstep, right into the heart of local people, so it was very personal as well as a very political thing. And my mother initially got involved in helping the marchers to come to the Common. My son was born just before the marchers arrived, and I went up there not long afterwards with a very small baby tucked in my windcheater, and was promptly told by a policeman that the baby should be at home and shouldn't be out and about. And gradually over time it became a women-only event, and as it became a women-only event I became more politicized by it. (Tess Ridge)

Another participant from the same generation took up the Greenham story:

We [a group of women in Bristol supporting the Greenham women] used to have big circular meetings, huge meetings. We tried this horizontal way of organizing, with mediated conversations, no real structure. But when the policing of Greenham became more acute we became more organized. We had telephone trees, and when something was threatened we would call people and rush off to look after the site at night in case the bailiffs came. I remember trying to break a fence down, it was incredibly liberating. Greenham did politicize us. We would try to go to pubs on the way home, but wouldn't be allowed in. This made us both angry and proud. We were angry and energized by just being women together. (Mary Upton, G2)

Sasha Roseneil spoke about her involvement as a young woman:

It was 82–83 and I was doing teenage activism. Then I started going to Greenham, and then I left school to go and live at Greenham. I'd been getting more and more involved, and I had been arrested a few times. It caused quite a lot of uproar at school and the school did actually ask me to leave. (Sasha Roseneil)

Sasha, who has written extensively about Greenham Common (Roseneil 1995; Roseneil 2000), spoke of how her experience there had influenced her interest in the everyday practices of living and ethical subjectivity:

being interested in everyday ways of doing, and being, and living, and questions of how we live together. (Sasha Roseneil)

She later became involved in feminist and lesbian politics in London: in helping produce the *London Women's Liberation Newsletter*, helping out at A Woman's Place and becoming part of the collective. But this was the later 1980s:

It was a time of vehement identity politics, race politics were absolutely raging. That wasn't the stuff that had been talked about at Greenham, so it was another education in feminist politics. (Sasha Roseneil)

These extracts speak to the importance, at that time, of separatist politics – of having a place in which a particular form of what Sasha terms a *'queer feminism'* could flourish. They also suggest shifts over time and the emergence of challenges to a politics that assumed the pre-eminence of gender and the neglect of class, race and other identity struggles. But the point I want to focus on here is the new genre of politics emerging from feminism and the peace movement. This, in turn, informed the practices of younger women, many of whom used the term 'anarchist' or 'queer' to describe their styles of activism.

Susan Pell grew up in Canada and went to university in what she saw as a conservative part of the country, but:

In the mid-1990s protests happened in response to intense cuts in Canada that culminated in the anti-globalization protest 'the battle for Seattle' in 1999. This was a hugely visible protest. I learned a new critical language. I was involved in some subcultural things, but they didn't resonate with me – they struck me as very masculine. I got more interested in women's issues and worked for Planned Parenthood for while. And I started to look at the value of alternative media – zines and things – for political activism.

I'm much more of an anarchist than a member of anything. And I feel like I'm always attracted to queer spaces – non-hetero-normative spaces ... I'm not gay myself but I find people there who are more politicized, less likely to make sweeping generalizations about the world that assume they know who other people are. (Susan Pell)

Susan and many others of her G4 generation came to politics through anti-globalization and environmental movements, and often brought considerable creativity to political practice. Alessandra Marino's research focused on forms of resistance through performance and theatre, and on 'non institutionalized' women's movements that mobilize women through writing: it is through writing, she argues, that people can intervene in the public sphere and expand the definition of politics.

Cecilia Wee (G3) described herself as an independent arts curator – a 'maverick' whose work was informed as much by political theory as art theory. She argued that cultural performance as a form of politics opens up new creative engagements in public spaces, museums and other sites that are fluid, sporadic and not easily contained. She organized collaborative events – *'spectacles of resistance'* – in public spaces and the public realm, describing with excitement how she brought a group of artists to the 2010 BP-sponsored Tate summer party to respond to the implications of the oil spill in the Gulf of Mexico earlier that year. She also worked with art students in the kind of relational and 'practical' politics discussed earlier in this chapter:

> *I'm helping them to connect with the rest of the world – whether through a guerrilla activity or a more structured performance, I try to provide a cultural context for what they do … I like to bring artists together, to make connections they might not have seen otherwise. But I am also interested in the audience – in their experience, how they understand what they see, how to open up their access to the creative process.* (Cecilia Wee)

The use of events, demonstrations and performances as a form of political practice resonated across many of the interviews. Dana Rubin was researching the Israeli occupation of the West Bank and recounted how she tried to bring the reality of the occupation into a Gay Pride march in Tel Aviv, under the slogan 'There is no pride in this occupation'. She also helped form what she termed *'the first queer group against the occupation'*. This was *'very intensive, and really questioned everything'*. And it was deliberately performative, theatrical:

> *We collected used weapons from the occupied territories and tried to march with them, but we got arrested. Then we set up something that looked like a checkpoint on a main thoroughfare, and marched with blindfolds made to look like those the Israeli army used with Palestinians, and so on. All of this was about trying to bring a different kind of politics, one that was both feminist and queer. We were trying to look for the connections between different forms of oppression.* (Dana Rubin)

These younger participants can be viewed as shaping and being shaped by a 'post-identity' politics. Sarah Lamble, another young researcher, spoke about the politics of feminist, queer, transgender organizing that *'doesn't organize around identity'* but that engages with anti-capitalist, anti-poverty struggles:

> *I used to think that politics was about doing things, now I think it's about building and sustaining relationships so that movements have meaning in people's lives.* (Sarah Lamble)

Such relationships are, in part, enabled by new social media – Facebook, Twitter, blogs and so on – that provide new vehicles for political connections and mobilizations, often across borders. However, as Sarah commented, communication alone is not enough: the dramatic political changes in North African and Middle Eastern nations took place through mass presence of protesters in public spaces, and *'in Facebook there can be a lot of* not *doing'* (Sarah Lamble; her emphasis).

But there are risks associated with performative politics. The arts can be accommodated and incorporated in what, in the 1990s, came to be termed the 'culture industries', and were put to use – 'functionalized' in the words of one participant – in government programmes of urban regeneration and community cohesion. In addition, Cecilia Wee's work, and that of the artists she commissioned, was fragile and vulnerable, subject to contracts, sponsorship, cuts and periods of unemployment. She spoke of wanting to move from *'creating very specific sealed off moments into creating art that has an idea of social change behind it'*. This meant finding funding for a larger, more sustained programme that could link the arts to green issues. Both areas however lack resources.

Hannah Berry, quoted earlier, has also faced difficult choices:

> *I first went to work for a research association which promoted ethical consumption and people saw it as selling out because it was about reforming capitalism, not fighting it, but the good thing was that it left me time to be an activist as well, and the subsistence wage fitted with my ideals quite well, too. Then going to work for the LSP [Local Strategic Partnership] women's network – suddenly my focus shifted to local politics – proper reformist stuff, going to forums, working on projects, and more than anything my current situation of being paid by the state to do research.* (Hannah Berry)

Of note here are Hannah's ambivalent feelings about moving between different kinds of activism. While Tricia Zipfel and others who came to politics in the 1970s felt that they were involved in changes that were revolutionary, for this younger woman being paid to do 'little projects' was unfulfilling. Hannah and others are less likely than women from earlier generations to be able find the kind of employment that will enable them to bring politics into their working lives. Their accounts bring into view the tensions between being 'inside' the system, and thus able to have direct influence, and being 'outside' in what some see as a more authentic political space. This inside/outside duality is one that runs through this book, but in the chapters that follow I show how the idea of 'spaces of power' confounds such clear distinctions.

Conclusion: mapping change

This chapter began by trying to show what has inspired – and continues to inspire – participants in this research to become 'political', and then moved to a discussion of how women enacted politics in different sites and through different repertoires. It has traced the significance of what some women termed a 'practical' politics, a politics which connected 'personal' and 'political' and that generated new capacities and resources. It has shown something of the ambivalence many women brought to their encounters with mainstream political institutions, but has also traced ways in which some sought to transform them. Finally it has highlighted the significance of more transgressive political repertoires that challenged the traditions of older political institutions and movements. As such it has offered a series of 'mappings' of politics and how it is understood, lived and embodied, and how such mappings are subject to change. The chapter has not set out to write a history of any particular movement or period; but it does offer at least three ways of conceptualizing political change.

The first concerns personhood and identity. The women on whose extracts I have drawn in this chapter grew up in different periods, witnessed different mobilizing events, encountered different political 'elsewheres' and met different political challenges. They were not, however, formed once and for all as political persons of a certain sort (x is a feminist, y is a Labour Party activist, z is an anarchist); not only were most formed through complex entanglements between different struggles, they also changed over time. Personal biography matters, and we will see in subsequent chapters individuals coming to perform politics in different ways across a life-course. And generation matters, too; we can see the kinds of narratives participants offered changing according to age and generation. Older women (generational cohorts 1 and 2, and some from cohort 3) offered more complete, rehearsed narratives and they were more embedded in connections to taken for granted assumptions about the characteristics of a particular period ways (this was the cold war, that was 1968, then there was Thatcherism); their stories, it often seemed, had been told before, to others or just to themselves, and had been honed in the telling. The stories of younger participants (especially generational cohort 4) were less sure, with more uncertainties (about what is going on) and ambivalences (about how to place oneself in it); their life projects were still in the making and their stories still being worked on.

A second way of mapping change over time centres on shifts in political performance. Political movements tend to be associated with particular performance repertoires – the campaign, the party, the small group, the gathering, the demonstration, the spectacle, the riot, the mass assembly. These change over time, not only as movements mature, fracture, speak to one another, become exhausted and perhaps reassemble, but also as new spaces of power emerge: Sasha Roseneil (G3), describing her feminist activism in the late 1980s, spoke of how:

> *I was very young compared with pretty much everyone else who was around, and there's a sense that it was all a bit past its peak, that the peak had been the 1970s and what was going on now was different, there had been a move into local government.* (Sasha Roseneil)

However, it is also possible to trace resonances over time. For example, many young activists engaged in dramatic, radical and disruptive performances have an image of older movements as rather dour, boring and conventional. Yet it is possible to map echoes and resonances between, for example, the dramatic occupation of Greenham Common, with its innovative communication channels and its theatrical and symbolic feminization of a military installation, and the activities of UK Uncut in 2011 as it occupied banks and other buildings and installed crèches, libraries and other public spaces, as well as the Occupy movement (see Chapter 9). There is also a resonance between the older Reclaim the Streets marches and the recent Slut Walks. This is not to say that the *politics* is the same; but that there are resonances in the political performances across different times.

Over time, shifts in accepted performance repertoires tended to create new insides and outsides to what was understood as activism; one participant noted how she felt an outsider at Greenham Common because she was not like the other women there, and another noted ambivalence about whether to continue on an established political path or move on, with the personal rejections that might follow. Shifts in performance repertoires also led to intergenerational hostilities and tensions. Alessandra Marino spoke of the problem of those who see themselves as representatives of a particular generation: *'the myth of 68,'* she argues, *'is a moment that can't come back'.* The power of this myth has meant that older activists tend to construct younger generations as passive. But it has also meant that younger activists have to redefine what politics might mean and how it might be practised. At the same time younger generations may view older activists as having become professionalized or depoliticized (see also the mother-daughter authorship of a text on shifts in feminist politics, Woodward and Woodward 2009; and Maskovsky 2009 on inter-generational stereotypes within the gay movement in responses to the AIDS crisis).

A third way of mapping change over time concerns the relationship between activism and the shifting political and governing projects oriented to managing populations, curtailing dissent and sustaining the legitimacy of hegemonic blocs. Such projects tend, in much of the literature, to be viewed as evidence of the expanding reach of globalizing neoliberalism (see Chapter 8). Activism is viewed as taking place outside and in opposition to these logics. But activists tend not to be active for the sake of it, but seek to contest the actions of the powerful at specific moments and to campaign for particular, historically situated, social and political reforms. At the same time the political and governing projects of the powerful often seek to draw on the resources, skills and practices generated by activist struggles and social movements. This creates what in subsequent chapters I term a series of 'perverse alignments', 'close encounters', 'modernizing logics' and 'critical engagements' whose effects cannot be read as simply the extension of neoliberal forms of governing. The stories we tell about change matter, not least for the ways they might inform the politics of the present and future.

3

Perverse Alignments: Women's Activism and the Governmentalization of Community

This chapter tells a twin story. One is of the flourishing of 'community' as the locus of a series of activist struggles and forms of political engagement. As the previous chapter showed, some participants in this research had been inspired by the radical community activism of Latin America or came to politics by participating in community-based struggles. Some had developed local resources to combat poverty, poor housing and rundown estates; others created small-scale cooperative and neighbourhood projects that brought 'personal' issues of childcare, women's health or domestic violence into the public domain; yet others participated in community-organizing as a form of oppositional politics. But a second story tells of the proliferating array of government programmes designed to regenerate, empower and mobilize community as a governable terrain. Participants in this research were ambiguously positioned in such programmes, sometimes confronting them from the 'outside' and sometimes seeking to draw on the resources they offered. Their work sometimes prefigured new policy programmes as governments sought to innovate or to co-opt 'what worked', but it also often contested the logics of those same programmes, as we will see.

Community is, of course, a highly contested concept, and an extensive literature highlights different perspectives, meanings and policy foci (Amit and Rapport 2002; Cohen 1987; Creed 2006; Mooney and Neal 2009; N. Rose 1999). It is the elasticity of meaning that renders community ambiguous, able to be mobilized – and appropriated – within different and often antagonistic political projects. It often implies a commonality of interest, place or identity that can be an unproblematic source of solidarity. As Jane Wills notes, this can be a rather old fashioned idea (Wills 2011); academic work on social networks has drawn attention to how sociability and identity are produced through networks, ideas and things, rather than membership of the shared space of belonging (Cresswell 2010); or as networked individualism rather than a bounded area (Wellman, Wong, Tindall and Nazar 1997). Nevertheless community remained, for many participants, both a common-sense descriptor of where they saw their politics taking place and a resource for their political agency. Such a politics sought not only to transform 'everyday lives' through informal and unpaid labour but also to challenge deeply entrenched patterns of inequality and disadvantage, poverty and exclusion. But work in and through community brought women into antagonistic relationships and close engagements with governmental power. This chapter begins by tracing a number of different 'imaginaries' of community articulated in the accounts of participants in this research. It then explores the governmentalization of community within the UK and how women 'worked the spaces' generated by different projects and programmes. It suggests different understandings of the gendered labour in new state spaces, and how women experienced their closure and the partial erasure of the politics they had enabled. Finally, the chapter offers ways of theorizing what I have termed the 'perverse alignments' between feminist-inflected activism and the governmentalization of community.

Imaginaries of community

Community was an attractive idea for many participants whose first encounters with political action were those of setting up playgroups, playgrounds, cooperative housing projects, advice centres and other resources for combating local issues of poverty and disadvantage. The experience of encountering such poverty was often hugely formative; Naomi Eisenstadt (G2), who later became Director of Sure Start, recounted how:

> So working in the nursery at [name of estate] was enormously formative and there was very little that happened in Sure Start that I can't say I can trace to work I did there. It was the true, the real experience. I was there for five years, and I still use stories from that time in speeches and everything. (Naomi Eisenstadt)

Particularly striking in this quotation is the reference to such experiences as 'the true, the real'. This, I think, carries a double meaning: first, community exists as an authentic space, untrammelled by the messy worlds of politics and policy, perhaps pre-modern in its sensibilities: a place inhabited by women, children, the elderly and those in need of care, and others not part of a modern public sphere. This, as Joseph (Joseph 2002 and others have noted, is a highly gendered image and one to which I will return. The second inflection of 'the true, the real' – and one closer to Naomi's meaning – is of community as the place where real poverty and disadvantage are lived. This meaning is echoed in other extracts: for example, in the following quotation from Carole Harte (G2), the coordinator of a women's advice and information centre in Birmingham at the time of our interview:

> Over recent years I have been doing something that was fulfilling an ambition, bringing grassroots women who were currently experiencing whatever disadvantage it might be, in this case poverty, into direct contact with those who

shape society to ensure that what we saw at the point of impact, where reality bites, where reality meets policy. (Carole Harte)

Although Carole is from the same generational cohort as Naomi, the 'real' here refers not to a past experience but to present actions, and designates places and populations untouched by the efforts of policy-makers of the 1990s to address issues of poverty, exclusion and disadvantage.

But community is not only the 'other', the 'real', but represents distinctive forms of work:

I guess that at a certain point of your life you have experiences that are hugely formative, form relationships that are incredibly powerful, and the really large network of people that I got to know in those years – I was only in the US for two years, but I got involved in a whole network of people who were doing community action, setting up playgroups, we got a better playground, working to create independent schools. I ended up working with the Black community, with the welfare rights movement. Because I was English it was more accepted – there was less suspicion of me than there would have been for white Americans. So it was a bit of a baptism of fire. At the end of two years my father died so I came back. So by that point I had done one year volunteering in England, involved in this amazing community work in Islington, one year at LSE stepping back and trying to do some thinking about policy, then two years in America, and I thought of myself by that time as a community worker, that's what I did. And to be honest if you asked me today what I did, who I was, I would say that, the same thing. I kind of feel that's what I've been. (Tricia Zipfel)

Such work tended to be unpaid or underpaid, but it was both a job and a style of politics – local, oriented to issues of exclusion and rights, and traversed by divisions of race and power. (Tricia's position as a white woman working on Black issues was, in the United States at that time, accepted because she came from 'elsewhere' so was not locked into local political struggles.)

Community also became a designator for a range of professions: community planning, community architecture, community education, community arts, community development and so on:

I was an architect with an interest in housing and an interest in social justice. I had worked for a while as a Community Architect but locally I was involved in the Community Forum, and was active in [name withheld] Residents Association. We wanted to get the area to be a general improvement area at the time but we didn't manage that, but other projects came in – for example an Area Caretakers project. I was also heavily involved in the Neighbourhood Centre as Treasurer and later became the Chair, and I did housing advice sessions once a week for ages. (Esther Boyd)

I worked with community groups in Docklands in the 1980s, with something called the Docklands Forum – a federation of community groups, employers, faith groups, trade unions. We were (in part) funded by GLC, and we worked on a People's Plan for the Royal Docks as an alternative to the planned airport. We did campaigning to ensure local needs were met and voices heard in the 1980s redevelopment of Docklands. But it was broader than that – we were both opposing some of the planned developments, but also trying to work for community gain in plans that were put forward. (Sue Brownill, G3)

My politics came from my interest in the arts, the visual arts. I went to a gap year in France, found out about community arts; I was in Paris, thinking about urban spaces, about shared spaces. So I spent time in community arts, then about five years ago worked out what I was supposed to do – which was working somewhere that was, well, challenging the norm, but that was also working with, supporting mainstream thinking to move on, supporting governance to change. (Sonia Khan, G3)

I worked in CDF [Community Development Foundation]¹ for ages. That was the time when they had projects on the ground so there was always a lot to learn, and there were always new projects. That's where I learnt about community development really. When I first got involved in community development, housing and planning were the important issues, but what people actually got when they went out and knocked on doors was play and childcare and stuff. But at the time these were not viewed as such important issues, and it was before the time gender issues were acknowledged – it was all about redevelopment. (Marilyn Taylor, G2)

These extracts show how roots in a community ethos formed the basis of diverse and mobile working lives that offered individuals the opportunity to generate significant spaces of power. But they also suggest something of the tensions. Some are implicit in the different conceptions of space and scale in these and other extracts; about, for example, whether community is a place or an ethos, whether it is exclusively urban and whether different scalar imaginaries can effectively be collapsed into a seemingly cohesive entity. Some are more explicit: for example, the tension between a focus on infrastructure and a focus on everyday lives (see also the extracts from Theresa Stewart in Chapter 2). The extract from Marilyn also suggests some of the limits of the class-based emphasis on poverty and disadvantage that informed the professionalization of community in this period: the neglect of gender and the silence on 'race'. Both came to the fore, however, in other accounts of political work, especially that promoted by some of the left-leaning local authorities in England in the late 1970s and through much of the 1980s, including the GLC:²

I came to the GLC as head of one of the sub-sections within the Women's Support Unit, so I was very involved in women's politics but now within the local authority. And outside of that we set up the Asian Women's Network as a resource centre, we had a little office in a building for women's projects, near Holborn. For several years I was quite active in that, there were several us, the idea was to have a central organization that supported local women's organizations. (Avtar Brah)

Avtar Brah was, as Chapter 2 recounted, primarily oriented to a politics of race, but came to inflect this with attention to the intersections of race, gender and other axes of disadvantage and exclusion. But what is striking in this extract is the ways in which gender and race politics were both brought inside local government through the development of equality units in the 1980s, and how the resources of the local state were mobilized to promote local activism and local facilities. Other organizations emerged that drew on a mix of state and non-state funding to promote community action and to try to influence policy: law centres, resource centres, housing action projects, community arts projects, women's centres, immigration advice centres and so on. Community activism became a form of collective political practice that was stretched to encompass 'inside' and 'outside' spaces. This form of practice required the knitting together different people and forms of politics:

> I suppose it was a kind of community entrepreneurialism. And there's a great debate now, isn't there, about whether this was killed off later by getting grants from the GLC, etc., and whether it [political action] might come back as we are about to lose all those grants. That takes us back to the stuff I'm doing now. But then you just had to run these things. (Jane Foot)

This speaks to how someone still active in the present reflects on the possibilities of community as a site of politics as government programmes and institutional logics have changed over time. One debate has been how far 'authentic' forms of community activism had become compromised as government grants – and, later, contracts – led to projects of professionalization and incorporation. But a second change has been the appropriation of community as a locus of new rationalities of governing: concepts of social inclusion, democratic renewal, active citizenship, responsibility, participation, decentralization and, most recently, the Big Society and other localization projects each seek to reconstruct relationships between state and citizen with 'community' as a primary resource for social action beyond the state.

> Then in the 1990s community came back into fashion, but in a way that I wasn't very happy with. I was going to Demos seminars on communitarianism and wanting to throw up basically, and the Americans were all discovering civil society, and everyone was saying how wonderful the voluntary sector was. (Marilyn Taylor)

The journey from community activism to community development and then to communitarianism[3] is a highly gendered journey; one in which women are viewed as the economic divers of change but at the same time become charged with greater responsibility for care and welfare (through voluntary labour) and called upon to be the bearers of ethical and moral responsibility. It is a journey in which the boundaries between public, private and personal are redrawn: the feminist claim that 'the personal is political' becomes realized in ways that both take on women's claims for the recognition of issues of childcare, domestic violence and inequalities within the household while the 'personal' – matters of conduct and behaviour – become taken up in public policy. I will return to these issues in Chapter 4, but here want to note how 'community' is traversed by multiple and often antagonistic political projects. Older models of community activism, inspired by the work of Paulo Friere and the radical politics of Latin America, sit uneasily with more recent developments from the United States, based on the community-organizing work of Saul Alinsky (currently favoured by the UK coalition government and source of inspiration for London Citizens; see Chapter 9). Community professionals (working in community arts, architecture and so on) often found themselves in conflict with community activists. And the politics of community were traversed and confounded by the politics of race, gender, sexuality, generation and other lines of social and political fracture.[4]

Governmentalizing community

The women quoted in this chapter all engaged, at some point in their working lives, with a succession of UK (usually English) government programmes: Community Development Programmes, Inner Area Studies, the Priority Estates Programme, Urban Renewal projects and the New Deal for Communities were all designed to contain potentially disruptive 'communities' and to invest in their renewal and regeneration.[5] These generated new spaces of power and opened up new prefigurative pathways that became inscribed in policies of the 'Third Way' governments of Blair in the late 1990s and the coalition government of 2010. But the alignments between community activism and governmental projects of development and containment were played out rather differently in successive programmes. Many remembered the early Community Development Programmes (CDP) as opening up extensive opportunities for local activism to flourish: Ursula Murray recounted how '*CDP was a very open initiative that drew in experienced activists. The Home Office* couldn't control it' (my emphasis). CDP was underpinned by radical political critiques of inequality and disadvantage. But such critiques generated high expectations of change that clashed with the more limited purposes of government.

Under New Labour community and active citizenship programmes proliferated: Education, Health and Employment Action Zones, New Deal for Communities, Neighbourhood Renewal, Sure Start, Social Inclusion projects and crime reduction initiatives. Such programmes looked to 'local communities', local partnership bodies and local neighbourhoods in ways that sought to bypass existing institutions, particularly local authorities, many of which had supported and housed radical left-wing and equality projects through the 1980s and early 1990s. Community was viewed as the place – locality was important here – where new forms of engagement between government and 'ordinary people' could be established (Clarke 2010a). They offered lots of spaces of opportunity but were not founded on the same kind of systematic collective critique as CDP and tended to work through an explicitly partnership-based regime that served to collapse distinctions between 'inside' and 'outside', so rendering critique more difficult:

> *Partnerships were invited spaces, and therefore the rules of the game were not those of the community, whereas you need popular spaces where people can find their own voice. And that's what I think was missing a bit under New Labour. The real change comes about from the dynamics between the popular and the invited spaces.* (Marilyn Taylor)

This extract sets up an opposition between the idea of community as a 'popular' space free from governmental intervention and the 'invited' spaces opened up as government projects and programmes invited community actors to participate. My interest, however, is in those actors who brokered between these different spaces, aligning different rationalities to open up new dynamics of change. Being part of a partnership or working on a government programme did not necessarily erase radicalism. Many participants lived through different regimes, taking critiques and political learning with them and adapting their strategies as they went:

> *Over twenty-two years the Priority Estates Programme was always interesting. The idea arose from the outgoing Labour government's concern about run down estates, then in 1979 the new Conservative government launched the project because they knew that Right-to-Buy [a tenant's right to purchase their council accommodation] would never work on the most deprived estates. So we were funded by a Tory government, working in mainly Labour authorities, championing the right of tenants and challenging [local authority] housing management services. We developed a cooperative housing model for public sector housing and then, in the 1990s, tried to apply it to other services. We were piloting a form of 'neighbourhood management', but struggled because it was before its time. We applied for a grant to do research on how to build on the housing cooperative model and apply it in a neighbourhood across a whole range of services.*
>
> *What we were talking about was neighbourhood management, we tried to pilot the model and it just didn't work – it was before its time. But when Tony Blair came in and set up the Social Exclusion Unit, with its amazing analysis of poverty, and neighbourhood disadvantage and inequality, that was just fantastic. I got very excited. I got involved in the PAT [Policy Action Team] on neighbourhood management and felt this was what Priority Estates Programme had been trying to do for years. This is why I went to work for the government in 2001 [on Neighbourhood Renewal] since I did feel excited by it; it felt it was a natural extension of the agenda we had been exploring and slowly developing for twenty years.* (Tricia Zipfel)

In the Blair years, programmes of development, participation and empowerment flourished, opening up new opportunities for many participants and benefiting from the relational and political skills they brought. They offered new spaces of power that drew women into governance arrangements while also offering them resources that they could sometimes divert in their efforts to promote social justice. Such participants, however, had to negotiate the contradictions between their own politics and those underpinning government projects of inclusion and renewal. These consistently privileged a communitarian rather than an adversarial politics of community, and sought to transform governance itself by looking beyond institutionalized interests to the 'ordinary people' of community and civil society.

As such those drawn into these types of programmes have often been charged with complicity in the rolling out of new logics of 'inclusive' Third Way neoliberalism (Bondi and Laurie 2005). That is, they are viewed as agents through whom neoliberalization could colonize potentially oppositional spaces. But I want also to suggest that participants themselves appropriated neoliberal projects and programmes. To explore this a little further I want to develop the idea of 'translation'. This appeared as a practical discourse in some of the interviews – a way in which women described what they did:

> You can probably – I can give you an insight into a real world and you can translate *that into an academic language which is what people in government, decision-makers expect to see – a language that's recognized by policy-makers. So we need each other, otherwise I might be talking to the Russians in French – it will have no effect.* (Carole Harte; my emphasis)

> Then I acted as a connector with the rest of the department, bringing civil servants in to meet with them (community forum members) about different issues, *translating what they were saying into documents that were acceptable and understandable to the department.* (Tricia Zipfel; my emphasis)

These are speaking from different positions, with Carole viewing me as an academic implicated in translating her ideas to policy-makers, while Tricia had, at that time, a Civil Service attachment in which translation between different stakeholder interests was a key part of her role. Responding later to this extract, Tricia expressed a discomfort with her use of the word 'translate' because:

> the whole point of the Community Forum was to enable them to speak directly and in their own words and in their own way to the minister and policymakers. We said that they should 'tell it like it is' and that's what happened. My role wasn't to 'translate' in the sense of 'interpret', to make more acceptable or palatable, but to facilitate the exchange and to support it by putting it into documents that civil servants then had to take note of. But it was important that it was me doing it because I totally understood where the forum members were coming from ... Lots of people have commented on the value of having 'people like me' on the inside of government, and it did make the Neighbourhood Renewal Unit different from the rest of government, at least for a while. (Tricia Zipfel)

'People like me' hold contradictory subject positions, both inside and outside dominant institutions and forms of rule. They were inspired by forms of radical community activism that sat uneasily in the culture of the Civil Service. Tricia brought her experience of Latin American participatory politics community activism into what she saw as the bland and technocratic participation promulgated by the UK Civil Service. The work of Carole, Tricia and others evokes the sense of translation as an active, agentive process, requiring the labour of summoning, mobilizing and – most importantly – combining elements into new assemblages (see Chapter 7). And, of course, translation was also needed between the rationalities and practices of different elements of government itself. Governmental projects of community development, community empowerment, the promotion of community cohesion and others tended to be situated outside mainstream service-delivery departments and in rather ambiguous relationships to them. They represented a shift towards more horizontal working, sometimes understood as 'network' governance, but were cross-cut by performance and accountability regimes derived from hierarchically organized 'silos' of government. They were ambiguously positioned between central and local government, valorizing the 'local' and the empowerment of local actors while being suffused with centralizing targets and measures. These contradictions were managed by participants, but also actively 'worked' by them to generate spaces of power in which radical agendas could be pursued. Their labour was sometimes co-opted by the various units of government established to promote community development and community cohesion.[6] These sought to transcend what were considered to be 'old' institutional, professional and political barriers by empowering 'ordinary people' as active citizens. Indeed, many government programmes picked up on ideas and practices that had been prefigured by radical projects, both in the UK and in international development work. However, government programmes also offered new spaces of agency, of power, that could be mobilized by participants. Here is Jan Etienne talking about working on projects funded from the New Deal for Communities and Better Government for Older People programmes:

> The bulk of my involvement in what I might call informal political activities has been working with women's organizations. One of them has been an older women's organization dealing with communities. You get this situation where they [the programme board] want to tackle the needs of particular sections of the community. They put out money for short courses so that people can participate on urban regeneration boards, committees and so on. I have provided a lot of this kind of training. I'm also involved in delivering equality training for various employers, but when I thought about meeting with you I was thinking to myself that one of the things that I really wanted to share was the experience that I've had, that I still have, of working with older women who are living on a council housing estate. This is the part of my work that I feel much more excited about. It's all voluntary, but it's a side of my life that I really get a lot out of ...

I asked her what it was that excited her:

> I've been working with an over fifties project in Brent for the last eight years. I'm not a borough organizer kind of person, but what it is about these women, they're probably one of the most multicultural sort of groups that I've ever worked with. I've never come across Irish, African and Caribbean working so well together. Most of them are involved in the Greater London Pensioners Association for which they are campaigning at the House of Commons all the time, equalizing the

pension, you know the whole thing about returning the link to earnings. Some of them are campaigners, some of them are working for Black disabilities. They have all sorts of skills and what I do with them I actually conduct … put on these little training exercises which are supposed to be about giving them the confidence to be able to challenge the local council. (Jan Etienne)

Carole Harte's empowerment work was not funded by any specific government programme but used the spaces generated by the turn to more participative styles of policymaking to promote active citizenship:

My first funding application – I asked for the money to help me to help women to participate in our society. What I was talking about was active citizenship I suppose. I wrote that I wanted them to stop being passive observers because that's what seemed to change for me when I went through a learning process. Getting more confident, etc. (Carole Harte)

As part of her work coordinating a women's advice and information centre she sought to enable community actors – predominantly but not exclusively women – to voice their experience to policymakers:

We secured funding for a workshop in which women were asked to focus on their own experience. Then I asked them to put them together into themes, then we would look at how those themes related to different policy areas. Eventually we honed it down to a set of recommendations which were presented to a group of minister and senior civil servants. They didn't keep up their end of the bargain (about who we would get to see). But it had a big impact on the women who participated. We're all of us in a bus to London: and some have never left [the council estate], and we go into the Houses of Parliament and it's like 'Wow!' And if you ask them they'll say it was actually brilliant. It's my job not to let them know the struggles we had to get them the bus fare, the childcare and all that kind of thing. (Carole Harte)

This is one of a number of examples Carole spoke about where she had mobilized women to take up 'invited spaces' in the policy process, responding to participation and consultation exercises, organizing focus groups to enable a response to consultations on 'stronger communities' and on crime reduction strategies under New Labour. But this mobilization also set agendas: an event on 'barriers that women faced in their community' was facilitated and broadcast by BBC3. This underscores the role many participants play in summoning and mobilizing 'community' and how they engage in active processes of translation within the spaces opened up by 'participative' styles of policymaking.

I want to juxtapose Carole's experiences with those of Hannah Berry, a young woman who at the time of the interview was working in a community empowerment project for Manchester Women's Network. With a woman from Venezuela she had set up GAP (Gender Audit Project) as a community-interest company, based in a cooperatively managed workspace, shared by several organizations, that Hannah had helped establish. The GAP involved other women in doing the audit research, enabling them to get accreditation for their skills. They conducted audits for bodies such as the then Local Strategic Partnership and Strategic Health Authority; they made recommendations, produced leaflets and, like Jan and Carole, offered 'empowerment' and 'training' programmes for women:

> *The audits show that there is a real lack of confidence among women to get involved in formal structures [e.g. those associated with the Local Strategic Partnership]. This helped us get funding for empowerment programmes for local women. We ran education workshops looking at things like what is gender, how are children socialized, looking at media images of women. We worked with the women to identify areas they were weak in and developed training to suit.* (Hannah Berry)

They also secured funding to do awareness-raising in schools, to work with women living in refuges, parents within Sure Start programmes, older women, asylum-seekers, the League of Jewish Women, women with mental health problems, the Red Cross women's group and research on women councillors:

> *We always work with existing groups. Our interventions are so tiny the idea is that any learning will be embedded – there will be some way in which they will carry on once we have gone away.* (Hannah Berry)

Although these three participants are from different generational cohorts, and come from different political backgrounds – Jan from anti-racist politics and Labour Party involvement, Carole from class-based politics, Hannah from anarchism and direct action on climate change – there are some striking similarities between their descriptions of their work. All described bringing women together to events in which they formulated policy and campaigning ideas; all saw 'empowerment' as a political activity; and all explicitly targeted women. And all worked the 'invited spaces' of governance to mobilize resources and promote social justice and equality. Finally, all used the language of empowerment, development and active citizenship.

These are however all difficult terms. Cruikshank (Cruikshank 1999), Sharma (Sharma 2008), Brown (Brown 2005) and others have noted their significance as technologies of neoliberal rule 'which help mould individuals into responsible citizen-subjects who fit the requirement of the prevalent governance regime and who participate in the project of rule by governing themselves' (Sharma 2008: 17). 'Women's development' and 'community empowerment', then, formed contradictory points of alignment between emerging governing rationales and participant's political work.

Ambiguous spaces and problematic politics

The expansion of spaces of power linked to governmental projects and programmes took place alongside the progressive 'professionalization' of many community-based organizations. Such organizations were particularly vulnerable to the 'contract culture' in which service-delivery contracts came to replace most forms of grant aid. Sukhwant Dhaliwal worked for women's refuges in Manchester and London, in neither of which did she find an outlet for her campaigning style of politics:

> Now [name of group] are incredible but for me it was all about service provision. I kept thinking the politics was coming, you know, I kept on thinking the politics was coming. To give them their due they had historically lobbied on social policy stuff, but they are pretty entrenched in service provision, I would say. But when I got to Southall Black Sisters there was a completely different culture. They talked about legislative reforms, they went and campaigned and lobbied for it.
> (Sukhwant Dhaliwal)

This contrast is one that resonates through the literatures on the 'professionalization' of activist spaces and voluntary-sector bodies as they are drawn into new relationships with the state (Bondi and Laurie 2005; Braig and Wölte 2002; McDermont 2010). The transformations of governance (see Chapters 4 and 5) that took place in the 1990s opened up a 'mixed economy' of service provision, an economy generated through the marketization of public services and the change of funding regimes for voluntary and not-for-profit organizations from grant aid to contract. As organizations with a tradition of activist and campaigning work came to take on service-delivery roles, so they became subject to quality, accounting and management requirements against which their performance was monitored – and on which future funding depended. Informal activities became formalized, complex roles became narrowed down in the disciplines of service provision, and the relationship between volunteering and managing shifted. As Sukhwant acknowledged, many such organizations continued to engage in campaigning and advocacy, but the balance of their work shifted and the demands of meeting the requirements of the contract rendered them less attractive for volunteers and activists alike.

Sonia Khan describes a similar experience but in a very different institutional and political context. Early in her career she had worked initially as a volunteer and later as an employee of Free Form Arts Trust, an organization rooted in the 1960s ethos of community education, community arts and community engagement as routes towards empowerment:

> So I spent four years in a community arts organization that had started off in the late 1960s; it was about bringing arts to the people. But it had evolved to match the times, so in the 1980s it did more around regeneration, then in the 1990s it was moving towards working on estates, supporting the statutory sector on social regeneration. And I have to say that as time went on in that job I got to feel that they weren't what they had been, they had lost some of their edge. And that wasn't necessarily a bad thing, but they hadn't worked out what they needed to be now. They had become more of an intermediary between community and the state, and in the end they weren't community-based and

they weren't rebellious – and that was fine, but I felt they needed a new vision for the 1990s. The strategic leadership were pragmatic people who wanted to survive as an organization, to keep artists involved – it was a kind of professionalization, I suppose. (Sonia Khan)

The contrast between politics and professionalization is a theme to which I return in later chapters, but here I also want to note that the language used by Sonia (strategic leadership, vision, intermediary bodies, professionalization, rebelliousness) is itself not innocent language but draws both on political critiques and on managerial discourse.

The literature on the fate of voluntary and community organizations has tended to focus on such processes of professionalization. However, community projects were also highly vulnerable to three rather different processes that limited their power to generate politicized subjects and activist politics. The first was one of *co-optation and containment* as activist conceptions of 'empowerment' became articulated with governmental notions of active citizenship and responsibility. After Carole Harte had suggested that she saw her role as being that of producing active citizens, able to speak back to government, I asked her, as government is now full of the language of active citizenship, how she felt about her material now being part of official policy talk.

The saddest thing was when I heard the leader of the Tory Party quoting back my own words – I thought what's happening here?

I asked her what had happened.

Well, I think that they've listened to the words, and they have sort of – they are coming back and biting us on the bum with them, saying well we've listened, this is what you have asked for. But, oh my God, we didn't mean that. (Carole Harte)

The laughter that accompanied this explanation was dismissive and ironic, but there was considerable anger, too. Similar sentiments were expressed by Jane Foot, in her comment that *'New Labour has stolen our language'*. This can be viewed as a reflection on the ways in which governmental projects and programmes – especially those of New Labour, but also those promoted and funded by the World Bank – draw on social movements or international development practice and resignify them in accordance with what some would term a neoliberal strategy of rule (see Chapter 8 and Newman 2012b). Empowerment and active citizenship programmes, whatever their 'origins', tended to become oriented towards producing new kinds of governmental subject, able to take their place in 'reflexive modernity' in general and economic development strategies in particular.

A second process, overlaid on the first in complicated ways, might be termed *empowerment as symbolic action*. Empowerment and community development programmes can be viewed as constructing disadvantage and exclusion as cultural processes that can be resolved by personal empowerment rather than through attention to structural and economic factors. Hannah Berry, reflecting on her work with women asylum-seekers, reflected that:

I can see actual positive benefits for individuals from what we are able to do. But these women [asylum-seekers] have got an active citizenship programme where they are not even allowed to be citizens. And all around me I see women who get their status only to have to go and work in Tesco's. The women are getting deported left, right and centre. But I also see them learning about how politics works in this country, and they are getting heard by people with power. We did this event and on the minibus on the way home there was a real buzz. (Hannah Berry)

The 'buzz' of women travelling on minibuses to speak to those in power resonates with the Carole Harte interview. But the work with women asylum-seekers points to the limits as well as the possibilities of empowerment work: such women were learning active citizenship while having no citizenship status. And it raises the question – empowerment for what? What forms of citizenship and what kinds of power are open to women whose economic and cultural capital within the UK was so low, even if they had avoided deportation? Carole faced similar contradictions – many of the women she worked with were likely to continue to experience domestic and street violence, to remain in low-paid jobs and to be among the most vulnerable to the effects of economic recession.

A third process is that of *erasure or abandonment*. The spaces of power opened up by government programme were temporary and fragile, and they offered highly contingent sites of employment (see Chapter 5). Most of the projects within which the participants quoted in this chapter worked have been subject to cuts and many have closed. While the GAP project and others indicated that women's empowerment had become something which statutory bodies were sometimes willing to fund, they occupied a highly precarious funding environment:

We were selected to get money, but a month later the Minister for the Third Sector cancelled the programme because he realized that electorally it would not look good to be seen to fund campaigns for Romany women and other unpopular groups. (Hannah Berry)

The women's advice and information centre that Carole coordinated closed in 2009 (she went on to work for a Voluntary Service Council in a different town), while the projects and programmes on which Jan Etienne worked did not continue after the coalition government came to power in 2010. But what is striking is that when some spaces were closed down, many of the participants moved on to others – up until a moment when someone had had enough, got ill or burned out, or when personal lives came to dominate over activist engagements for a while because of childcare and other responsibilities. Yet others became involved in the later twists and turns of policy as governments turned to 'active citizens' and communities to take on responsibilities formerly provided by the state, making decisions, providing services, managing assets and promoting the well-being of their 'communities'. Community groups and organizations were invited to bid for contracts to deliver services formerly provided by the central or local state, health and education services, thus offering citizens an apparent 'choice' and breaking the 'producer dominance' of the public sector.

The processes of what many view as the professionalization and incorporation of community activism are currently being paralleled by emerging models of community organizing, represented in the work of London Citizens and other citizen organizations and assemblies. Drawing on the United States, and inspired by the work of Saul Alinsky, the model seeks to build on existing institutions (predominantly faith groups) and to generate new models of leadership:

> It's about finding islands of social capital, putting them together by finding shared interests and then putting a positive alternative on to the table. So it's about doing public politics – putting people into the public arena, putting them into public relationships with each other, then generating the public performance of politics. But it's always very practically grounded. (Jane Wills)

The political work undertaken by London Citizens includes what Jane terms 'rescaling the process of identity making', subordinating issues of difference to a superordinate category that people can identify with despite differences; and 'reproducing the collective memory' of the organization at each assembly to overcome the problem of highly mobile populations. London Citizens has had considerable success in challenging government and local government, notably in the Living Wage Campaign. But as Jane reflects, its very success in mobilizing populations makes it vulnerable to co-option (Wills 2011).

Participants also became involved in developments linked to the idea of the local community as a source of assets that could, it was assumed, displace the need for state resources and institutional support. 'Asset based' community development, an approach originating in the United States, proposed a focus on mobilizing community assets rather than on meeting needs 'from above', challenging the relevance and value of professional and state interventions. One participant described a local 'community-mobilizer' scheme as a route towards enabling community members – mostly women – to 'run things for themselves' rather than being reliant on professionals being 'parachuted in' to the area. Asked to describe the work of community mobilizers, she described them partly as 'professional neighbours' and partly as resource mobilizers promoting educational development. The aim was 'resilience building':

> It gives confidence to people who would not have challenged authority. I mean this woman was saying that in the course of the last few years one of her children has been diagnosed with Asperger's syndrome and she's had quite a hard time

with getting that recognized, and the confidence that she's gained through working with the mobilizer enabled her to tackle that effectively, so the child now has proper provision. One way of getting proper provision is going to an agency and getting somebody to help you do it; but she's managed to do that herself. (Kate Simmons, G3)

This has some similarities to Jan Etienne's description of how her work within a Neighbourhood Renewal programme was helping to build the confidence of women and to Carole Harte's work mobilizing women as active citizens. But there is a crucial difference: while these aimed to give women the confidence to 'speak back to power', the community-mobilizer scheme was oriented towards giving people the confidence to do things for themselves. Such initiatives are, of course, multi-vocal. They draw on radical ideas of associational democracy, women's empowerment and greater local autonomy. But they are readily aligned with developments that look beyond welfare services towards responsible communities: the installation of the coalition government's conception of community mobilizers across the UK was a key plank of David Cameron's ambitions for a Big Society. As Kate Simmons commented, the ill-defined notions of volunteerism presented by Cameron did not fit well with the well-organized, funded versions of community mobilization seen in the localities with which she was involved.

These inflections of community became increasingly prominent following the financial crash of 2008 and the attempt by many governments to cut services and reduce the size of the state, devolving responsibility away from government. Paradoxically the forms of local connectedness and agency propounded by government policies of localism and active citizenship bore remarkable similarities to those generated by the political movements and alternative practices of the 1960s and early 1970s, and by their continued development in marginal spaces alongside – and in uncomfortable alignment with – governmental programmes of intervention, containment and concern. Governmental discourse can be seen as once again stealing the language of feminist-inflected activism, not least in the valorization of local connectedness, mutuality and participation, seeking to re-inflect each with a communitarian ethos and to strip them from the politics that had generated them. These attempts are, however, not necessarily successful, as I will show.

Perverse alignments?

Participants across different generations worked for and against a succession of governmental projects that sought to constitute community as a governable space. Community became a resource for new forms of service provision and was saturated with discourses of empowerment, participation and active citizenship. These in turn were reworked around notions of responsibility (for oneself and others) and (market-based) choice. The slips and slides towards communitarian politics, the recasting of governance regimes to favour so called 'faith' communities and the privileging of the 'local' community as the site of depoliticized forms of participative governance all make it difficult to imagine community as an autonomous space of political agency and antagonism. Despite the imaginaries of community as something 'other' (Joseph 2002), the arguments of this chapter suggest that such spaces cannot be viewed as autonomous spaces beyond the reach of dominant projects and protected from the imperatives of both state and market. Rather, they show how deeply implicated community activism and governmental projects and programmes have been, not only in the UK and some other European nations but also in the development projects promulgated by the World Bank, NGOs and other agencies. One consequence has been what many view as a professionalization of activism; the translation of activist commitments into a series of technical skills that need to be acquired and performed in order to secure funding, contracts and stakeholder legitimacy. However, this does not necessarily erase activist commitments: as Larner and Craig report on their work on partnerships in New Zealand: 'This gaining of professional and technical expertise was complemented by hearty political engagement, powerfully motivated by anger over the impact of neoliberalism' (Larner and Craig 2005: 409).

This continued capacity for anger and engagement is often sidelined or ignored in the literature on the governmentalization of community, depicted as a singular process in which 'authentic' expressions of community are subordinated to new regimes of power:

> What distinguishes the contemporary spaces of community [is that they] have been objectified by positive knowledges, subject to truth claims by expertise and hence can become the object of political technologies for governing through community. And these political technologies involve the constitution of new forms of authority of this new space of natural associations, and the instrumentalisation of new forces in the government of conduct. (N. Rose 1999: 188–9)

From this perspective the emphasis on community engagement in successive government programmes can be viewed as a way of tutoring citizens through forms of participative governing, rendering potentially unruly populations compliant through the production of new forms of self-governing subject. These strategies of rule have been widely criticised (N. Rose 1999; Newman and Clarke 2009: ch. 3; Cruikshank 1999). Less visible are questions of ambiguity and tension. What comes into view through the interviews is the multiplicity of different governmentalities, rather than a singular form of rule. While 'participation' and 'empowerment' are common discourses, they are articulated with other rationalities – development, containment, inclusion, choice, localization, resilience and, most recently, new conceptions of 'the social' (of the 'Big Society') as displacing or supplanting state welfare.

Such discourses may at times be linked to the turn to the market and the valorization of entrepreneurial selves; at others (or rather, in other voices) they may be articulated with a Freirian pedagogy through which political subjects may be produced through processes of 'conscientization'; and yet others may draw on development discourses that look to Latin America and the global south for inspiration. But they may also become bureaucratized, part of the instrumental rationalities of a managerialized politics of the global north, especially the United Kingdom, or inflected with the social capital focus of some versions of US politics.

How can we understand the ways in which these different perspectives, projects and practices are combined? Masson argues that community policy should be viewed as 'a co-construction, or more exactly as a compromise, the result of collaboration as well as of conflicts and tensions between community/women's and governmental actors' (Masson 2009). This gives it a 'hybrid' quality that cannot be encompassed in general narratives of cooption of social movements or the governmentalization of community. Such narratives, she suggests, are both politically immobilizing and theoretically problematic. Similar hybridities are evident in the United Kingdom. We can trace across the accounts the problematic alignments between 'professionalized' spaces and 'authentic' spaces of activism and campaigning; between 'grassroots' and 'policy'; between participative politics and managerial logics.

Each of these examples of hybridity suggests the problems of aligning elements that are understood as diametrically opposed. That is, they are constituted as binaries (authentic space/governentalized space, invited space/popular space, professional/political, 'elsewheres' such as Latin America and 'here'). But more than two elements may be at stake. In her study of Mahila Samakhya, a gender and development programme in India, Sharma points to four empowerment frames, which 'stem from different ideological perspectives and arose out of diverse spatial locations and historical moments' (Sharma 2008: 22). In the Indian context these included a feminist strategy to engender social transformation; a Freirian liberatory struggle against oppression; a Gandhian order of moral self-rule; and a neoliberal project that fosters individualized conceptions of market empowerment in order to solve poverty and reduce big government. These alignments, she argues, serve to give neoliberalism, and the World Bank itself, a 'social and ethical spin' (Sharma 2008: 20). We can see, then, how empowerment strategies in India encompassed both hegemonic and counter-hegemonic frames, but all sought to mould behaviour and so all must, Sharma argues, be viewed as governmental projects. But they diverged in terms of the social subjects they wished to create and the kind of society they sought to establish, and so did not determine the subjects summoned to power: 'Even as development attempts to create and regulate disciplined individuals and collective bodies, it also breeds subversive tactics and unruly subjects who protest their subjectification and subjection, who test the state and unbound it from presumed limits, and who resignify development' (Sharma 2008: xxxv).

The value of Sharma's work is that, by drawing attention to four different ideological projects, she helps challenge the 'in or against' duality of activist politics confronting governmental power. In the context of the United Kingdom we might point to forms of community activism inspired by Freirian notions of empowerment; to critiques of professional power and the shift, within many professions, towards notions of participation and co-production; to the movements demanding greater devolution and local control; to feminist practices of cooperative and collaborative working; to democratic movements advocating more associational or deliberative forms of engagement; and to communitarian ideas of interdependence and reciprocity. Each has offered ideas and resources that have been drawn on by governmental programmes that might be termed neoliberal in their intentions. 'Empowerment' and 'co-production' slide inexorably towards governmental notions of responsible, active citizenship, and of welfare users taking greater responsibility for their own health, care and well-being, but also offer discursive framings for counter-hegemonic projects. Associational and deliberative forms of democracy offer new ways in which the state can draw citizens into participative and pedagogic relationships, but also spaces of politicization (Barnes *et al.* 2007). Devolution and localization might be viewed as helping constitute the public sphere as a series of bounded spatial entities separate from the wider polity and amenable to self governance,[7] but also summon new actors to the politics of negotiating new state forms. Cooperative and collaborative working are integral to the effectiveness of governance regimes based on networks and partnership, but are also integral to social movement politics. And the notion of community itself can empower new constituencies: the emergence of 'faith' communities reminds us that community encompass projects of the right as well as the left, religious as well as secular; they are readily aligned with communitarian politics (Fraser 1999; Fukayama 1999; Robinson 2008) and traversed by patriarchal/paternalistic politics of gender.

It is this hybridity of community, as Masson argued, that produces ambiguity. It enables activist struggles to be resignified by government, but this does not mean that the original meaning is erased. The spaces of power opened up by participants in the governmental turn to community were those in which multiple rationalities and resources had to be assembled. This generated the need for forms of work involving translation (working across different systems of meaning) and alignment (bringing together different political projects). In the United Kingdom community projects had to be aligned with funding regimes; new technologies of participation had to be aligned with traditional political spaces of representative government; local innovations had to be aligned with central government targets and evaluation regimes; politicized forms of agency had to be aligned with logics of governance that privilege managerialist conceptions of effectiveness; and so on.

But the multiplicity of different ideologies and projects condensed in governmentalities of community also opens up spaces of contestation and contradiction. The extracts in this and the preceding chapter show how participants have worked the borders between activist commitments (inspired by both feminism and community politics) and governmental projects and programmes. By being drawn in to such programmes they became responsible for delivering governmental agendas and developed professional skills that potentially distanced them from those they sought to represent or mobilize. But they did not thereby necessarily become depoliticized: the women referred to in this chapter all spoke of continued activism and sustained strong political identities. They continued to look to what they often term the 'grassroots' where, in Carole's terms, 'reality bites', for inspiration. They may sometimes have felt defeated as programmes become undeliverable (Tricia, Jane). They may have become depressed about the compromises that had to be made as community based agencies turn to service delivery (Sonia, Sukhwant). Working the spaces of power can be painful, can lead to disappointment and to the experience of having one's voice – the very words one speaks – taken away and made to mean something different. But participants were not just passive pawns in the governance game. Moving into 'invited' spaces of governance enabled them to lever resources and to extend the reach of their influence. And they brought considerable political, as well as professional, skills. At one point Carole invited me to become linked to a virtual organization she had set up that had no formal ties to any voluntary or statutory body, and that offered a private forum in which views could be shared, ideas formed and strategies developed. Its privacy and anonymity operated as a smokescreen behind which participants could regroup and strategize. Carole, and others, became highly skilled at working the borders between governmental power and political agency.

How far might the production of community as a locus of gendered action prefigure wider possible transformations of social and political life – including those imagined by notions of well-being, the good society and even of the Big Society? Jane Foot, who appeared earlier as a 'community entrepreneur' forging new ways of conducting politics in and through community in the 1980s, later became more of a policy entrepreneur, using her skills to engage in policy research and advice. In a phone call in October 2010 she bewailed the fact that:

> So much of what I have done is now happening again – it makes me want to reprint all the reports of the CDP and other projects I was involved in. We are just back in the 1980s again, engaged in the same arguments. (Jane Foot)

The governmental context in which she operated was very different to that of the 1980s, but Jane could see many resonances between the Thatcher governments and the 2010 coalition government determined to reduce the size and reach of the state and to install forms of self help and mutualism that would enable a Big Society to flourish in its place. At the time of the phone call Jane was active in promulgating an 'assets-based' approach to social and civic renewal, health and well-being, and was attempting to align this approach with an implicitly socialist conception of the role of the state in redressing inequalities. She reiterated the need to keep the idea of being simultaneously 'in and against the state'[8] in view: resistance to the current period of cuts and the shrinking of public services and public institutions should not take the form of defence of the status quo.

Jane, Carole and all of the women quoted in this chapter offer a rich repertoire of resources for alternative forms of policy and practice. The extracts indicate not only that radicalism was alive and well, but also that governmental programmes could offer resources and spaces of agency that were able to support alternative political projects; and that government itself can be challenged by new models of community organizing. What is less certain is what might come next. Neither governmental projects nor activist commitments are unchanging; each draws on, borrows from and adapts to the other, and each is configured through wider social and political transformations. Many of the accounts in this chapter show how government projects and funding streams offered spaces of power that women could lever to enable those experiencing poverty and disadvantage, exclusion and marginalization to 'speak to power'. The current political shifts in the UK towards a smaller state buttressed by an image of self-provisioning communities is likely to not only reduce these possible spaces of power but also to intensify inequalities and social divisions. I take up this theme towards the end of the book but first I want to turn to a different set of potentially perverse alignments: those between activist projects and the transformations of policy and governance that took place in Britain in the 1990s and beyond.

4

Close Encounters: Feminism, Policy and the Remaking of Governance

This chapter traces what happens as women bring political commitments and campaigns into policy and governance roles. This is a terrain littered with stereotypes – the governance feminist, the femocrat and other demonic figures who, as they take on new forms of power, become distanced from the politics that formed them and separated from those whose interests they claim to represent. However, the evidence of this research does not support such stereotypes. It shows how participants moved in and out of policy roles, in and out of politics, in and out of campaigning roles and in and out of different 'sectors', gathering political experiences, building relationships and accreting skills on the way. The legislative and policy reforms they won led to the acceptance of lesbian and gay civil partnerships; brought about improved provision for children and families; secured women's legal and financial independence; and opened up new policy foci on health, well-being, safety, care, parenting, disability, mental health and other issues. But participants also raised concerns about what happened next – how policies somehow became detached from the politics that inspired them, and how strategies of mainstreaming and monitoring failed to deliver the transformations they promised. Each 'success' was partial and conditional, and each can be situated in wider narratives of depoliticization and mainstreaming.

To explore some of these paradoxes this chapter traces how participants sought to influence policy and monitor its impact. It asks how far 'close encounters' with policymaking led to the incorporation of activists as they engaged with dominant forms of political and institutional power. It shows how policy was shaped by women bringing activist commitments into policy roles in the Civil Service, NGOs, think-tanks and local government. It also traces what happened as activist commitments were institutionalized through processes of 'mainstreaming' and monitoring. Throughout the chapter my focus is on the different 'spaces of power' that participants opened up and mobilized, and on how 'insider' and 'activist' roles, while often viewed as separate and antagonistic, were connected in multiple ways. Such connections did not erase antagonism but perhaps make us think again about what a policy is and how it is performed.

Gender agendas and social policy

Feminist influence on social policy has a long genealogy that can be traced through different inflections of 'feminism' and through different formations of welfare states (Fink and Lundqvist 2010; Gordon 1990; Guy 2009; G. Lewis 2002; Newman and Tonkens 2011). Within the United Kingdom the second-wave women's movement generated extensive critiques and new forms of provision (for example, health and maternity services, childcare provision and elder care carer support, provision for women experiencing domestic violence) designed to transform the paternalistic and patriarchal assumptions inscribed in welfare services (Charles 2000). The feminist challenges to the maternalism of post-war social policies were – selectively and conditionally – accommodated in social and public policy, enabling Walby to suggest, in 1999, that: 'Gender relations are being transformed. A new gender settlement, a new social contract between women and men, is being created. These arrangements are potentially more equitable, productive and socially inclusive for both women and men. Government has a crucial role in supporting this new settlement. Especially a new Labour government with an ethos of modernising and reducing social exclusion' (Walby 1999: 1).

This quotation reflects the optimism of a period in which New Labour had just entered government with a much higher proportion of women MPs and a policy platform that appeared to take account of the 'gender agendas' raised by feminist campaigns of previous decades. However, reflections that look back at that period talk of the assimilation and deflection of feminist agendas (Annesley, Gains and Rummery 2010; McRobbie 2009) or imply that the achievements of women's liberation in projects of 'empowering' women merely served to enable us to take our place as full worker citizens in the 'Social Investment State' (Lister 2001; Lister 2002; Lister 2004).

To assess such claims, I want to use the accounts of participants to show what happened as social policy came to be inflected by feminist struggles and claims. Hilary Land (G2) spoke of life as a campaigner, an academic and a member of a number of review bodies, including the Cabinet Office Policy Review Staff to which she was seconded in the 1970s, initially under Labour and subsequently under the first Thatcher administration (during which time the group was abolished). These engagements with policy were all informed by her involvement in the 1970s women's liberation campaign for legal and financial independence for women (in which Ruth Lister was also active):

> *We developed a critique of the male breadwinner model out of our own family experience. We used our professional bourgeois skills to send evidence off to policymakers, working on issues of taxation, pensions, child benefit, family law, domestic violence and so on. In the 1970s there was a concern to improve the lot of women; and in some ways it was as if we were pushing at an open door.*

It got harder in the 1980s: it was quite hard to get a handle on Thatcher – the paradigm had shifted, the door had slammed and we had far fewer networks with policymakers. The YBA Wife campaign and Rights of Women emerged out of the original financial and legal independence campaign, and my involvement in the Women's Budget Group [WBG] is a continuation of these in some respects. I have worked on issues of childcare and social care, maternity provision, work/life balance etc, and the WBG always comments on pre-budget reports and writes submissions to the Treasury on their impact on women. There were some ministers and civil servants who were happy to use our arguments but you trained them up and then they moved on to another policy area. We had some successes and the last New Labour government finally accepted the value of gender impact statements. However, the label comes off a policy proposal as soon as it gets into government – it's very hard to trace a specific policy back to its origins. You just sow these little seeds and hope that something grows from them. (Hilary Land)

Ruth Lister worked, initially, from a different kind of space: she spent some sixteen years in the Child Poverty Acton Group (CPAG) before becoming an academic. She served as a member of the Commission for Social Justice, set up in the early 1990s by John Smith to advise the Labour Party; was a member of the Commission on Poverty, Participation and Power, with a focus on the participation of people in poverty in decision-making (Commission on Poverty, Participation and Power 2000); and a member of the Fabian Commission on Life Chances and Child Poverty, the National Equality Panel, and many other boards and campaigning groups. She described her work as being focused on securing legislative and policy reform:

Because of my work with CPAG, I have always had a parliamentary focus, trying to get change through Parliament. Even in the Women's Liberation Movement, we were campaigning for legislative change to ensure women's legal and financial independence. But we also tried to live the future in the present, modelling the kind of society we wanted. CPAG worked a lot both with people in government and the opposition – we had good links with the Labour Party in opposition. We did seminars at No.11 [home of Chancellor of the Exchequer] on child poverty through the Smith Institute. As an academic my work on feminist perspectives on citizenship has informed policy interventions on lots of issues, including parental leave, and the work on poverty also fed into the work of the Women's Budget Group, one of the main intermediary institutions. (Ruth Lister)

Sue Himmelweit was the first Chair of the Women's Budget Group, a think tank which does gender audits of budgets, financial statements and expenditure plans as well as response to particular consultations. This is part of a wider transnational movement promoting gender impact assessments which has had a considerable impact within the EU and on agencies concerned with international development. In the UK the Women's Budget Group comprises a small core group – all working voluntarily – and a wider network of women bringing different forms of expertise. Sue described how, under New Labour, its work contributed to the political climate which led to the introduction of legislation requiring public bodies to conduct gender impact assessments of policies and services (the Equality Act 2006). As Sue argued, these were not extensively implemented before the change of government in 2010, and the potential impact of the legislation has subsequently been weakened as the Treasury sought to pass responsibility for assessing the gender impact of budgetary measures (including public service cuts and changes to benefits) to local authorities or individual ministries. Nevertheless the Women's Budget Group played a significant role in drawing attention to the likely impact of the then new Coalition government's 2010 spending review, showing how cuts to benefits and services would impact disproportionately on women (Women's Budget Group, 2010). The Fawcett Society then used this evidence to challenge the government, through a process of judicial review, on its failure to conduct a gender impact assessment of its June 2010 Emergency Budget when first elected. This challenge was not successful, but the Treasury acknowledged that it was regrettable that such an assessement had not been done and subsequently conducted a limited gender equality impact assessment on the following year's budget. The work of the group continues.

There are several points I want to pull out of these accounts. First, although these are individual interviews there is a very strong sense of a feminist community: the interview transcripts are littered with the names of academics, policy actors, campaigners, equality activists, elected politicians and civil servants who had known each other for a long time and who had collectively learned how to link feminist politics, campaigning and policy interventions to good effect. Sue noted in particular the significance of women such as Fran Bennett, and Hilary Land recounted with some pride how twenty-five years on from the original 1970s campaign, 'we had a party of members of the original group and all of us had kept feminism going in our working and personal lives in various ways'. Such networks, at the time, spanned the civil servant/activist/academic boundaries and challenged any clear distinction between 'insiders' (those working inside policy circles) and 'outsiders' (campaigners and activists). However Sue Himmelweit noted how relationships with Treasury ministers and officials, never as open to outside influence as other government departments, had, in 2012, shifted from the period in which the WBG had been regularly consulted and in which it has been possible to foster networks with government advisers and occassionally with sympathetic ministers.

Second, the spaces of power were both relationally constituted and, as the life stories of Hilary, Ruth and Sue show, stretched over time, opening up and closing down in different political contexts and having constantly to be remade as policy actors moved on. And successes were ambiguous, with policies tending to become detached from the feminist politics that informed their making, but sometimes leading to a strengthening of feminist activism (as in campaigns around the Coalition government's economic and social policies). Third, there is no single gender agenda. We can see how the nature of the struggles moved on from challenging the 'male breadwinner' model to helping shape 'family-friendly' policies, working to prioritize issues of poverty and care, participating in the formation of New Labour's national childcare strategy, working on parental leave and so on. However in 2012 feminist academics and campaigners were highlighting the implications of proposed benefit changes – in particular the introduction of a universal benefit that would be means-tested on household income and paid for the whole household to a single household member. This, it was argued, would reverse the idea that women should be treated as independent economic actors and potentially lead to the return of a 'male breadwinner' model (even if framed in gender neutral terms). This was, at the time this book went to press, being challenged by Sue's work in the Women's Budget Group and by Ruth's attempt to bring feminist perspectives into deliberations on a new welfare reform bill in the House of Lords.

The wider body of interviews suggest the breadth of feminist issues and agendas that campaigners pursued, the links between different struggles and the intersections of multiple-identity claims. They also show the significance of the network of feminist institutions and lobby groups that the second-wave and gay liberation movements had generated, including the Women's Budget Group, Fawcett Society, Stonewall and campaigning organizations on contraception, abortion, domestic violence and the treatment of victims of rape and abuse. What is at stake here is the relationship between broad social movements that operate in what Nancy Fraser (Fraser 1990) described as 'counter-public' spaces – spaces in which new identities and solidarities could form, separate from and in opposition to the mainstream public sphere – and more 'professionalized' interventions in the public sphere to try to bring about change. But this distinction suggests a binary between 'counter-public' and 'public' that is not sustainable here; the 'close encounters' with which this chapter is concerned took place in spaces of power sustained by personal connections to collective groups and wider political projects.

The work of Angela Mason (G2) suggests something of the power of such projects to influence legislative change. Angela had been active in trade union and Communist Party politics, and had been tried and acquitted in the Angry Brigade trials of 1972. She was an early member of the Gay Liberation Front and of the gay rights group Stonewall, of which she became Executive Director in 1992. She described Stonewall as a 'professional lobbying group' on gay agendas, on legislation on the age of consent, on the recognition of civil partnerships and on the repeal of legislation banning the teaching of homosexuality in schools:[1]

I mean if you take some of the [legal] cases that we did. The first big case I did was on the age of consent, and actually that was a hard issue because it was the age of consent of sex and sex is always quite a tricky issue, although the press always like sex. We were always concerned in whatever we did, whether it was campaigning for a vote in Parliament or taking a legal case, we tried to do it in such a way that increased public understanding.

So in all our legal cases, whether on the age of consent or later on civil partnership, we tried to find articulate and sympathetic claimants, and we sort of put them out in the public media. Because one of the secrets of campaigning is that campaigners can talk all they want but they are never quite believed as much as the people who are actually feeling the pinch. You have to beware of the sort of lobbying voice, and you have to try and organise things so that the alternative voice – the voice of experience – comes through.

I mean to be fair those sort of politics were actually rather different from the Women's Movement – the Women's Movement wasn't very practical or strategic at all, so I don't know quite how it managed to get the changes it did. I think sort of being a lawyer probably helped a little bit, and then having that work professionally, and that helped a bit as well, and I think perhaps my vast [Communist] Party background might have helped a bit. (Angela Mason)

Angela's work shows the power of pragmatic political skills, honed both through radical activism and Communist Party membership, allied with legal and media skills, and she has had considerable impact on the equalities landscape through her work (see also discussion in Hunter and Swan 2007). The power she describes is tactical, strategic; indeed, she makes an explicit contrast with the Women's Liberation Movement that was 'never very practical or strategic at all'.[2]

A rather different perspective is offered by Davina Cooper, from the G3 cohort, who served on the Women's Committee of a London borough as an elected councillor and spoke about the tensions associated with working in equality roles:

The approach I took was to enter institutional spaces but without compromising politically too much. These weren't easy spaces, and any power I had was short-lived because I wanted to work ethically according to my principles and political commitments. But I was working in a decision-making terrain that was of course already hugely structured and constrained, and I was too young maybe, and didn't have the skill to turn my commitments into practice – people talk about working through networks, creating alliances, constantly building up support ... but certainly then I wasn't a good networker, though I had one success – as chair of Community Development – I did manage to stop the council pulling funding from an Asian community centre. (Davina Cooper)

There is a suggested contrast here between the extensive political skills and tactical use of power depicted by Angela Mason and the strong ethical stance and unwillingness to compromise in Davina's account. But such a contrast is too stark; both were highly skilled women who successfully pursued social and political change, but from rather different spaces of power (Angela continued in high-profile equality and party political roles while Davina later became an academic). And many women combined strong personal and political commitments with tactical skills. Theresa Stewart (G1) became involved in Labour Party politics before the days of the second-wave women's movement, but later brought an explicitly feminist politics into her political roles in local government, working on health, education, contraception and community development, all of which are critical issues in shaping the quality of women's lives. Jane Foot, from a later generation, combined strong socialist, feminist politics with different forms of 'state work', supported by a collective ethos of working 'in and against the state'. She was very involved in a range of practices that linked critical perspectives to campaigns for better provision:

> *I think it's that thing of – where do you think the critical points are for women? I became very strongly involved in housing, and the kind of welfare state I suppose, because for me the poorest women – their quality of life was not only determined by their wages but by issues of housing, of benefits, of domestic violence, the quality of their home life, their family life. And that's where I saw that as socialist feminists we could be most powerful, and that analysis about the role of the welfare state – we were part of a women and housing group, I was very active around council housing, and that for me was about the quality of life for women. Actually, a really good quality social housing sector would be the greatest contribution you could make to the quality of life for women. And it was quite hard, it was a hard argument to make at the time, when it was all about wages and equal opportunities – the welfare state was not seen as a really important site of struggle for feminism. I think now that understanding is much more widespread, but in the mid seventies, if you look at the big campaigns we had they were about equal pay, abortion, it wasn't council housing. (Jane Foot)*

This is, however, a very UK-centred depiction of what were the critical spaces for women. Ida Susser's work on supporting women organizing in response to the AIDS epidemic in Africa tells a different story (Susser 2009). She helped form Athena: Advancing Gender Equity and Human Rights in the Global Response to HIV/AIDS and, as well as work in Africa, worked within the United States to defend budgets for AIDS preventative programmes.

These extracts illustrate the very diverse spaces of power from which women sought to influence social and political change, and something of the range of skills and political orientations they brought to that work. They suggest the breadth of the agendas being pursued, from benefits to care, from domestic violence to parenting, from housing to work/life balance, from campaigns to make contraception available to unmarried women to campaigns for the legal recognition of civil partnerships. They also show the multiple feminisms at stake and the complex entanglements between them. I return to the work of some of these participants in subsequent chapters, showing how their work evolved to address different constraints and opportunities. But first I want to focus on one set of issues that intensified the focus on cross-cutting work and the delivery of complex policy outcomes: issues of children, families and parenting.

Remaking governance

We saw in the previous chapter how policy spaces were generated in the UK during the Thatcher years, and how some women elaborated a politics of 'in and against the state' to inform their critical engagements with state power. Here, I show how women mobilized spaces of power within the proliferating policy initiatives of New Labour. These enabled many participants with backgrounds in community-based, voluntary, charitable and campaigning organizations to become powerful policy actors. I focus in particular on three participants. Naomi Eisenstadt (G2) had gained extensive experience in the voluntary sector, culminating in the directorship of the National Council for Voluntary Organisations (NCVO). This, she reflected, gave her the opportunity to establish powerful networks, but *it wasn't for me – defending a sector held no interest for me, I knew I was interested in women, children, sex education – I wanted a cause*. This led her to the Family Service Units (see Chapter 5) then to two major government programmes addressing poverty and exclusion under the New Labour government: Sure Start and the Social Exclusion Unit. Mary MacLeod (G2) was part of the emergence of second-wave feminism in Edinburgh, working on issues of domestic violence and helping establish women's refuges. After training as a social worker she worked for Barnardo's, which at the time was mainly a provider of children's homes. She went on to teach social work both in Edinburgh University and North London Polytechnic; became involved in the charity ChildLine, where she ran a twenty-four-hour counselling service for young people; and then went on to head the National Family and Parenting Institute (now Family and Parenting Institute, FPI), *an organization that's involved in policy research, voice, information – all the things I was involved in at ChildLine*. Lisa Harker (G3) worked for the Daycare Trust, the Child Poverty Action Group, the Save the Children Fund and the left-leaning think-tank, the Institute for Public Policy Research (IPPR), before working as an advisor to the Treasury on the development of New Labour's ten-year childcare strategy and then becoming the government's Childcare Czar.

The appointment of these three women to roles that carried considerable power and influence reflects a number of related shifts in governance that took place in the 1990s and beyond. The 'governance narrative' (Rhodes 1997) tells of a shift to a plural polity and more reflexive style of governance. This narrative has been widely criticized: as I have argued elsewhere (Newman 2001; Newman 2005a) there was no clear shift from government to governance or from hierarchy to networks. But three issues are worth noting. The first reflects the strong New Labour policy focus on children and families. This can be understood as emerging out of the success of feminism in the transformation of social policy addressed in the previous section. The second generated shifts in the policy process itself. External stakeholders were drawn into policy circles, 'expertise' and evidence became valorized, think-tanks and advisors were drawn close to politicians and the Civil Service, and there was a new emphasis on public participation. Third, the institutional architecture of government changed; Sure Start, the Social Exclusion Unit, FPI, a long-term childcare strategy and a Childcare Czar signalled not only new policy foci but also a new way of 'doing' policy. Governments established multiple projects and initiatives, looked to local partnership working as a key lever of policy delivery, and devolved some responsibility for managing and evaluating policy to other agencies.

Participants in this research both helped generate these shifts and mobilized new spaces of power within them. Sure Start was a 'cross-cutting' policy agenda that encompassed issues of childcare, parenting, early education, health and family support, with an emphasis on collaborative working and local involvement of both stakeholders (professionals working in the field, funders, local governance bodies) and parents, grandparents and local communities. It was overseen by three different departments of government and was an early example of an attempt to deliver more 'joined up' governance. Naomi described the experience as follows:

> I think what you bring from the voluntary sector is an understanding of coalitions, and just working with the grain of what people want, which is very counter-cultural. In the Civil Service you work to a minister, and you work to a department, but working across departments seemed to challenge people. What was most interesting about it all was that I had no idea how different all this was. I didn't know that working across was a problem. I didn't understand about departmental policy. There was so much that was completely innovative about Sure Start but at the time I didn't know it was unusual. (Naomi Eisenstadt)

Each Sure Start project was shaped by local actors within the overarching requirements of the programme, and provision was usually through a partnership body comprising local authority, voluntary sector and professional stakeholders. This marked a profound shift in central/local relations, albeit one that was not sustained (Anning and Ball 2008; Belsky, Melhuish and Barnes 2007; and Naomi's own account, Eisenstadt 2011).

Mary MacLeod's work helped generate a shift towards more participative styles of policymaking. ChildLine raised issues of bullying, the position of children in care, child abuse, family relationships, and children and the law. Mary used evidence they had gathered from children in presenting evidence to an intergovernmental commission on children in care, and organized a major conference on 'Children and the Law' in 1999 that marked a shift towards enabling children's voices and interests to be inscribed in policymaking and legal practice. She drew extensively on this experience of bringing the voices of children directly to policymakers in her work at FPI:

> There's an assumption that professionals know best, and that professional intervention is by definition benign. But when you hear from children themselves about what they need in order to live their lives differently, and how they see

services as a kind of juggernaut coming into their lives, taking things over, you get a different view and a sense from the children themselves that it's always possible to change things. (Mary MacLeod)

FPI was one of the organizations pushing for a stronger place for public consultation and involvement in policy, and:

Well, I think it's all over government now in the sense that they have to consult parents and families. Some years ago there were lots of policy documents that didn't have such consultation, so we set up parent/politician events with lead politicians. I don't think that [consultation] would exist in the same way without us. (Mary MacLeod)

It is fruitful to compare this focus on consultation to the work of Carole Harte and other community-based actors discussed in chapter 3; while the spaces of power are very different, both were concerned with bringing population groups excluded from power into direct communication with policy actors (see also Barnes *et al.* 2007).

Mary also typifies the paradoxes associated with the 'close encounters' of this chapter. She described her role at FPI as trying to be the 'voice of reason' on family policy and described her work as:

the everyday business of trying to influence the public and political conversation on 'the family' and to make it less punitive about particular families: not only those that were not two-parent heterosexual, but those with working mothers. And it was about the attempt to get into the public domain recognition of the effect, not only of poverty, but of other influences like the commercialization of neighbourhoods, the absence of play, long working hours, all the issues that are now bundled into 'family-friendly' policies. We were trying to fight the 'blame the parents' narrative. (Mary MacLeod)

This public conversation was conducted with other feminist academics (those at the Centre for Care, Values and the Future of Welfare[3] as well as women associated with the Women's Budget Group and Fawcett Society); with policy actors who had been touched by feminism; with some voluntary organizations and NGOs, and so on. They took such conversations not only into policy circles but to the media, party conferences and the wider political landscape. This was remarkably successful: the term 'family-friendly' policy was adopted by politicians of all political persuasions in Britain. But there is something of a paradox here. Family-friendly policies secured substantial benefits for women struggling to combine care and paid work responsibilities, or to survive on low incomes. It also brought benefits for men as fathers. But the price was that the phrase became stripped of its feminist associations and used in conjunction with other political projects, for example, those that valorized 'hard-working families' and denigrated other population groups. At the same time, as Mary remarked, the tendency to blame families for problems of crime, ill-health, poor education and worklessness continues, sharpening considerably in the aftermath of the disturbances in English cities in August 2011.

Think-tanks were a rather different contributor to public conversations. They were not usually a space for 'progressive' politics, but often provided spaces of power through which participants could exert influence. Lisa Harker described how the think-tank role had advantages over campaigning organizations in that think-tanks got listened to where other agencies might not. She also contrasted her role with that of FPI:

> Mary would have to get into a lot of detail because of her area of specialism, she must be official, she must have a strong commitment to the department she faced. Whereas I think there's a lot more freedom around the special advisors, and the political journalists, and that sort of whole world of rather murky ... all the other ways of influencing to get where the power is, particular under Blair. I mean the departments became less powerful (apart from the Treasury), and the special advisors in and around No.10 wielded a lot of the power, so I guess in short I think think-tanks know how to wield power in those environments rather than having to use the formal channels which many organizations would have had to focus on. (Lisa Harker)

I asked Lisa where she got her ideas from.

> Largely from other people so actually a lot of ideas aren't really new ideas. One of the success stories would be the Child Trust Fund, which was invented in an IPPR handbook. Actually the idea came from the United States. So yes, you get your ideas by scouting around for other people's ideas. And the thing that I think we could do very well was to try to broker a way forward between different opinions in different parties. So if you're working on environmental issues, for example, Greenpeace would take a line and say 'no more gas or coal-fired power stations', and the government line might be 'we have to do that, or it's the nuclear option'. IPPR would disengage with both sides, and try to find a way through that was a balance between those two principles. And I think that made us sort of unpopular with purists who would stick to their fundamental principles, but it's a way of ensuring that any policy that gets made isn't as bad as it might have been. (Lisa Harker)

There are some stark implicit contrasts here: between the independent broker role which she attributes to IPPR and the role of campaigners who have a clear position on an issue (though Mary also spoke about being the 'voice of reason' between different interests); between the 'murky' world of politics where influence can happen and 'official' channels; between practical politics and 'purists'. The extracts also point to two different kinds of work: one concerned with generating new things (the Child's Trust Fund, for example) and the other mediating between different interests in order to make policy 'less bad' than it might otherwise have been.

These accounts suggest something of the changing nature of the spaces of power participants generated and they ways in which these produced 'close encounters' with policy and governmental actors. The period of the Third Way governments in Britain and beyond saw the emergence of 'joined up governance', 'partnership' and 'participation' as dominant policy discourses. These spaces emerged in part from the styles of 'doing' policy and governance that had been developed by women 'knitting together' people, movements and campaigns in multiple spaces of power. They came to greater significance as those who had worked in voluntary sector or community-based projects took on governance roles in an expanded and plural policy. This was no accident – women with fractured working lives were less likely to climb an established occupational ladder than to find spaces emerging from and constitutive of 'new' governing rationales. That is, women were highly active in new governance forms but also used the new spaces of power these offered to initiate new pathways and projects.

Many such pathways and projects focused on the complex policy problems that arose in the aftermath of Thatcherism: urban deprivation, child poverty, social exclusion and other 'wicked issues'. In turn, they opened up space for new cross-cutting agendas to be raised: on health and well-being, domestic violence, community safety, obesity and nutrition, climate change and so on. Such problems were 'wicked issues' in that they had no clear and agreed definition, were associated with multiple interlocking causes and could not be resolved by any single agency or department of government alone. 'Partnerships' opened up particularly significant spaces of power, not least because of the ways in which relatively junior actors and senior institutional and policy actors were brought to the same table. This did not eradicate power differences but did generate contingent spaces of opportunity. The next example is taken from the account of Julia Lowndes (G3), a local government worker who used her post as lead officer on a community safety partnership body to develop and improve provision on domestic violence and sexual health:

> I went to a conference in London about domestic violence, and it was about the health responses that we were all shouting about at the time because they were so dreadful. Towards the end there was a kind of opposite number to me working in Community Safety [in a London borough], and she talked about their 'Snapshot Project' which provided cameras to the local Women's Aid for women who didn't want to go to the police, so that they could photograph their injuries and keep a record, and I thought, 'My God, that's a good idea' so came back to [Birmingham] and worked with a group called Healthy Gay Life [serving men who work in the sex trade] as well as Women's Aid, Victim Support and others to get funding to get that started. All these groups had been in competition with one and another for funding, and now we're together, they'll be getting the cameras for free, together with training from the police. It's been about bringing the third sector in and getting the statutory sector to think outside of the box; getting the police to provide training for the voluntary sector when they knew that people wouldn't come to them to report crimes like domestic violence or homophobic crime, and they stuck their neck out there because we put the seed money in and convinced people this was a good idea. (Julia Lowndes)

Such work shows how ideas are 'pulled down' or 'translated' from other places and people and made to work in a new context. This offers a rather different sense of translation from that discussed in the previous chapter, where community-based claims, needs or languages were 'translated' in ways that rendered them acceptable to policymakers. Here the process of translation is one in which issues are resignified or rebadged so that they could be levered into existing policy programmes and resource streams. The extract from Julia hints at the work of resignification: here a process in which domestic violence comes to be represented as a health issue, thus rendering it a suitable issue for funding and coordinated action in order to represent the views of marginalized citizens to government.

This work can be viewed through Larner and Craig's study of partnerships in Aotearoa, New Zealand (Larner and Craig 2005). The 'strategic brokers' they identify tend to be community activists who move into more formally recognized roles as local issues become politicized and partnerships become a favoured technology of governing. They emphasize that women are disproportionately represented in these brokering roles, but the political context of their work remains fraught. Brokers are required to translate their political goals into technical processes and to emphasize collaboration over conflict. And while the process skills they offer are significant assets, these are severely stretched to deal with the multiple pressures of their role (see also Newman 2001). Larner and Craig view such pressures as arising from the work of joining up the fragmentation arising from a previous phase of neoliberalism: 'In this way, the neoliberal state gets to have its cake and eat it too, courtesy of the expanded domestic domains of feminised strategic brokers' (Larner and Craig 2005: 27). But the paradox is that such brokers can also mobilize the spaces of power that partnerships offer to secure 'other agendas' and alternative political projects.

The politics of 'mainstreaming' and 'monitoring'

The previous section showed how activists worked with policymakers and mobilized new governance arrangements in which the borders between politics and policy became blurred. Here, I turn to how participants sought to make their achievements and successes 'stick' by rendering them into governance technologies that were less dependent on the willingness of specific actors to maintain them. 'Mainstreaming' equality and 'monitoring' global patterns of exploitation were, in different ways, examples of the tensions this generated.

Mainstreaming

Equal opportunity work was not a primary focus of my study, but the accounts do open up important questions about how such work is remembered and currently understood. Lisa Duggan (Duggan 2003), writing about the fate of feminism in the context of the rise of neoliberal economic policies in the United States, argues that the neoliberal endorsement of 'equality feminism' and 'gay normality' were part of a process of mainstreaming associated with 'Third Way' rhetoric, a process that acknowledged diversity as a means of appropriating identity politics. McRobbie (McRobbie 2009) builds on this to trace what she terms a 'cultural process of "undoing"' (McRobbie 2009: 30) of the politics of feminism. She describes the emergence of a 'gender aware' governmentality that takes feminism into account (McRobbie 2009: 140). But it is only liberal, 'equality feminism' that was taken into account at the expense of radical feminism's concerns with social criticism. The decline of feminism, she suggests, goes in parallel to the mainstreaming of women's issues. She is highly critical of Sylvia Walby's support of mainstreaming strategies:

> Gender mainstreaming can be thought of as a non-conflictual accommodating kind of programme or schema which follows a path which has some equalising potential, but which in essence can be absorbed and taken on board by the structures and institutions of capitalism. When, earlier in this book I have talked about 'feminism being taken into account', it is this strain of feminism which permits offices of government to claim that women's interests are indeed being looked after. The vocabulary of gender mainstreaming is 'modern', managerial and professional, a programmatic approach, with all kinds of tools for evaluation and assessment of outcomes which can be enrolled as marks of good practice within corporate as well as state and public sector institutions. (McRobbie 2009: 154)

In a similar vein Angela Mason came under extensive criticism for her work at Stonewall from gay rights lobbies who depicted her work as a professionalization of sexual politics and as promoting a 'normalization' of heterosexual models of partnership and marriage (e.g. Richardson 2005). These are convincing critiques, but operate at a high level of abstraction that separate governance technologies from agency. I will return to such debates in Chapter 8, but here want to draw on the accounts of early practitioners of mainstreaming working in particular spaces of power (left-leaning institutions) at a specific political/cultural moment (the 1980s). Marion Macalpine (G2) held a post as an Equal Opportunities Officer within the GLC:

> *There were 20,000 GLC staff, and my role was to set up programmes in FE [further education] colleges that would allow access to interview to good jobs in the GLC at different levels. It was a big scheme with lots of places on it, and it was targeted to women, ethnic minorities, lesbians and gay men, and people with disabilities. Class was not mentioned but it was all about second-chance education. Obviously all of us in the Unit were involved as well in setting up and developing all those recruitment and development procedures, which have now become totally formulaic and discredited. However, at that time it was a huge shift, wasn't it? It did feel amazing to be in at the beginning of that. But now they've now become formulaic and wrongly used.* (Marion Macalpine)

Avtar Brah, of the same generational cohort, also worked on equality issues in the GLC; after its closure in 1985 she went to work at Birkbeck, a college within the University of London:

> *My job was an unusual one. I was a lecturer in multicultural studies, expected to develop education programmes that would attract students who wouldn't normally come – second-chance students. There wasn't resistance to developing the work – but they wanted me to speak to large meetings (of the whole faculty) about multiculturalism. But I said I didn't want to be the multicultural specialist, that something had to be done across the board. And the Director was behind me. Politicking was key; we had to be creative. I think the most creative part of my work, with Jane Hoy, Mary Kennedy and with five or six other women, we decided that we would try to mainstream it within the faculty. We set up the first equal opportunity group, we asked every section of the faculty to look at the nature of their students and what kinds of tutors they had. This was the most difficult part of the work but because we had backing people had to do it. Lots of creative things were done, some very creative courses were developed. I don't know what's happened since – directors change, the politics moves, but for a few years we had a very active kind of EO policy and practice programme. (Avtar Brah)*

The extracts show how the 'invention' of mainstreaming was possible because of positive alignments between activist concerns and a sympathetic institutional climate: the GLC (a left-wing local government body) and Birkbeck (an education institution historically committed to attracting students from a wide range of class backgrounds). Both participants referred, prompted, to its impoverishment over time. I noticed that Avtar used the word 'mainstreaming' and asked if it was around in the 1980s:

> *No, that came afterwards. We were doing it [mainstreaming, widening participation] before there was a word for it. Now, of course, it happens because of legislation as well as because senior management have been made responsible for widening participation. But it's a different kind of ballgame now. Some of the creativity is lost as it goes beyond the special moment when we were working with grassroots women, part-time students. Now it comes from the top, has a different kind of impact. (Avtar Brah)*

Similarly, Marion reflected on how equality procedures had become 'formulaic' and 'wrongly used'. What had been lost, in part, were the 'close encounters' that sustained political momentum. Looking back to the notions of translation introduced above, equality politics had become one, and only one, element of new assemblages of actors, laws, policy guidelines, committees, job descriptions, management practices, appeals procedures, training handbooks, performance management systems and audit mechanisms. And as Tania Li has argued, in a different context, the process of assemblage can serve to render an issue into a technical matter and thus depoliticize it (Li 2007b; see also Newman and Clarke 2009).

Viewing mainstreaming as an assemblage of diverse elements draws attention to its ambiguity. What happens in any particular time and place cannot be predicted since elements can be combined and recombined in new ways, with unpredictable outcomes. I want, then, to point to two rather different assemblages of equality work that took place some years after the pioneering work of Avtar and Marion. Here is Adi Cooper talking about her work a strategic director in local government in the 2000s:

> There's never been any kind of focus on LGBT [lesbian, gay, bisexual and transgender] work in the borough, and someone from the police force wanted to set up a forum. My role was to support that and it is now established. The approach was for all of us to make personal pledges to support this issue and work for change. That's using my power [as a strategic director]. And in terms of the sort of formalized equality standards within the council, my bit of the council is ahead of the rest because I think I'm pushing people all the time, asking what they are doing, what they could do. (Adi Cooper)

Angela Mason, whose work as a political campaigner in Stonewall was described earlier, later took up a post in the Blair government, heading what was then the Women's Equality Unit:

> Ministers control the whole thing but I think you have to generate enthusiasm. You have to sort of have a vision that this is possible and persuade others of that position, and so you don't get sort of ... because there's more stuff in the Civil Service that will knock you back absolutely all of the time. Much more than if you're a director of a small organization where you can say, 'I'm going to do this', and then you do it and if it works then you get the sort of glory of it, whereas in government you have to stick to your guns but you do have to enthuse people. Both Bills I was involved had a lot of stakeholder input, and involved a lot of working across government departments. So you have to build relationships, actually. I mean when you're trying to persuade Conservatives to come on board with gay rights or persuade other departments not just put a block on it. That's what you have to stop them doing, and you do it through building relationships, I think. (Angela Mason)

I told Angela that this had come through very strongly with everybody to whom I had talked, and asked what kind of stakeholders she had involved in the preparation of the Bills.

> Well, we had a lot of discussions, listening to the gay community, partnerships, and then with the EHRC [Equality and Human Rights Commission]. We had a Stakeholder Task Group, which we took quite seriously trying to arrive at key decisions about the shape of the new Commission. Even so far as some of the parliamentary drafting we did with stakeholders – that was quite a first. (Angela Mason)

I asked if there was much resistance.

> Oh, there was enormous resistance – I mean there really was a sort of root and branch opposition. But I think by the end of it we had created quite a good platform. (Angela Mason)

These extracts from Adi and Angela show how equality work was not simply a set of bureaucratic instruments used to deliver 'mainstreamed' programmes but remained political work; and also show how it adapted to the 'new governance' style of policy work noted earlier, based on partnerships and high stakeholder involvement. But each also drew on technologies (the 'personal pledge'), policy scripts and equality discourses. They each reassembled elements of past actions and events: in Angela's case, of prior attempts to institutionalize equality at the centre of government; in Adi's case, the legacies of a police service's responses to earlier charges of 'institutional racism'[4] and its subsequent attempts to forge equality partnerships. They each also signalled new elements of equality assemblages: the shift to 'human rights' discourse and the inclusion of bisexual and transgender issues.

At the same time mainstreaming itself was becoming mainstreamed as institutional practice, being taken up in the governance instruments of the European Union, the International Labour Organization (ILO) and other global, national and regional institutions. The New Public Management of the 1990s offered new instruments, including performance measurement, target setting and audit procedures that were readily appropriated by activists. Gender mainstreaming predominated over other possible axes of equality policy and as a result some – but only some – feminist agendas were acknowledged within social policy and some women were included in policy circles and in governance institutions. But, following McRobbie's argument, these inclusions concerned the progress or improvement of the position of women in an otherwise unchanged social order. Those elements of feminism that had transformational potential remained 'outside' the mainstream, and not incorporated into policy and practice.

There is much to agree with here, but I want to raise a few concerns. One is the idea of a clear distinction that can be made between liberal and radical feminisms: many of the women interviewed seemed to work across these categories. For example, Theresa Stewart, a lifelong Labour Party activist, was strongly associated with mainstreaming women's issues within Labour Party politics and within the local authority of which she served, for a period, as leader. But she also successfully campaigned on extending the availability of contraceptive advice for unmarried women. Angela Mason, who used her political skills to campaign for radical and revolutionary political agendas, also worked to secure 'liberal' changes such as the recognition of civil partnerships. She reflected, somewhat ironically, on having herself become mainstreamed as the issues about which she was concerned were acknowledged in policy, and it is certainly the case that in her later roles in the Women's Equality Unit and the Equality and Human Rights Commission she had become deeply entangled in government. But she continued to offer radical perspectives on power and agency and, at the time of the interview, was continuing her political work as Deputy Leader of Camden Council.

Second, processes of appropriation and resignification are not unidirectional: spaces of power are those in which actors can mobilize governmental resources and appropriate governmental discourses. The inclusion, development and empowerment programmes that proliferated under New Labour drew extensively on feminist praxis. Funding streams could be co-opted to generate rather more politicized subjects and assertive actors than public policy had envisaged. In addition, we can see how this work sought to transform not only the subjects involved but also the agencies concerned. Equality mainstreaming can co-opt activists, but perhaps can also be viewed as a process through which social movements can co-opt the state, its functions, powers and resources. I do not want here to celebrate their success: my focus, rather, is on the paradoxes that arise in such 'close encounters'; how such paradoxes are differently experienced and lived in particular, time-specific governmental projects; and, over time, how the focus shifted from questions of 'how could policy change be secured' to 'how could policy provisions be monitored and institutionalized'.

Monitory power

Monitoring was a key element of equality policy, but was also used in contexts where national or institutional policy had insufficient reach. Keane (Keane 2009) has drawn attention to what he terms the rise of 'monitory democracy' – the public scrutiny and control of unaccountable power. His argument is that contemporary, especially global, dynamics and flows of power now reach into areas in which democratic institutions can only play a limited role. Monitory power takes place through media scrutiny, blogging, congresses and through new forms of cross-border institution. It is central to the work of the Women's Budget Group, discussed earlier, and to the wider movement promoting gender impact assessments. It is also exercised through a proliferating array of standards and codes of conduct.

The growing significance of monitory power is situated in contemporary problems of accountability and legitimacy in plural systems of governance. It has given rise to a huge proliferation of institutions concerned with quality, inspection, audit and evaluation (Power 1994; Newman 2001). These developments have been widely criticized. The nature of 'evidence' is always open to contestation, and the instrumentalism of measurement and monitoring practices detaches data from the experiences out of which campaigns and other forms of activism emerge. But, like mainstreaming, monitory power can also be appropriated and levered by activists. Social movements across the globe have used measures such as audit and measurement, monitoring and reporting both to bring particular forms of inequality to public attention and to secure forms of redress for those who have experienced breaches of laws and other policy instruments.

It is interesting that two of the participants in this research, Sukhwant Dhaliwal and Sasha Roseneil, from different generations and from very different political backgrounds, had both been involved in Newham Monitoring Project, formed in the early 1980s as a community-based anti-racist project in the face of the failure of statutory bodies to address racist attacks and to monitor police harassment of the Black community. The Gender Audit Project on which Hannah Berry worked is part of an international turn to audit and evaluation of equality goals, and its promotion by bodies such as the ILO. And the challenge to the 2010 UK coalition government budget by the Fawcett Society represents a significant use of audit and scrutiny to check government action. While the Fawcett Society's bid for judicial review of the 2010 budget did not succeed, its actions brought the likely effects of the budget on women and others into the public domain and generated considerable debate.

Monitory power is also inscribed in a proliferating array of review bodies, public enquiries, and the appointment of 'independent' lay and expert representatives on boards, trusts and commissions. Marian Barnes (G3), a social policy academic and activist promoting service-user involvement and rights, was invited to become a Mental Health Act Commissioner, and she became particularly interested in the position of women detained in high security facilities. In the early 1990s she gave evidence at a public inquiry into the treatment of patients, in particular women patients, at Ashworth Hospital; the inquiry was one of the factors that eventually led to the decision that women should no longer be admitted to such high security facilities:

> This [being a Commissioner] was for me a very important experience. I did very much feel that being involved in MHAC [Mental Health Act Commission] was an opportunity to influence 'from the inside' even though many regarded MHAC as toothless. And the experience of women in the special hospital system was extreme – an issue that rarely gets made public. I felt I was bringing together research-based knowledge with a commitment to women who were in highly powerless situations in a context in which I had a route to power. And in doing so I was making an alliance with a woman on the inside (as in working in the system) who needed an ally because of the awfulness of the experience of working there as well as because of her commitment to the women who were patients. So one of the issues for me was that it was an experience of being able to be more effective in influencing policy thinking through involvement in what was a statutory regulatory body, rather than through research. (Marian Barnes)

I will return to Marian's account in Chapter 6, where I explore the turn to evidence and expertise in public policy more fully; but of particular interest here is the alliance between external 'experts' and internal 'whistleblowers' in bringing issues of exploitation and abuse to public attention.

Finally, monitory power is associated with the growing significance of global struggles for social justice. The human rights lawyer Camilla Warren (G3) describes how, in her earlier CND work with women's groups in Asia and Africa:

> *we were trying to work towards global labour standards to stop companies subcontracting in ways that exploited local labour forces across different supply chains, going to the lowest standards to expand their profit margins. We tried to build on commonalities, on the common experiences of people working in these various supply chains, people who happen to be women in usually part time work. We linked up with trade unions and tried to exert pressure so that all of the workers in a particular supply chain, whatever the country, could have common legally enforceable labour standards. But the NGOs that were involved – the politics was rather wishy-washy, they didn't have a strong enough critique and couldn't form critical blocks, and the trade unions were a bit all over the shop as well. So it was co-opted by an institution called the Ethical Trade Union Initiative, which was a partnership of companies, NGOs and trade unions, and it ended up with companies dominating it. It became all about auditing when I think it should have focused on campaigning for a living wage, that's what women need. It all became around health and safety and social audits, which at the end of the day they never really do that much. Anyway companies are constantly squeezing factories on price in order to get cheaper and cheaper goods here [the UK]. It doesn't matter how many audits you do, because the conditions are just getting worse anyway.* (Camilla Warren)

This extract draws attention to the limitations of monitory power, limitations that resonate with my earlier discussion of mainstreaming. That is, it can be co-opted and detached from the politics that generated it. Camilla explicitly contrasts 'auditing' with 'campaigning', emphasizing the weakness of the former. Kate Raworth, who worked for Oxfam on global supply chains and women's work, was also doubtful about the power of standards and codes of conduct:

> *Well you know these factory managers are incredibly difficult to regulate, so retailers were hiring NGOs to go round trying to monitor them, and it was all about enforcing the code of conduct and making sure the factory manager behaved – a very policing role. And the whole NGO debate was about how do you monitor effectively, and do you do surprise visits or not. What we tried to do in our campaigning – and I'm very proud that I feel we did it successfully and it really did shift the terms of debate – was to say to the retailers, 'It's not just about monitoring what's going on in the factories, you need to look at your own terms of trading, your own purchasing practices.'* (Kate Raworth)

I asked Kate for an example.

> *Tesco's, for example, has somebody whose job it is to talk to suppliers about its code of conduct, to monitor its implementation, but then they have a buyer who might say, 'Well, I want it 30 per cent cheaper, I want it delivered faster, and I'm going to give you less regular, less advanced notice.' So monitoring the code of conduct is divorced from the purchasing practices. And you can see how the supermarkets are passing the costs and risks of business down the supply chain. It's called lean manufacturing, and it's a wonderful business model for supermarkets,*

working with minimal stocks, fast turnaround and just-in-time delivery. But we showed that this results in incredibly insecure working conditions for women on the farms and in the factories, hired on temporary contracts, pressured to work overtime, or left standing at the factory bus stop each morning, not knowing whether they will get any work that day ...

The work we did looked at how pressures were passed through the supply chain in twelve countries, focused on the garment and fresh produce sectors. We showed how the principles of lean manufacturing were translating into poor terms and conditions particularly for women employed in these sectors. And the report had a significant impact. Certainly in the UK it shifted the terms of debate amongst retailers within the Ethical Trading Initiative from talking about codes of conduct to talking about their purchasing practices with their suppliers. It was fascinating when we first met with retailers and said, 'Tell us about how you ensure labour standards in your supply chains.' Oh, they had lots to say about monitoring their codes of conduct, and then we said, 'Well, what about your own purchasing practices?', and we were met with an absolute silence – they didn't know what to say, they'd never thought about it. That was how we knew we had hit on something. (Kate Raworth)

Both Camilla and Kate highlight the importance of political work alongside mainstreaming and monitoring standards. But both examples also show how the links between activism and policy work have been – in part – reconfigured to take account not only of the spread of new knowledge media but also the shifts of power within and beyond nation states. This speaks indirectly to, and perhaps adds a fresh perspective on, debates about the mainstreaming and monitoring of equality goals that have tended to dominate much feminist literature in recent years. It suggests how codified standards need to be set alongside more politicized concern with how and where power is exercised. It also suggests the need to set concerns about the employment rights of workers within a nation state against a more global sensibility of how patterns of exploitation are reconfigured as capitalist enterprises shift production sites to places where such rights may not exist.

As these examples show, the concept of monitory power is used to categorize highly diverse forms of power and agency. It is associated with government bodies of audit, inspection and quality assurance that seek to exert control over professional autonomy and judgement; with transnational NGOs that seek to secure new forms of global governance; with human rights lawyers and activists who seek to challenge governmental and corporate abuse and exploitation; with researchers seeking to generate and use knowledge as a political and policy resource; and with individuals bringing private actions within institutions into public view, either overtly (bringing information to the attention of the media) or covertly (through alliances with those with a respected public voice). We might extend this list to encompass academic research, citizen journalism and the use of the web as a means of generating new forms of public scrutiny. Condensing all of this into a single form of 'monitory' power that is – or is capable of – supplanting democratic power, as Keane claims, is problematic. The examples I have drawn on suggest highly different forms and uses of power, based on highly diverse forms of expertise and with differential access to resources that might generate publicity and action. Nevertheless, they point to the significance of transnational and transdisciplinary lines of communication and action; and to the importance of 'knowledge-work' as a form of political agency. I return to these themes in Chapters 6 and 7.

Conclusion

This chapter began with the question of how far 'close encounters' has led to the incorporation of activists as they engage in policy work that enmeshes them in dominant forms of political and institutional power. But in the course of the analysis a second question has opened up about how far 'success' in bringing about policy shifts and legal reforms is compromised as the issues become mainstreamed. Two dimensions of mainstreaming have been examined. The first concerned the mainstreaming of 'gender agendas' in what has been termed the 'social investment state', while the second centred on the incorporation of equality agendas into 'mainstream' institutional practice.

The feminist challenges to the maternalism of post-war social policies led, in the United Kingdom, to significant policy shifts. But these were, in retrospect, vulnerable to appropriation by Third Way governments seeking to modernize welfare states. Gøsta Esping-Andersen (Esping-Andersen 2009) was a leading proponent of the turn from protection and welfare to the promotion of work as the route to female equality, together with the advocation of social investment strategies that viewed children as the citizen workers of the future, able to take their place in the global knowledge economy. Women no longer need to struggle for equality, his analysis suggests, since modern states now depend on their equal participation in the workforce and should therefore make every effort to enable them to do so. States should invest more in education and in improving the life chances of children as the citizen workers of the future, thus enabling women to participate more fully.

The ideals and practices of the social investment state appropriated and resignified feminist arguments – not only did the 'label come off' as campaigns and claims led to policy adaptations, but government actors invented their own labels inscribed with a distorted image of what gender equality might look like and how it might be achieved, diluted their own policies and attempted to pass responsibility to subordinate tiers of governance. However, the spaces of power that women opened up and mobilized were not simply governmentally determined spaces – as Brah suggests (Brah 1996: 181), spaces occur at the point of confluence of different political, cultural, organizational and personal projects. The work of aligning these multiple and competing projects was the gendered labour of the women on whose accounts I have drawn here: those who brought feminist perspectives, children's or human rights discourses and alternative cultural practices into their 'close encounters' with the policy process, whether as academics (Hilary Land, Ruth Lister, Sue Himmelweit, the staff of Care, Values and the Future of Welfare [CAVA]), as leaders of campaigning organizations (Ruth Lister at CPAG, Angela Mason at Stonewall), as directors and workers in charities and NGOs (Mary MacLeod and FPI, Kate Raworth and OXFAM), or as human rights lawyers and independent commissioners (Camilla Warren, Marian Barnes). The incorporation of gender agendas into social policy cannot, then, be simply attributed to forms of economic neoliberalism dominated by the search for cheaper, more flexible and less unionized (female) labour. Even within the economic agenda, ambiguities arise: as Ruth Lister comments, it is dangerous to assume unity or integration in these new state forms: 'Such ambiguities mean that there are spaces, such as around childcare and poverty, that civil society actors can exploit to argue for a more genuinely child focused and also more egalitarian approach' (Lister 2004: 176).

The participants in this research are evidence of precisely the ways in which actors can exploit such spaces. However, this is not a celebration of their agency, nor of the benefits that mainstreaming equality agendas secured. Spaces of power, as I have argued, are specific to the political-cultural formations of particular times and places. Much of the work of those quoted in this chapter looks back to a particular period of Third Way governance, a period in which many feminists were drawn into policy circles and in which partnerships proliferated. In the political climate of austerity following the banking crisis and subsequent recession, many of the achievements of the women discussed here are being reversed. The process of welfare state retrenchment and public service cuts are producing new landscapes of inequality that are highly gendered, classed and racialized. And new policy architectures are potentially taking us back to the formations of welfare that led to earlier campaigns for women's financial independence.

In such a climate debates about incorporation, professionalization and mainstreaming seem rather dated; as activists move back out to the streets to protest against cuts and austerity, and to challenge global capitalism and its agents, the bankers, so the fate of equality legislation and of those who enacted it in organizations can appear to be yesterday's agenda. But the work of such women has had a lot to say about politics and political skills: the importance of coalition building, of networking, of translating and of brokering between different sites and scales of power. The work of all of the women discussed in this chapter can be understood as traversing multiple borders between central and local government, between different departments of government, between different sectors, between different stakeholders and interests. But they also worked the borders between activist networks and policy actors, bringing their political commitments and activist experience into their 'close encounters' with government (see Chapter 9 for examples of how such work continues).

The relationships, separations and tensions between campaigning 'outside' and taking up such spaces of influence are now evident in a range of contemporary struggles: on environmental governance, interventions on global supply chains and human rights as a new hegemonic global discourse. Each of these is, of course, subject to incorporation and depoliticization; but they form crucial sites in which struggles over meaning and practice are currently taking place (Collins 2003). Each draws extensively on feminist praxis: the *how* of politics and policy as well as the *what*. And each has to engage with institutional sites of power and authority: the focus of the next chapter.

5

Modernizing Moments:
Work, Organizations and the
Entrepreneurial Self

Women's work is positioned rather ambiguously in contemporary narratives of the transformations of economy, work and organizations. As I argued in the previous chapter, second-wave feminism opened up new ways of 'doing' politics and policy as well as bringing new issues into the policy domain. As such it forms a significant element of the narratives of modernity and the emergence of a new 'spirit' of capitalism that transformed organizations and their management:

> Hailing from leftism, and especially the self-management movement, they ['neo-managerialists'] stress the continuity between the commitments of their youth and activities that they pursued in firms, following the political turning point of 1983, with a view to making working conditions appealing, improving productivity, developing quality and increasing profits. Thus, for example, the qualities that are guarantees of success in this new spirit – autonomy, spontaneity, rhizomorphous capacity, multitasking (in contrast to the narrow specialisation of the old division of labour), conviviality, openness to others and novelty, availability, creativity, visionary intuition, sensitivity to difference, listening to lived experience and receptiveness to a whole range of experiences, being attracted to informality and the search for interpersonal contacts, these are taken directly from the spirit of May 1968. (Boltanski and Chiapello 2005: 97)

This list of skills and capacities is remarkably similar to those valued by the women I interviewed. Furthermore, the 'spaces of power' I described in the previous chapter might be viewed as characteristic of the institutional transformations linked to the 'new spirit' that Boltanski and Chiapello depict. This is one version of a series of grand narratives that link feminism to the emergence of new political, economic and social orderings of power. Second-wave feminism has been implicated in the shift to 'reflexive modernity', by helping to challenge tradition and by constituting the flexible, reflexive subjects required by modern forms of capitalism. It enabled development agencies to turn to women as the bearers of responsibility for economic development in the global south, leading to a plethora of women's 'empowerment' and development programmes (Cruikshank 1999). Feminism, in short, was 'seduced' by capitalism into providing the resources for the further exploitation of women (Eisenstein 2009).

However, such narratives flatten complexity. 'Past' and 'present', 'tradition' and 'modernity' are depicted as singular entities that neatly succeed each other rather than being co-present. This leads to a number of difficulties. First, modernity is depicted as a period rather than, as Marcus argues, an ethos (Rainbow and Marcus 2008). Second, such narratives hide differences of class and race (the work of most women, even in the global north, is not particularly 'reflexive' and they have little chance to be creative). Third, they mask differences of place, assuming that the rationalities associated with a mythical cosmopolitan centre represent the new norm: differences are merely a question of evolutionary time lags or perhaps stubborn refusals of some places to become modern. But, more importantly in the context of this book, they blame women for their own exploitation, erasing the struggles for social justice in which they have engaged; or suggesting that their radical critiques of capitalism were 'placed in the service of forces whose destruction they were intended to hasten' (Boltanski and Chiapello 2007: 97). This chapter sets out to offer a more nuanced account, highlighting the ambiguities that arose as women's labour generated new organizational forms and new ways of organizing.

The chapter moves through a series of 'modernizing moments'. The first section, 'Challenging "tradition"', focuses on the lives of two women who, in very different ways, became the markers of modernity-to-come in the early 1960s. 'Challenging professions' takes us to the 1970s and early 1980s and the ways in which some professions responded to social movement, class-based, community and 'multicultural' challenges. 'In and against the (local) state' depicts women entering local government in the 1980s, bringing their socialist feminist commitments into the difficult work of contracting-out services. 'New managerial times' shows women taking up new spaces of organizational and managerial power, and 'Entrepreneurial selves' traces the experience of women crafting their own – often fragmented and precarious – working lives.

This temporal sequence is designed to situate the account of each 'modernizing moment' in its political, economic and governmental context rather than to tell a linear history. This is not, then, a story of a shift from Fordist to post-Fordist or from bureaucratic to post-bureaucratic organizational forms (see Lash and Urry 1987). Nor is it a complete story: the rise of the 'managerial state' in the twentieth century and of the transformations of public services in the twenty-first have been told elsewhere (Clarke and Newman 1997; Newman and Clarke 2009). Similarly I have not attempted to retell other gendered histories, whether of discrimination in the workplace (Coyle and Skinner 1988; Cockburn 1991), of women's place in 'culture change' programmes (Itzin and Newman 1995), in management (Kerfoot and Knight 2004; Maddock 1999; Marshall 1984; Marshall 1995; Newman 1994), in the professions (Barry, Dent and O'Niell 2003) or of shifts in patterns of women's economic activity (Molloy and Larner 2010; McDowell 2009; Mac an Ghiall and Haywood 2007; Walby 2009; and others). Rather, my aim is to offer a series of episodes or snapshots – moments that capture something of specific processes of change at particular times. And the story I tell is in part my own story. I have inserted myself into the account at various points, though like many other women my story has spanned transformations of work in 'community' and 'policy' as well as in organizations. The spaces in which we worked, responding to different cycles of reform and reorganization while also engaging in what we hoped were transformational projects of our own were, as I will show, not necessarily comfortable spaces. But they have nevertheless to be viewed as ambiguous spaces of power from which challenges to dominant orthodoxies could be voiced.

Challenging 'tradition'

Here I recount the experiences of two very different women, both born in the 1930s, and thus the 'oldest' of the participants in this study (from generational cohort 1). Neither was born in Britain and both are somewhat famous. The organizations in which they found themselves early in their working lives in Britain – the Civil Service and the broadcast media – were exclusionary, hierarchical, male-dominated and predominantly white, untouched by the equalities legislation to come.

Dame Steve Shirley entered the UK from Germany in 1939 as an unaccompanied child refugee. She joined the Civil Service because she thought it would provide stability after her damaged childhood but also because in her family *'that's what you did, you worked for the benefit of the public'*. Her first boss was a *'bully and a sexist'* and *'things were very tough'*. She spoke of how women were on different pay scales to men, and of the barriers to women's promotion and advancement: *'It really was a different world, and some of it I think led me to really battle for the empowerment of women, but also the empowerment of any minority.'* She began developing software for the fast-growing computing industry, and *'suddenly found that outside the Civil Service my salary doubled'*. In 1952 she set up her own company – F-International – employing a women only workforce:

> A service company is nothing but its people, and I was recruiting from that 51 per cent of the potential workforce that nobody else was offering anything to, so I was getting the cream of that and the calibre of my colleagues was really incredibly high. It was a crusade rather than a money-making thing. At one point I had in fact investigated whether to run it as a charity. So we had a high quality, very high motivation and after a few years decent management. We had six women on the Board, when nobody else was having women at all, so we were breaking through. (Steve Shirley)

The main issue I want to pull out of this account is the construction of 'spaces of possibility' for women trapped by the maternalist ethos of 1950s

Britain: women who, in Dame Shirley's terms, were 'wasted talent' and who needed new opportunities for themselves and whose 'flexible labour' could benefit the company. The setting up of F-International might be viewed as prefiguring the later shift from an industrial to a service economy in Britain, as well as the emergence of employee share ownership. But the company was also prefigurative in a different sense: while Dame Shirley did not claim the term 'feminist', there was an implicit valorization of women's management practice that predated the 1980s debates about 'women in management' and the corporate benefits to be gained from women's leadership styles. In the early years she fought against the image of F-International as a 'women's company' in case this became a competitive disadvantage, but then decided that her success in building it could serve as a role model for other women.

There are other features of this account to which I will return, but before doing so I want to introduce a second woman of this generation – Beverley Anderson. She was born in Jamaica, went to study in the United States and then joined the Jamaican Foreign Service (in 1963) because *'I wanted to understand how political decisions were made.'* She later served in the Jamaican Embassy in Washington where, as the only woman, her posting caused resentment among male colleagues. She arrived in England to train to be a teacher, and came to visibility as one of the first Black women local government councillors. She was invited to appear on a series of short TV programmes from which she went on to host the Channel 4 series, 'Black on Black':

> *'Black on Black' became a sort of success, and most of the children on my council estate then were white, and they got to stay up till 11.00 at night to watch it, and of course next morning back at school walking up the corridor the caretaker said, 'The toilets are flooded', and we deal with school again. For me this was a really healthy mix because most of my time I was doing something that I thought was worthwhile. I always had mixed feelings about broadcasting, and therefore it was very nice for me to get back to blocked up toilets.* (Beverley Anderson)

There is ambivalence about 'holding' power here – Beverley decided not to continue as a diplomat or as a high profile face in the media. The emotional resonances that ran though the interview all concerned issues of access and empowerment through education:

> *I did a lot of interesting things, and many of them were about gender and race, but you know the thing that excites me most is education. As a Head Teacher I felt that I could use my authority to share it with people who didn't feel that they had a right to any power, were afraid of power, didn't understand how useful they could be as partners in power, and it's all true [she laughs].* (Beverley Anderson)

She then went on to work at both local and national levels on opening out access to higher education and served on a number of boards (the Arts Council,

The British Film Institute, the Oxford Stage Company) as well as becoming Chief Executive of the Book Trust:

> *I was seen as a grey-haired Black woman and I used to call myself a threefor...*
> *They get three for one, they get the grey hair, they get the woman and they get*
> *the brown skin, so there's absolutely no question that in some of the things I was*
> *asked to do, I knew they were asking me because of the colour of my skin. And*
> *I thought, 'Well lucky them, they actually get somebody intelligent as well, I will*
> *do it.'* (Beverley Anderson)

Both women moved out of 'blocked' hierarchical organizations (the UK Civil Service, the Jamaican Foreign Service) and constructed their own life projects – projects that linked personal commitments and public action. Both created spaces of possibility for others – whether the women employees of F-International, the pupils of inner London schools, the young people supported by the charities that Steve Shirley went on to found or the cultural openings in the established artworld opened up by Beverley Anderson.

These accounts also demonstrate something of the exclusionary and oppressive qualities of traditional organizations characterized by hierarchy, patriarchy and whiteness. Both women rejected the institutions that they saw constraining them, choosing to move on to other forms of influence. Of course, both were privileged, well-educated women who were affluent enough to be able to make such choices. Less visible is the work of those stuck in organizations with entrenched gendered and racialized divisions and in highly exploitative forms of labour. But the accounts suggest some of the ways in which these began to be broken down, whether by creating alternatives such as F-International, by changing them through 'presence' (being a Black woman in a white media), through 'empowerment' (challenging the hierarchies entrenched in professional expertise) or through the development of other women as leaders, managers and members of governing bodies. The accounts, then, can be situated in a politics of access and inclusion that sought to overcome gender segregation and inequality in the workplace. Despite the efforts of women working on campaigns for gender equality traced in Chapter 4, we might argue, with Boltanski and Chiapello, that (male) hierarchy only began to be seriously challenged as organizations came to valorize new, more flexible and responsive ways of working and thus opened up spaces of possibility for women, or to value 'diversity' as an organizational asset. We can also see the symbolic capital that both female and Black leaders offered to organizations seeking to open up new markets and appeal to new audiences and customer groups. But these are rather functionalist readings that overlook the agency of women trying to open up new spaces of possibility for others. They also overlook the specificity of the ways in which 'pre-modern' orderings of hierarchy, patriarchy, whiteness and 'modern' rationalities are articulated in particular spaces at specific moments; and how the tensions and contradictions are lived and managed – or not.

Challenging professions

The story of the role of professions in the political and cultural transformations of the 1970s has focused extensively on radical social work (Lavalette 2011). This had its own forty-year celebration in 2010 and its political trajectories, divisions and contradictions closely paralleled those of the second-wave women's movement. Radical movements within medicine, schooling, planning and other professions also emerged, alongside a series of 'new' professions and professional identities. But I want to focus here on librarianship, arguably less radical, not only because it evokes my own history but also since it brings into view the difficulties faced by cultural institutions – public broadcasting, museums and galleries, including the television companies that employed Beverley Anderson – as they attempted to respond to social and cultural differentiation while struggling for survival in a shifting policy and spatial landscape (Barnett 2003; Morley and Robbins 1995). Librarianship, along with teaching, nursing, heath visiting, social work and other occupations opened up significant 'spaces of opportunity' for women. These were, of course, subordinate professions – law and medicine remained predominantly male enclaves of power until much later. But these female-dominated professions also enabled many women to bring social movement and other political commitments into their working lives.

In 1962, at the age of seventeen, I began work as a library assistant in my local branch library. Apolitical and relatively uneducated I entered an organizational world of professional and bureaucratic hierarchy, much as in the Civil Service of Steve Shirley's day. Although a predominantly female profession, men were at the top, holding both professional posts in the branch and with a solidly male hierarchy of supervisors, inspectors and chiefs above them; women assistants were the bottom, with women cleaners somehow falling into a kind of underclass. I remained in this clerical role for some years before studying for a qualification and gaining a political education on the way. The service I re-entered in the early 1970s was ripe for change as the cultural, social and political transformations of the day began to bite, making me feel – rather arrogantly – that most of what we did 'at work', serving an old, exhausted culture, was pretty irrelevant.

In the 1970s and 1980s I became part of new groupings of children's librarians and community librarians then on the edge of the profession. As we began to engage in 'outreach' activities in order to reach non-traditional library users, we inevitably came into contact with very different publics and attempted to carry their voices back into the centre. I – and colleagues who I later went back to interview – remembered the personal impact of taking services into the local mosque, of reading stories to children on a glass-strewn playground in a rundown council estate, of giving talks about books to groups of teenage mothers in a family centre, of trying to develop a service to support community action groups and a local immigration advice centre, of developing Black studies collections and projects at the time of the inner-city racial disturbances in Birmingham. Each served as a fast and sometimes brutal form of political education. And each produced more dynamic and contested conceptions of the public that challenged professional assumptions of universality, neutrality and openness of the public library's role (Newman 2006).

Commenting on the changes taking place in some parts of the service in the 1970s and early 1980s, one of my former colleagues reflected that much of what happened would now be considered patronizing, but it marked a key stage in our evolution as cultural critics of the mainstream service and our attempts to model different forms of professional practice that prefigured notions of the 'coproduction' of knowledge (see Chapter 6). We also engaged with the turn to 'partnership' and 'participative' styles of governing discussed in Chapter 4, working with family centres, Community Development Programmes, 'free' schools, youth organizations, education authorities, health clinics, play schemes, prisons and other agencies. But such projects were limited; we were also symbols of what came to be viewed as 'progressive' practices and left-wing political projects that became targets for the New Right politics to come.[1]

In and against the (local) state

The spaces of power described in the previous section were spaces opened up by the profound cultural and social shifts of the period; shifts that fractured the post-war social, political and organizational settlements. A decade later, however, the British welfare state had become the target of New Right vilification and the focus of Thatcher's modernizing reforms (Clarke and Newman 1997). My focus now turns to the forging of connections between the class politics that intensified in the 1980s and the changing organizational logics of local government as it became subject to legislation requiring local authorities to submit much of their manual workforce, including school cleaners and caterers, to compulsory competitive tendering (CCT). Jane Foot, who appeared as a 'community entrepreneur' in Chapter 3, became a local government worker in the 1980s as she sought to bring her socialist feminist politics to the defence of low paid (predominantly female) workers. She drew on her experience of working in a trade union-funded resource centre in which:

We did lots of things about improving services in order to make them more defendable through CCT. So I did a big piece of work with Sheffield school cleaners and school caterers – sort of to work with them to improve the services before they had to be put out to tender. That was interesting, there were big campaigns about school meals, with linked stuff about nutritional issues – this was often the only hot meal kids would have. That was a perfect piece of socialist feminist work, really. And Jamie Oliver has proved us right! [She laughs.] (Jane Foot)

But the trade union resource centre wasn't sustainable financially and eventually she moved from campaigning from the outside to managing the CCT process within a local authority.

> *Loads of us went from those trade union resource centres, law centres, SCAT, into local government, either at the GLC or Labour-controlled councils. There was no local government profession for CCT, it was a completely feminist- and women-dominated area of local government. And I still have dinner with them all twenty years on. Some of them went on to become directors of DSOs [Direct Service Organizations, in-house contractors], and some became the first women local authority Chief Executives.* (Jane Foot)

Ursula Murray was one of the other women mentioned by Jane and her account is very similar. Before joining local government she had worked on school meals projects that aimed to revalue women's skills in the context of 'early noises' about privatization:

> *The Tories had got rid of nutritional standards in school meals, and we wanted to do something. We worked from a socialist feminist perspective, working with working-class women on a women's employment project. But by 1986 there was a sense of dismay – there was a feeling that change had been possible in the era of political funding and sponsorship [for campaigning organizations], now it was all about income generation.*
>
> *So I got a job as team leader of a public services team whose task was to 'roll back the frontiers of the private sector' in order to extend the public and voluntary sectors. But this only lasted two weeks: then Labour lost the [local] election and the task changed to preparing the council for CCT. Nothing had been done, apart from a working party opposed to privatization. There had been no attention to CCT by the Chief Executive, but thousands of women's jobs depended on it. That was my job for the next ten years. The brief was to keep us legal while defending the council and council jobs from privatization.* (Ursula Murray)

I asked Jane and Ursula whether the move into local government was opportunistic, with jobs opening up as the organizations that had previously supported them had their funding cut, but both saw it as a collective intervention:

> *In my view – you were challenging the state, this was the time of 'in and against the state', but also you had to defend it. This was in the period after the miners' strike, the abolition of the GLC, so local authorities were then at the front line. It was not that you sought the job but you were drawn or pushed into it out of a sense of duty.* (Ursula Murray)

> *I think we thought we would change the world. This was all the 'in and against the state' stuff. That group was very influential.* (Jane Foot)

I also asked them to describe something of their work. Jane responded:

> *I think we thought we could go in, we could help councillors resist [CCT], and the lessons from SCAT and the work in Sheffield was that we could win. In my time in Camden we never lost a contract. We kept a lot of those services in house, and*

we did improve them. There was a lot of ducking and diving going on. But there's a theme about relating, I think – between those who need the services and those who provide them. And both are very often women. Local government tends to forget that a lot of its staff are also its users. All that stuff about the client-contractor split and the provider focus – some of that is absolutely justified, some of what went on was completely scandalous. But we really threw out the baby with the bathwater in a big way. (Jane Foot)

I want to pull several things out of these accounts. The first is the ways in which changing political contexts – here Thatcherism and the 'contracting out' imperatives on local government – opened up new policy and management spaces for women. There were, as Jane notes, no existing staff with the skills and experience to undertake this work. But, second, it was the political commitment to working-class women, and prior experience of campaigns on women's work, that led both women to 'move in' to such roles. As such campaigning and activism became ambiguously aligned with state practice, with women engaged in extensive 'border work' roles as they linked inside-outside identities and forms of action (see Chapter 7). Third, the extracts point to contradictions in the process of public service reform. CCT was in part designed to challenge entrenched practices, especially in male manual work, and to disrupt the alliances between male-dominated trade unions and male councillors that at the time were, in Jane's words, *'completely scandalous'*. The role of the women who came into local government, bringing their socialist feminist commitments with them, was not, then, simply to defend the status quo. But the unravelling of entrenched and often corrupt practices through new competitive practices *'threw the baby out with the bathwater'*, opening the way for successive rounds of market-making and the entry of multinational companies into public service provision.

The final point is the emphasis from both participants on the collective nature of their interventions and the power flowing from the solidarities this generated:

The old girls network was very powerful in local government. The CCT girls' network was very influential; we were given a lot of respect. We still meet, still have dinner sometimes. There was a similar network in regeneration and in personnel management. (Jane Foot)

Women played key roles in all of this – there were a lot of women involved in key positions at that time. When you came in you recruited people, you had to spot, grow, fast-track people. All of us had come out of the voluntary sector. The voluntary sector equipped us to be light on our feet, and we had learned how to pull people together. In the work around school meals it was all about working collaboratively. The women's employment project – we still keep in touch. And there's still a bond between the women in local government who shared the experience of CCT. It was very heavy stuff. How did we live the risk? Always being on the end of legality. In terms of survival, what really mattered was a sense of collectivity. It was deeply shared. (Ursula Murray)

The spaces of possibility occupied by Jane, Ursula and others were characteristic of the Labour-controlled local authorities who saw themselves as in opposition to the Conservative governments of the day. But the skills developed in this period by women working 'in and against the state' helped equip them to take on later roles as consultants, members of think-tanks and workers on development projects. Some, including Ursula, began taking on research roles and later moved into post-experience teaching. Others, like Jane, were well-placed to participate effectively in Blair's 'joined up government' agenda. But both opened up spaces that younger women came to occupy – including the many women who took up management roles in local government and the wider public sector from the mid-1980s.

New managerial times

After 1992, and the local elections, there was a change of Chief Executive. New Labour had come in. It was like a tap that had been turned off but you hadn't known it had been there. Previously there had been political people meeting all over the place. Suddenly it was all new public management. (Ursula Murray)

The processes of public sector reform in which Ursula and others found themselves were linked to what John Clarke and I termed the rise of the 'Managerial State' (Clarke and Newman 1997). Just as women were gaining a foothold on organizational power bases, it seemed, so power was being dispersed, managerialized and made subject to an array of competitive and performance pressures. Writing about the new managerial order, Höpfl noted the evangelical qualities of the discourse that was designed to challenge the 'established church' of traditional management (Höpfl 1992). New managerial and leadership orders in which women participated helped challenge the old church of tradition and hierarchy, moving from an emphasis on compliance to a search for commitment through the use of 'soft power'.

There are no easy generalizations to be made about the experience of women taking on managerial work. Managerial images of the 1980s and 1990s centred on the heroic business leader able to cut through defensive practices to render organizations 'lean and mean', fit for the global marketplace of health and other 'public' commodities. Some commentators have argued that women brought something rather different. Sue Maddock, for example, describes the new generation of women managers who had been politicized in the 1970s and seasoned in management in the 1980s as bringing 'post command, post market and post modern' approach (Maddock 1999: 219). However, there were considerable differences of approach and style among the women I interviewed, and they occupied very different spaces of power. Those who had come through professional hierarchies were able to extend the reach of their influence in 'hybrid' professional/managerial roles in which different forms of authority and expertise were – often uncomfortably – aligned. Some of those who had worked in 'support' professions such as personnel or accounting moved into more powerful roles as they were drawn into the corporate centre, though on the edge of what continued to be club-like decision-making networks. Women who had been stuck on the low rungs of ossified bureaucratic or professional career ladders could find themselves becoming 'business managers' of devolved service-delivery units, with all of the tensions this generated. Some, including many involved in CCT, moved from community-based or non-governmental activism into relatively powerful policy positions from which many stepped into chief executive posts. But others moved out of the public sector to take up roles as entrepreneurs providing services under contract as a result of the introduction of purchaser-provider splits and marketization. Some applied new managerial methods to voluntary organizations. Others became consultants, trainers and developers, offering services to organizations relentlessly searching for new skills and assets.

The new spaces of organizational and managerial power opened up to women were, then, paradoxical spaces that were inhabited by different women in different ways. Management was understood as both a paradigm that needed to be challenged (because of its instrumental, technocratic process) and also as a means of bringing about what was perceived to be needed reform. Sue Richards (G2) recalled how:

> *The Civil Service was viewed by Thatcher as an irresistible force, an immovable object. And I was right in the middle of it, in this club like, closed institution. From what I was observing I felt that we desperately needed change to the Civil Service, and she [Margaret Thatcher] was going to bring it. But I also felt that you could want that radical change but not for her purposes. Her sort of hatred of bureaucrats fuelled her commitment to policies to change them. I do think that had a huge impact – there are still echoes of that earlier past there, still very much in place. It's this that made me aware of the relevance of having someone who understands the machinery of the state, but is committed to different critical agendas, broadly socialist labour, whatever. And so it kind of began to feel like that was my contribution in life professionally, and it has shaped how I have put together the different routes, in different circumstances.*
> (Sue Richards)

This nicely captures the paradoxes of the period. The pre-managerial, bureaucratic, inflexible and often unresponsive public sector was a focus of change projects – in the spirit of 'in and against the state' – by many of the participants I interviewed. But when the changes introduced by Thatcher came along we were tempted to say, with Carole Harte in Chapter 3, 'Ah, but we didn't mean *that*.'

The managerial imperative rapidly spread from government to the voluntary sector. Naomi Eisenstadt describes her role in transforming one voluntary organization – the Family Service Unit – into an organization that prefigured New Labour's style and approach, before her subsequent move to Sure Start:

Interestingly enough the organization was most powerful in Old Labour strongholds. It had had a very radical beginning – it was originally the Pacifist Service Unit set up by people who had been conscientious objectors during the war. But my impression was that the people doing the work needed the organization as much as the people who they were serving needed it. And that culture permeated the organization, and I wanted to stress the needs of the people who we were serving, not the needs of the people working there. People were fantastic, people did amazing work but there was no managerial structure. We paid someone to be our union rep, and we had 300 staff and didn't have an HR person, so it was classically old Labour. The fundamental fieldwork was amazing, the management structure was not. And really I came in as a Tony Blair to make it New Labour basically. (Naomi Eisenstadt)

Such reforms were those that closed some of the spaces of power for the women cited in the previous section; as Ursula Murray commented, the introduction of a New Labour culture into an 'old' Labour leaning local authority was 'like a [political] tap had been turned off'. And managerialism was key to the 'professionalization' of many voluntary bodies. Stella Semino had worked as a social worker for another left-leaning local authority – Lambeth – during the 1980s while also doing volunteer work for the Migrants Resource Centre in Victoria. After she left her social service job she was invited on to the Migrants Resource Centre's Management Committee. But:

The organizational circumstances were awful. The building – passed over from the GLC – was derelict; they had huge debts to the Inland Revenue. Then most of the staff left. So I invited a group of friends to work on restarting the centre. This was very successful, I'm so proud. (Stella Semino)

She became a part-time volunteer again, but later the organization started to professionalize:

We had to get funds to cope with the needs of the building and to meet our debts. But constraints came with funding – we had to do things we didn't necessarily want to do. Now the organization is a service provider not a community organization any more. We give advice and do a lot of public relations. The people on the management committee are now professionals, not people who are volunteers. And the organization doesn't really consult with volunteers anymore. (Stella Semino)

These two experiences – those of Naomi and Stella – can perhaps be understood as mirror images of the impact of managerialization on voluntary and civil society groups at different 'modernizing moments'.

Managerialism was not the invention of New Labour, of course – *The Managerial State* (Clarke and Newman 1997) addressed the reforms of the Reagan/Thatcher years. But managerialism certainly intensified under the 'modernizing' programmes of the Blair governments. Public management became a contested terrain as modernizing pressures collided with ideas about how a reformed management could be used to deliver 'progressive' organizational and public goals. This was the ethos of the management development and MBA programmes I worked on during the 1990s from a base in a School of Public Policy at Birmingham University; such programmes were proliferating at the time as professionals sought managerial qualifications, but also as those squeezed by and critical of the impact of managerialism and privatization in the public sector searched for alternative paradigms. As Sue Richards, a colleague of that time, explained:

> *I have been driven by the idea that public management could be more than the tool of the New Right. I've always felt very ambivalent about the term 'new public management', because that was a stereotype, an impoverished version of what actually was happening. The strands of it, the elements that I thought were important, remained submerged.* (Sue Richards)

I asked Sue what were her submerged strands:

> *Well, some of it is to do with the people who work in the organization being treated as human beings and finding fulfilment and self-actualization and so on, rather than being characterized as wasteful bureaucrats, so there's that side of it, but it's more a kind of innovative focus, I think. I go back to my own earliest roots and the story I told you about my dad, and how he felt and what he became. The sense of so much wasted talent, and so little self-actualization and so much pain and drudgery, and how it need not be like that ... it is about a degree of control I think.* (Sue Richards)

I wondered whether she thought that public services could do that:

> *Yeah, I think so and I think that would be important for it to able to generate that kind of wellbeing with people. Public servants should be driven by those ideas, along with stuff about serving the public.* (Sue Richards)

Adi Cooper, at the time of the interview a strategic director in local government, described how she *'went in at the bottom'* but quickly moved into management because, she recalled, she looked at what was going on around her, and above her, and thought *'I could do that differently'*:

> *The most difficult transition for me was from a front-line practitioner to front-line manager. I found it very difficult to take on that challenge of being able to tell people what to do, and being accountable for them, and performance managing them, and not being part of the front-line. That was really hard, really, really hard, but once I'd made that transition it was easier on some levels to go up. Some other stuff I took was from working in collectives – it was about real respect for whatever people do. I don't know, it's about the interpersonal stuff ... I try very hard not to abuse that power, the positional power of being a very senior manager. And that comes from my politics.* (Adi Cooper)

There are important resonances between Adi's account and the image of public management offered by Sue: the importance of values, the focus on humanizing the workplace and of public service. In the 1990s such discourses became central to organizational programmes of 'culture change', while the relational dimensions of their work took on new significance in the turn to 'joined up government', 'partnership' and 'participation' in the rhetoric of public policy (see Chapter 4 and Newman 2001). This turn in public policy drew many women with experience of voluntary sector and community-based activism into policy and management roles, and brought some of those with experience of CCT into senior management:

> I was responsible for policy, quality, the internal market and other things – equality, community safety, the drugs action team – I worked to nine different committees. What's notable is that all of these things were cross-cutting – I wasn't responsible for any service departments. I had to do policy through partner agencies or by influencing service departments. And negotiation skills were really important. There were always allies – you find the people within the departmental hierarchies who agree and you support them. I really valued the services, I knew there were people out there who needed them and I had respect for what they were doing. Feminism helped – you find the feminist in the housing department who you could trust. But the job was undoable. (Jane Foot)

This extract suggests how the later focus on policy outcomes and 'cross-cutting' issues enabled new alignments between multiple agendas; these were less explicitly political, less explicitly feminist, but did generate spaces of power which women such as Jane could occupy, with all of the resulting tensions and stresses – 'the job was undoable'.

In previous research (Newman 2005c) I showed how senior women managers occupied the new spaces of power constituted by the emergence of 'leadership' discourse, selectively amplifying government policies on social exclusion, public involvement, community capacity building, preventing ill-health, restorative justice and so on, and rearticulating them with counter discourses, including those of feminism, anti-racism and with redistributive concepts of social justice. An 'expansive' – or even colonizing – conception of public leadership was, then, rooted in the possibilities offered by New Labour's own discourses and was readily taken up by women sympathetic to notions of participation, distributed power and a strong ethical and value base. As I emphasized in Chapter 3, I do not want to romanticize the agency of individual women; each worked in landscapes of antagonism in which reconciling personal and political commitments with modernizing imperatives was often problematic and painful, and fraught with contradictions. It is no surprise, then, that some decided to move into roles with rather more capacity to control their own labour through different forms of entrepreneurship.

Entrepreneurial selves

This chapter began with the story of a woman business entrepreneur – Dame Steve Shirley – but has mainly focused on women's labour in projects of transforming the state and public services. However, the processes of 'modernization' at the core of the chapter raise significant questions about the state/business, public/market and bureaucratic/entrepreneurial binaries. The stories with which this chapter is concerned show a triple process. One is of entrepreneurial labour within the state ('intrapreneurship'). All of the participants on whose accounts I have drawn have been innovators and their capacity for innovation, I want to suggest, came from the ways in which their difference (of gender and race, of career route, of values, of experience, or of networks) disrupted taken for granted ways of working. They often worked on the 'edge' of existing structures (the partnership coordinator, the project worker, the in-house trainer, the policy officer, the equality worker, the director of a new programme or policy). This enabled them to mobilize new spaces of power and to deliver changes that often prefigured more widespread shifts in economy and polity.

Entrepreneurship of a different kind – 'moving out' – is evident in accounts of participants with a background in state work who left to form businesses or become consultants. This looks back to Steve Shirley but also to the (sometimes permanent, sometimes temporary) moves made by Marion Macalpine, Sue Richards, Tricia Zipfel and others. The turn to self-employment was often made by women who had come through the GLC, Inner London Education Authority and other radical spaces: see, for example, the accounts of Sonia Khan, Jan Etienne, Sue Beardsmore and Munira Thobani. Jan and Munira ran equality programmes for public sector bodies, while Marion worked with Sheila Marsh[2] as consultants running leadership and management programmes with a particular focus on partnership working and participative and 'distributive' notions of power:

> *In terms of being self-employed basically I'm an educator and an enabler. I think that's my core skill really, and I really enjoy that. It felt that I could influence quite a lot of people in a positive way – being a consultant but working with an academic body and a public sector client, and there was a political alignment there.*
>
> *There are horror stories about being self-employed and the number of women who chose to be self-employed, and it had some disadvantages. One of the ones that I've really experienced is not being in a union. [But] what was wonderful was we could choose what we worked on. We could choose who we worked with.*
> (Marion Macalpine)

Sue Beardsmore G2 came to consultancy work through a very different route:

> *By the end of the 1970s I had become disillusioned with the Communist Party and decided to have a rest from politics. I worked in community arts, had a job with the Musician's Union, organizing conferences and things, then got a teaching qualification and worked at Cockpit, a youth project that brought the arts into community development work, looking at how groups not in the mainstream could express their voice. But I was never entirely comfortable in*

local government – for every thousand things you want to do, you only ever get five done, and that's by breaking the rules.

Then at the end of the 1980s I did a course in organizational development, and became a freelance consultant. Initially I worked with Voluntary Action in Leeds, offering consultancy to groups getting into the contract culture. But what I wanted to do changed over the years, I became more interested in group dynamics and conflict management, and that's what I did in lots of different places – for example, I was part of a delegation to Bulgaria from Northern Ireland trying to pass on the lessons from local conflict resolution programmes to other parts of the world. (Sue Beardsmore)

The spaces in which Marion, Sue and many other self-employed women worked emerged from the state transformations of the period: the contract culture and purchaser-provider splits, and other features of the New Public Management that required the development of new workforce attributes and skills. Sonia Khan showed the difficulty of clearly delineating the difference between 'inside' and 'outside' spaces in this new economy. She appeared in Chapter 3 as someone involved in community arts, and spoke of always wanting to work *'on the edges, in alternative spaces or places'*, rather than in organizations *'that were just the norm, where there was no vision'*. This took her to the Whitechapel Art Gallery where she was a project development worker, then to the Development Trust Association where she had a regional role trying to help arts organizations with self-financing:

I linked new and emergent projects up with those who had, for example, set up successful community-run organizations that were proven to be self-financing, or part of the mixed economy, enterprising. This was the time, 2000, when it was all thrown open by the election of New Labour, there was a bit of a naive sense that everyone should be running their own organizations. It was a free for all. There was no sense of framework in which the state would do this, the private sector should do that – it was a free for all. But within that there were some very interesting things happening. (Sonia Khan)

Here Sonia is referring to the emerging 'mixed economy' that the earlier programme of CCT and later development of purchaser-provider splits had prefigured. But what I find interesting in this extract is the ways in which the mixed economy and the new emphasis on social entrepreneurship produced a *'free for all'*, while at the same time the work of Sonia and other development workers was involved in processes of market-*making*. Later, Sonia moved to a further education college in a role managing what she termed *'creative sector development projects'*. While there she led a partnership of the tenants of an arts centre to develop a proposal to take it over when the company running it went into liquidation:

This was about bringing the management skills in that I'd started to develop and combining them with partnership skills, because this was a partnership project. So it brought together an understanding of communities and of partnership but also brought in front-line delivery as well – managing the business support and so on. So it was very interesting. I worked on this for a couple of years, but left before I had intended to. Because the process of being involved in the arts centre closing and then taking it on was exhausting, and it felt like somebody else should do the next bit. (Sonia Khan)

This extract resonates with the experiences of other participants involved in trying to run organizations (women's centres, women's refuges, community businesses, projects floated off from mainstream organizations) where they had to combine management skills, business skills, funding skills, and an understanding of partnership working and community/stakeholder involvement. Here is Tricia Zipfel speaking about the end of the programme (Priority Estates Programme: see Chapter 3) that had been funded under the Conservative governments of the 1980s:

In 1990 government decided to bring the programme to an end. After eleven years they felt it ought to be able to sink or swim on its own merits. By then we had become a huge organization, employing around fifty people, and had to shift from being 100 per cent grant-funded to being 100 per cent self-financing within three years. We made the transition without losing any staff, and I was very proud of that achievement. But this brought me personally into a head-on collision with the whole thing of running a business and operating in a quasi-private sector way. We were not-for-profit but suddenly had to start monitoring everyone's time and expenditure, had to put all sorts of systems in place to manage the business in a completely different way. The challenge was how do you combine that sort of hard-headed business approach to being a consultancy within a market place that doesn't provide a huge amount of money with an organization where the motivation of everyone was a commitment to a vision of transformation and supporting very deprived communities to become more resourceful and vibrant. That's why people came to work for us. It was a struggle, but we managed to do it for a long time. I always describe it as trying to land a jumbo jet on a sixpence by the end of March every year. (Tricia Zipfel)

Many such spaces opened up as 'in-house' services were contracted out and as groups of professionals set up organizations to provide services to particular client groups that had traditionally not been served well by the public sector. These offered scope for new ways of working: for example, high-involvement support services to learning disabled people living 'in the community'. And the 'joined up government' agenda not only spawned new partnership bodies but also new forms of organizations that did the joining up: for example, trusts that brought together health, social care and housing workers. Those moving from 'inside' to 'outside' did not necessarily make huge shifts in the kind of work they pursued or the relationships that sustained them. But they did speak of having greater freedom to define the purpose of their work and of the attractions – as well as the risks – of working both independently and collaboratively in a period where the business ethos and managerial forms of control were intensifying within the public sector.

This takes me to the accounts of women working in entrepreneurial spaces, particularly those associated with what have been described as the 'information society' or the 'creative industries'. However, these labels do not really reflect the range of ways in which women crafted their work. The consultancy work of Marion, Tricia, Sue Richards (who was a founder member of Office of Public Management), Sue Beardsmore and many others quoted in this chapter can all be described in terms of entrepreneurship. But I have selected extracts from the accounts of two women here, beginning with Jan Etienne. In Chapter 2 we saw Jan coming to politics through trade union and party, having worked in a factory in her early working life. She later found ways of combining her aspirations for a political career – both in the United Kingdom and in her country of birth, St Lucia – with part-time teaching and community-based 'empowerment' work (see Chapter 3). She spoke of deliberately working on multiple part-time teaching and consultancy projects through choice:

> I'll tell you why. It's through choice. It's because for many years now my political life has been a priority for me, and this is why not having a permanent, full-time job is convenient for me right now. What I do at the moment – I'm teaching at a Sure Start Centre and teach sociology at Aldwych. But I also deal with the mainstream life of Birkbeck, working across four different programme areas, and teaching courses from six to nine in the evening. Sometimes I teach day courses so emotionally it is ... a lot of people would say that it's a doddle working in this kind of way, but it's hard keeping it all together. And I'm active in South Kilburn project, I'm active in the Labour Party Black Social Society, again attending meetings all over the place, and currently when I'm in a selection [to be chosen to represent a constituency in a parliamentary election] then I have to devote full-time to the constituency. (Jan Etienne)

I ask Jan if the community projects she works on pay her as well:

> No, not at all. Everything that I do with the women is voluntary, except training and then I get a consultant's fee. I am also a consultant for ACER [Association of Colleges for the Eastern Region,] and once again I am there on their books delivering training because as a sessional lecturer you don't get that much money. (Jan Etienne)

I ask her what she will do if all the sessional lecturer work is cut out:

> I know, I would say my consultancy work will probably take centre stage then. (Jan Etienne)

This extract from our conversation hints at issues confronted by many other participants who followed insecure and often poorly paid employment paths. Many speak of such paths as offering both greater freedom (less pressure from the performance regimes of public sector work) and more opportunity (to pursue 'other agendas'). These other agendas may be parallel (parenting, care work and, in Jan's case, the exigencies of party politics) or may by integral to the work itself (finding spaces of power to pursue activist agendas; in Jan's case, empowerment work through her community-based consultancy work). Such pathways bring huge benefits: a feeling of choice, the accretion of skills and experiences that can be carried to new spaces, growing networks and the intrinsic rewards of the work itself. But they also carry huge costs. As well as concerns about earning enough money to live on in the present and securing adequate pension entitlements for the future, we can, in the extracts from Jan, see the emotional strain of, in her words, *'keeping it all together'*.

The next extract echoes some of these concerns but from a very different institutional space. Cecilia Wee, of the fourth generational cohort, and introduced in Chapter 2 as an independent arts curator, reflected on her life trajectory:

> *When I was younger then I wanted to do a PhD and go down that whole academic route and become a professor but when I started doing my PhD I realized that I didn't want to just do one thing, and I found out that academic work was too abstracted from a lot of the things that I was interested in. That's why I work with performance and live art, relishing all of those moments when the audience comes together with what you're doing, when audience and artists meet and confront each other. I like that live-ness and I like to see what the reaction is, and that process of reflection and questioning. I ran live projects for quite a few years with some friends and since then I've kind of been questioning what I really want to do, but luckily off and on having jobs that ensure that I can keep living. But now I feel I really know what I want to do and I don't want to waste anymore time working for other people when I could be working for myself and achieving what needs to be done. (Cecilia Wee)*

Such freedoms come with a price. Cecilia spoke about her work for a major art gallery that employed her to curate events from time to time:

> *You know, as an independent person working with the largest institutions, there's a lot of challenges, as you can imagine, to try and get the right person to deal with the Health and Safety stuff, and all of that. We basically got everything that we wanted and the thing is that once that relationship had finished, and once the event had finished then that's it, there is no continuation. As an independent I don't have any chart or any kind of structure as such. So for every event that you do then you invest a lot of time and labour, most of which is unpaid – because the fee that they give you is OK for the event itself, but not for all the relationships, networks, equipment, other things. So the people who programme those events are basically subsidizing the gallery in a way. (Cecilia Wee)*

This is a very different kind of entrepreneurship from that of Jan, but there are some resonances – for example, about holding things together and about finding ways of 'making a living' in order to pursue the things she really wants to do, and of patterns of exploitation. But the difference is in the choice of an entrepreneurial career path as one that enabled her to bring her passion into her work.

What is striking in these accounts is the way in which participants have actively crafted their own work and career path: they each have a sense of possible futures and each is highly aware of the dilemmas they face. They are vulnerable to shifts in the economy and in changes in the market for training and consultancy, for creative products and for 'empowerment' and development work. Contemporary sociological theory has offered a number of different phrases or concepts to capture changing career paths and the growth of entrepreneurial work: portfolio careers (Handy 1989), social entrepreneurship (Leadbeater 1996), the information society (Castells 2000) and the 'new precariat' (Ross 2009; Standing 2011). The latter is a term that, in particular, has been used to depict what are viewed as new forms of cultural work:

> Precariousness (in relation to work) refers to all forms of insecure, contingent, flexible work – from illegal, casualised and temporary employment, to homeworking, piecework and freelancing. In turn precarity signifies both the multiplication of precarious, insecure, unstable forms of living and, simultaneously, new forms of political struggle and solidarity that reach beyond the traditional models of the political party or trade union. This *double meaning* is central to understanding the ideas and politics associated with precarity; the new moment of capitalism that engenders precariousness is seen not only as oppressive but also as offering the potential for new subjectivities, new socialities and new kinds of politics. (Gill and Pratt 2008: 3; original emphasis)

This seems to depict the position of many of the participants on whose accounts I have drawn here. Their work can be described through a number of the concepts offered by Gill and Pratt from their distillation of the literature: temporary, intermittent and precarious jobs; long hours and 'bulimic' patterns of working (periods of high intensity followed by periods of no work); the collapse of the boundaries between work and play; and passionate attachment to the work itself (Gill and Pratt 2008: 14). But one might question, given its resonances with accounts from multiple generations, the novelty of precarious labour; it seems that many women in my study from G2 and G3 have combined work and politics in this way. Women have always done immaterial and affective labour, but the focus on precarious working practices only came to attention as it began to impact on male workers in the post-industrial flexible job market (Fantone 2007). Many of the ideas on which notions of a new precariat are based – those of the knowledge economy, risk society, 'immaterial labour' and a post-Fordist economy that has displaced older forms of organizing – have been critiqued by feminist commentators (McDowell 2009). But such concepts nevertheless offer a vocabulary that can speak to some of the ways in which participants described their working lives.

Conclusion

The predominant focus on state work in much of this chapter is significant. In the period with which I am concerned the (local and central) state was the primary target of political projects of modernization in which women stood both as a marker of modernity and as the barrier to modernizing projects. That is, the (partial and conditional) inclusion of women at senior levels of the professions, public service management, policy work and some areas of governance signalled that Britain was a modern state, committed to equality and justice and clearly distinguished from 'less civilized' nations in which women were less able to take on public roles (see also McRobbie 2009). But at the same time the welfare professions and public services that were the target of modernization programmes were largely staffed by women; and the care and welfare they provided were discursively linked to a pre-modernized 'nanny state' that induced dependence and over-mothering.

The chapter has shown how participants were positioned in this confluence of differently gendered modernizations. They were both models of change for the wider economy and polity, and the agents of change. That is, they brought something 'new' to the party, whether the flexible and resourceful labour needed for the changing economy, as in F-International; the symbolic presence of 'new' kinds of citizenship represented in the 'Threefor' of Beverley Anderson and multicultural libraries; or the relational and generative skills required to produce more fluid and responsive organizations. But they were also the agents of change, reordering the professions from within, working to 'empower' and 'develop' excluded or marginalized groups, introducing new person-centred management and participative leadership styles, and developing new spaces of possibility for others.

This would all seem to support the Boltanski and Chiapello propositions with which I began the chapter, i.e. that feminism and other movements of the 1960s and 1970s were complicit in the emergence of a new form of capitalism. It is possible to read these changes through the sociological narratives of the shifts from modernity to reflexive or liquid modernity (Beck, Giddens and Lash 1994), through the political-economic accounts of the shift from Fordist to post-Fordist organizations and the significance of 'immaterial labour'. But a rather different narrative into which the changes traced in this chapter might be understood is the Foucauldian narrative of the shift from liberal to advanced liberal forms of rule (N. Rose 1993). Advanced liberal forms of rule are conducted through forms of 'soft power': consultation, negotiation, empowerment and activation, precisely the practices espoused by participants. Governmentality scholars would tend to view the proliferation of such programmes as evidence of the emergence of new orders of rule through which the 'conduct of conduct' was regulated. The process of 'empowerment' through which workers were freed from the old hierarchical order was accompanied by the explosion of audit, scrutiny and measurement processes (including, perhaps paradoxically, those developed to try to ensure the implementation of equality policies). New discourses of devolution, managerialism, leadership and partnership were associated with the production of new kinds of 'self-regulating' subject; and the empowerment, development and pedagogical processes which many participants worked to install could be viewed as the instruments through which such subjects were produced. Women entering management could be viewed as doing important work in softening and humanizing organizations in ways that made them fit for service-based rather than industrial, Fordist production processes. The emotional, the relational, the personal were significant resources in the generation of new governmentalities that tied subjects more tightly to emerging orders of rule than had the instrumental and transactional forms of control of bureaucratic modernity. The empowerment and development programmes on which many women worked generated new logics that, it might be argued, helped constitute reflexive and flexible selves. Rather than the bureaucratization of feminism associated with state work we can see its continued *productive* power.

But such narratives, whether of the new spirit of capitalism or the shift from liberal to advanced neoliberal rule, flatten context. That is, they occlude the contested political rationalities associated with each of the different transformations described in this chapter; the logics associated with particular 'modernizing moments' are not displaced by succeeding reforms but continue within them. The contradictions between different temporal modernities created tensions for those trying to reconcile them in a particular place and time: trying to do new 'joined up' work from within a bureaucracy or trying to bring 'public' rationalities into a market-driven regime. We can see patterns in which some of these contestations produced new orderings of dominance, with 'old' rationalities perhaps becoming residual. In some examples we can see one side emerging as a 'winner': Thatcher defeated left Labourist local government and other alternative power bases through processes of vilification, abolition and reform. But others were more ambiguous. And even where some spaces were closed down, the actors who generated and peopled them often moved on to others. What most of this chapter has shown is the significance of the commitments that sustained individuals through different cycles of change. This is not a story of individual heroism but of collective endeavour, and of the living out of contradictions, uncertainties and personal dilemmas through different forms of collective practice. But it is also the story of the importance of the particular spaces of possibility associated with different political conjunctures. By focusing on the situated agency of participants in different places and moments, we can see ambiguities in new technologies and practices of rule.

6

Critical Engagements:
Knowledge-work as Political Practice

As I noted in Chapter 1, one of the inspirations for this book came from encounters with young scholars bringing activist commitments into their PhD studies and research projects. My conversations with them led to a broader engagement with 'knowledge-work' as a form of political practice in the professions, in development work, in teaching and training, and in policy communities. Across these categories the interviews showed how the acquisition of knowledge enabled participants to negotiate with and perform effectively within dominant ruling relations (see Chapters 3, 4 and 5). But the interviews also show how knowledge-work was viewed as means of *transforming* those same ruling relations. Such practices drew – implicitly or explicitly – on feminist scholarship:

> [F]eminist scholarship, like most other forms of scholarship, is not the mere production of knowledge about a certain subject. It is a directly political and discursive practice in that it is purposeful and ideological. It is best seen as a mode of intervention into particular hegemonic discourses...... It is a political praxis that counters and resists the totalising imperative of age-old 'legitimate' and 'scientific' bodies of knowledge. Thus, feminist scholarly practices... are inscribed in relations of power – relations that they counter, resist or even perhaps implicitly support. There can, of course, be no apolitical scholarship. (Mohanty 2003: 19)

This chapter traces a number of different interventions that sought to transform 'legitimate' and 'scientific' bodies of knowledge. It begins by tracing how some of the younger participants that were introduced in Chapter 2 saw research as a form of political engagement. Their accounts generate questions that are pursued in later sections, where I widen the generational and occupational focus. In the section titled 'The politics of recognition', I show how some participants sought to elicit experiential, affective and emotional 'ways of knowing' that traditionally had little place in the public sphere, in professional practice or in the academy. 'Close encounters' assesses knowledge-work at the interface between research, policy and practice. Finally, 'In and beyond the cultural turn' shows how participants engaged with post-structuralist forms of theory that drew attention to the generative power of knowledge-work: its power to constitute and perform what Gibson-Graham[1] term 'other worlds' (Gibson-Graham 1996b).

Knowledge-work as political practice

Your research has to make a difference to more than yourself and your own life.
(Alessandra Marino)

I'm doing a PhD that, because of the experience of politics I bring to it, I hope
can be an inspiration for other women. (Stella Semino)

Despite such commitments, many young scholars were ambivalent about the
relationship between activism and research:

I've always seen studying as part of my activism – gaining the knowledge to
support what I do. But there are lots of people doing politics through theory, but
without caring about how to present it – how to make their thinking meaningful
to others. So I had a five-year gap, a break in my studies, following a crisis. The
crisis was about modes of academic talking, their detached mode of presentation,
with them not wanting to communicate with people who didn't talk the same
language. (P.G. Macioti)

[Doing a PhD] I'm worried about being disconnected from reality because I read
a lot of pieces by people that on a theoretical level make a lot of sense but at
the level of actually reflecting reality in local neighbourhoods, really reflecting
political trajectories and the things that have happened, or the problems of doing
politics, and the kinds of decisions that you have to make doing politics, I don't
find that reflected in much material. (Sukhwant Dhaliwal)

I'm not a good activist, and I'm not sure I'm a good academic, and I'm certainly
not sure how they go together. In particular, I'm not sure that being an academic
is useful. When I did the PhD I wanted it to be useful, to be politically relevant.
But I'm not sure it was. Then I got the scholarship to come to England to study
more. Personally benefitting from my research made me really uncomfortable.
(Susan Pell)

Each of these extracts refers to concerns about how to make research
meaningful and useful to the movements to which participants were committed.
One response was to use research to give voice to groups experiencing
marginalization and exploitation:

The role of many people in the academy is to change the ordering of knowledge.
Our main point [in research on sex work and migration] is to ask: why don't
you ask sex workers what their experience is? Why do feminist abolitionists
or policymakers always think they know better? That's a very feminist point.
(P.G. Macioti)

The focus on experiential knowledge was closely linked to forms of activist
engagement with voluntary and/or political organizations. Participants
attempted to use research to raise awareness about the issues at stake, and to
try to 'give something back' to the movements or groups that they studied. For
example, P.G.'s research draws on x:talk, a sex-worker led project providing
free English classes to migrant workers, and mobilizing migrant sex works to

claim rights; Sarah Lamble's research on prisons drew on her activist work connecting LGBT prisoners to the wider queer and transgender communities through a pen-pal scheme (the Bent Bars project, http://www.bentbarsproject. org); Susan Pell's postdoctoral research centred on the study of how social movements create their own archives and collective social memory. The latter raised difficult methodological and ethical issues. Susan recounted how:

> *When I was doing my PhD I kept having the problem – what kind of stories do I want to tell? Where is it fair to make them open to public analysis? As a researcher I feel like a bit of a voyeur; I thought that people might look at me as though I had an ulterior motive. So as an academic I now feel like I have got to be an advocate for a particular kind of methodological approach concerned with questions of who do we study and how, and what should we make 'public'.* (Susan Pell)

Political commitments influenced not only methodological choices but also modes of engagement with different audiences:

> *There is something about the academy that is different from activism; activism has to be much more responsive. I want to combine both; without some form of activist engagement, being an academic doesn't make sense. So I want to write for activist groups – like I did a report for the Women's Coalition for Peace back in Israel, called 'Who profits?' about the industry of the [Israeli] occupation.* (Dana Rubin)

Similarly P.G. recounted how she had worked on a report on the impact of anti-trafficking laws on sex workers. But Sarah Lamble spoke of the 'perennial problem' of linking activism and academic work: '*academics will find it too activist and activists will find it too conceptual*':

> *I go back and forth on that. Sometimes I think that when I come to publishing I probably won't try to speak to both audiences at once, but will try to use the same material and publish it in different forms. Because as much as I want to say those two things can come together, if you are going to make it acceptable to non-academics it's probably not going to count in research terms given all the pressures of impact and stuff. I mean, I do want my research to make an impact but certainly not in the way that government envisages impact. So you have to make choices.* (Sarah Lamble)

Some participants who had set out on the PhD route did not continue, for a range of reasons. Lisa Harker, whom we met in Chapter 4, became impatient with the academic route and moved to other spaces of knowledge-work – NGOs and think-tanks – where the temporal cycle of research, policy and impact was shorter. And Cecilia Wee, who went on to become an independent arts curator, told how:

> *When I was younger I wanted to do a PhD but when I started I realized I didn't want to only do one thing. The academic life was too abstracted from what I was interested in – that is how audiences and artists meet and confront each other, encouraging processes of reflection and questioning.* (Cecilia Wee)

These participants all clearly wanted to create productive relationships between research and politics. As such they had to negotiate a series of dilemmas. One was how to re-imagine the relationship between researcher and research subject (as in P.G.'s comment on involving sex workers in the research process and enabling them to give voice to their experience). A second was that of how to find a theoretical basis for work that could not easily be situated in existing academic hierarchies and disciplinary repertoires. If your research is on India, the West Bank, Argentina or China, how can you do this within western traditions of liberal theory? If you are working on questions of culture and identity, how can this be accommodated in modernist social science? Most of the young scholars I spoke to were working beyond the cultural, linguistic and post-colonial 'turns' in social theory. But this led directly to a third dilemma, highlighted in the comments from both P.G. and Dana: how to overcome the limitations of academic styles of presentation, and respond to the imperative to make research meaningful and useful to those for whom the outcome might matter. Finally, the extracts show young researchers wondering how to engage in research as a form of collective practice that, in Alessandra and Stella's terms, made a difference to more than yourself. This was extremely difficult in an academic climate that valued and rewarded individual achievement, which viewed PhD study, in particular, as a singular and lonely endeavour, and in which research directed towards policy and practice tended to be valued less highly than 'critical' and theoretical work within the academy.

These concerns speak to each of the questions that structure the chapter. They reference wider debates about the transformations of knowledge and power that have been addressed in other literatures on the ethics and practices of research (Edwards and Mauthner 2002; Hollway and Jefferson 2000; Lather 1991); on the relationships between social science and government (Bevir 2010); on changing professional practice (Bondi, Carr, Clarke and Clegg 2011; Dent and Whitehead 2002); and on the neoliberalization of the academy (Cannan and Shumar 2008). My aim in the rest of this chapter is more modest. I want to draw on the accounts of participants to show how knowledge-work and politics are differently and multiply entangled in individual working lives.

The politics of recognition

Nancy Fraser famously argued that, 'The struggle for recognition is fast becoming the paradigmatic form of political conflict' (Fraser 1997: 11). Her analysis was situated in a feminist critique of political economy, but speaks to a range of claims for recognition that challenged the prevailing knowledge-power orthodoxies across the professions, organizational management, political practice and the academy. However, the recognition of diverse personal experiences and forms of voice potentially brings more of the 'person' into the governmental domain. I want to illustrate this paradox by drawing on examples of the reordering of knowledge and power within the professions, in development work and in the academy.

The social movements of the 1960s and 1970s challenged the professional monopoly of expertise, seeking to appropriate, translate and construct knowledge in ways that spoke to people's experience and which could be used in projects of social change. This was most marked, perhaps, in challenges to the orthodoxies of a powerful and male-dominated medical profession, which exercised control over reproduction, sexuality and bodily and mental health. This was a key focus of the burgeoning women's health groups of the 1970s and of AIDS activism in the 1990s (Maskovsky 2009). *Our Bodies Ourselves* (http:// www.ourbodiesourselves.org) – a feminist self-help resource first published in 1970 – emerged from one women's health collective and was widely circulated and used by women's groups. Ann McPherson (G2) was one of those involved in the Our Bodies Ourselves (OBOS) collective, and in her later role as a doctor in general practice she continued her interest in democratizing knowledge:

> *Well, I've always been interested in patient experience because, for example, the book on miscarriage I wrote was based on interviewing people about their own experiences. This began when I had breast cancer, which was fifteen years ago, and I met up with a colleague who had a new knee and we both wanted to know other people's experiences. And rather than have just the heroic or someone who has done something extraordinary we wanted to have this wide range. We started by doing a questionnaire, but a questionnaire isn't a really good way of doing it because people tend not to write lots about their experience. So then we came round to realize that we had to go and talk to them, and later we started to video them. We always used to interview between forty and fifty people from all over the country, different backgrounds, different experiences, and we've now done this for fifty-two different diseases. We managed to get a bit of funding from the Department of Health and also set up a charity. We found some very supportive people at the Department of Health and we set up DIPE [Database of Individual Patient Experiences].* (Ann McPherson)

Ann later developed a resource for young people (Teenage Health Talk On Line) that prefigured the more general turn to the internet and the use of new social media as research platforms; but more importantly, for my purposes, it was a pioneer of emerging models of practice in health and well-being based on co-production, peer-based support (for example, in the Expert Patient scheme in the UK) and personal experience, though Ann herself was highly critical of current health policy. She saw herself as a campaigner and policy actor;[2] she pioneered the generation of online resources through which groups – including young people – could share experiences of ill-health and learn from their peers; and had an influential policy role through participation in Department of Health innovations. But the extract above also demonstrates other political dynamics of knowledge-work: the significance of research methods (only some of which would enable a focus on surfacing experience); the evolution of research projects (from tiny and particular to major programmes) in a parlous funding environment; and the links between personal experience and publicly focused research (it all began with *'a friend's new knee'*).

Recognition, this suggests, is not simply a matter of a cultural acceptance of voices and experiences that had been hidden or marginalized, and adding them to the available stock of knowledge. It can also be transformative of 'mainstream' knowledge. This takes me to a second example, this time from international development work. In Chapter 5 I discussed how Marion Macalpine and others developed new forms of leadership and organizational development that privileged participative and 'distributed' notions of power. Here, Marion describes her work on an international programme that brought African women with expertise in gender and development together with UK practitioners of management and leadership education:

> *It was a fantastic education for all of us really. But there were lots of dilemmas around being a white person going out with big suitcases of books and ideas from the West, and I spent an awful lot of time thinking about it. And I think we developed a way of providing frameworks so that people could create their own content. Our role was enabling and facilitating; we tried to tackle the kind of power involved. I think the kind of development stuff fed directly into all the work that we did with British managers, so there was always a global context. We wrote a paper called 'Choosing the Knowledge We Carry' about contesting the hegemony of managerialism.[3] And we did quite a lot of work looking at individual managers' responses to the legacies of colonialism, the role of the World Bank and so on, which was all hugely powerful.*
> (Marion Macalpine)

Interestingly both sets of innovations were taken up by academic, governmental and charitable bodies. But the process of valuing experience was not without its own difficulties. Marion and Ann's work highlights the significance of mediating practices through which experience was elicited, codified and communicated. This suggests something of the power dynamics at stake between facilitators /researchers/teachers and those whose experience is elicited: in Ann's work, the power dynamics of professionals/clients and between generations, both of which she was trying to unravel; and in Marion's case the legacy of colonial power.

Within the academy the focus on experience presented challenges to academic hierarchies and objectivist conceptions of knowledge. Marian Barnes's work privileged care as a dimension of struggles for social justice; Marilyn Taylor was committed to projects of community and user empowerment; Helen Sullivan (G3) worked on public policy and local governance. Each valued experiential knowledge, and each sought to collaborate with the subjects of their research to produce frameworks and concepts that might help make sense of that experience:

> *I find it hard to pin down who my work is for. Much of what I do is for a practitioner audience – front-line workers who are trying to negotiate the difficult*

stuff. I also work with service users themselves, finding ways of introducing some of the theory I work with in ways that enable them to make sense of what is happening in their own lives. It's working these borders that is exciting and rewarding. (Marian Barnes)

Research has taught me that life is more complicated than theory tells you. I tried to find theories that worked 'on the ground' – theories that linked governmentality to the possibility of agency. I was interested in how domination was not the end of the story, how people could still have and use power. (Marilyn Taylor)

There's something very seductive about being the expert and I strove for a long, long time to become the expert. And I realize now that's not what it's about, it's about how you approach the issue, how you work out with people what the questions are. That's how your expertise, in as much you have any, is expressed; it's not about being anything, it's about becoming. (Helen Sullivan)

Each stressed the importance of research and teaching that speaks to the experience of those with little formal power, and emphasized the value of participatory methods and action research. Each also spoke about the importance of working across the academic/practice boundary and of being able to communicate what they did:

When I write I'm always thinking of the people that I was interviewing. If they were going to read this stuff it wasn't going to be their favourite bedtime reading, but at least it had to make sense to them, and I always felt that my first accountability was to the people I'd interviewed, basically. (Marilyn Taylor)

The politics of recognition opened out a concern with democratizing knowledge; not only making it more widely available but also introducing notions of the 'co-production' of teaching and research.[4] But it also opened up dilemmas, many of which emerged in my conversation with Catherine Durose (G4) and Liz Richardson (G3), both university-based researchers working on policy-related agendas – at the time of the interview, issues of 'community' and 'civil society'. Liz spoke about being a facilitator extracting knowledge from those she interviewed and then 'giving it back' so that they – and others – could make sense of their experience. Catherine spoke of being able to reflect on people's experience and of having:

a responsibility to sort of present their experience to the wider world because there's some bigger things you can learn from what they've done. That's why I also think I'm an advocate for people even if they haven't nominated me. (Catherine Durose)

Both spoke about the value of the 'co-production' of knowledge between researcher and researched: not only did it lead, they suggested, to better data to inform policy, but it also changed the power dynamics inherent to the research process. But both drew attention to some of the difficult power dynamics at stake.

It was, they suggested, difficult for academics to 'unlearn their privilege'. There are also methodological issues of authenticity and representation, and of communication:

> You have to ask if we restrict our ability to co-produce research because our comfort zone is text, and text isn't the comfort zone of many of the people you are researching with. (Catherine Durose)

And Liz raised the issue of how far the chosen methods of researchers working with experiential data enabled them effectively to 'speak to power' in a context where more 'scientific' methods – such as the randomized control trial – were privileged. But experience-based research and co-produced research raise questions that go beyond methodological concerns: they have deeper resonances with patterns of inequality and disadvantage, access and voice. These encounters take place in what Askins and Pain term 'contact zones'(Askins and Pain 2011, drawing on Pratt 1992): zones of interaction across difference that are material as well as epistemological. The interviews show participants wrestling with questions of how far to cede power and how far this might be possible. They suggest that the valorization of experience and authenticity may serve to undermine the perceived expertise of the academic and her ability to speak to power.

But there were other dilemmas and dangers at stake in the preference, by many participants, for more experiential and participative methods. Some spoke of how enabling 'ordinary people' to challenge the power of professionals and service-providers could feed into governmental challenges (and cuts) to the public sector. Sarah Lamble spoke about being reluctant to mix her research and her activist work because of the dangers of appropriation, either in the academy or, more importantly, by government:

> A lot of the work that I do now is trying to get prisoners' voices heard. The tensions that I have are around wanting to do work that would support and assist in the kind of anti-prison organizing work, but not to do the kind of criminological research that might get used by governments in ways that I didn't want it to be used, or to kind of advance my own career on the backs of prisoners. (Sarah Lamble)

Tess Ridge, a social policy academic who works in ways that seeks to get children's voices heard on issues that are problematic for them, also expressed concern about how her research might be used:

> I have to be very careful about my research. I think that's true of all of us who work with people who are vulnerable. I know that's totally the wrong term because they're not vulnerable but actually tremendously resilient. But if you say they're resilient then people think, 'Oh, poverty is not a bad thing, people are so resilient.' What I've tried to say all the time is 'children are really activated, they're imaginative, they're sparky, they're clever, they're smart, low income kids really try to get a lot of stuff solved'. But if you take that into a policy perspective it is assumed that they can have agency to overcome their problems. But they can't, poverty is so constraining. (Tess Ridge)

Bringing personal experience into the public and policy domains, then, is double-edged: it, too, is vulnerable to forms of appropriation in which research results are detached from the complexity and ambiguity of the findings, and in which policymakers can appropriate them to legitimate policies that are antithetical to the intentions and commitments of researchers. It also, by bringing more of the personal into the public and policy domains, opens up governmental projects of improvement and responsibilization. But collaborative teaching and research also opened up powerful alliances and vocabularies through which activist struggles could be pursued.

Close encounters: research, policy and practice

These dilemmas and ambiguities were intensified as researchers brought commitments to practitioners into the research process and were drawn into a series of close encounters with government. Many crossed the practice/policy/ political boundaries in the course of their own working lives and brought a commitment to conducting research across those boundaries. For example, Helen Sullivan had worked for local government before becoming an academic, while Sue Richards worked in the Civil Service, a consultancy organization, a school of public policy and the think-tank, Institute for Government. Ruth Lister, who had worked in the voluntary sector before becoming an academic, spoke about how *'I never wanted to do abstract stuff, I always wanted my work to be grounded'*. But I want to begin the discussion with the work of Davina Cooper, who had served as a local politician before becoming an academic. Davina spoke of trying to work across the boundary of academic theory and those engaged in 'practical politics' – often as gay and lesbian workers inside local government but also a wider audience of social movements. But this presented difficulties:

> *My academic writing comes out of my political commitments. I wanted to explore what the radical potential of the state might be. I got very interested in the mid 1980s about how these limits were being tested; many people [with radical backgrounds] were entering local government and doing what, theoretically, shouldn't have been possible within a capitalist state. My book,* Sexing the City, *came out of that experience. And I wanted it to be practically useful to those who had also been involved. But engagement in more practical politics often means tackling different problems and questions to those that can animate work as an academic. I have always been looking for crossover spaces where debates across these differences can happen.* (Davina Cooper)

Sue Brownill, speaking from a different history, spoke of how:

> *Always as an academic I try to engage with wherever I am [living/working]. This started with my work in Docklands, where I used my experience to write my thesis on popular planning. But ever since I have tried to keep my feet on*

the ground, especially being involved in policy and planning stuff. So I have always been involved locally – working with community organizations, housing associations and so on. Academically one of my areas of research has been public participation in planning and regeneration. I've done research for ODPM, the Royal Town Planning Institute, the GLA [Greater London Authority], etc., on this as well. That's where the Big Society comes in. I started with an interest in neighbourhood plans – there was a pilot not far from where I lived. But it was really low key, not much happened. But what was developing was a campaign around cuts which showed up many of the issues, so I followed that. (Sue Brownill)

There are important resonances between these experiences and those of the women cited in the previous section. But the desire to make research 'grounded' and meaningful to those engaged with 'practical politics' can be disappointing. This takes us back to Dana's and Susan's comments, in the first section of this chapter, about the different temporalities and languages associated with academic work and activism, and their experience of the difficulties of 'working across' the research/activist boundary. This is especially the case, Davina acknowledged, where theoretical work is involved:

With others, I tried to shape the Centre (the AHRC-funded Centre for Law, Gender and Sexuality) in ways that enabled it to do work that was intellectually and theoretically innovative, that was critical and interdisciplinary, but that would also engage with policy and with community activists. So it would look outwards and would cross over the academic/non-academic divide. But it wouldn't do that at the expense of theoretical innovation. (Davina Cooper)

I asked Davina how she managed that tension.

I think it was the hardest thing. We tried to do crossover work, and looked at different formats for discussion, for expressing our views, different modes of communication, and started to build up networks. But a lot of our work didn't translate easily into community activist interest, and it was too critical for many public policy makers, and that's the difficulty. It was the same with Sexing the City. There's always that problem of how, if you do more critical and theoretical academic work, the problem isn't necessarily the accessibility of what you're saying, it's about the interest of what you're saying. Often the questions and the problems you're addressing are different ones. (Davina Cooper)

Helen Sullivan's 'crossover' work was rather different. She began her working life in local government, and developed a strong commitment to addressing issues of poverty and disadvantage in particular local communities and in enhancing local democracy. After becoming an academic she worked in – and later led – teams engaged in evaluating large government programmes, including Health Action Zones, Local Government Modernisation, Local Strategic Partnerships and Neighbourhood Regeneration/Management. These programmes were situated in shifts in both government and the academy. The New Labour governments of the 1990s funded a number of large-scale evaluation studies as part of the 'What works?' agenda in public policy, seeking to find objective methods and evidence, and to embed a more 'scientific' approach to policymaking (Bevir 2010; Nutley, Walter, and Davies 2007; Newman 2011a). This movement towards evaluation supported the growth of new academic units, often located in business schools or schools of health or public policy (some of the very few areas of expansion in higher education in that period).

> When we did the evaluation of the local government modernization agenda government was in the grip of its 'What works?' phase; it was 'This is a policy, does it work or not?', and the question that never got asked was 'Is this the right policy?', and to what extent are you constructing the evidence on the basis of the policy that you've already set in train. In the earlier evaluation of Health Action Zones, which Marian [Barnes] led, that was more open in the sense that the policies for service modernization were still trying to address inequalities. This was back in the days when those sorts of things were still cared about. I think as the New Labour emphasis became much more on modernizing services, and choice, and empowerment, then evaluation became less about whether policies could have anything to do with the most disadvantaged people in society, or whether they were going to make any difference to structural inequality. (Helen Sullivan)

But evaluation programmes, she suggested, could also be bent to address wider questions. Marian Barnes made a similar point:

> There are spaces; you can make spaces in doing contract work, you can develop more critical spaces; you can both deliver what's expected and open up more critical perspectives. For example, in doing the Children's Fund Evaluation [for which she was co-director of the national evaluation] prevention was already a mainstream policy and practice discourse so we said, 'Let's take that seriously, push it, interrogate what that might mean.' In evaluation projects there's something about recognizing the impossibility of achieving the objectives that officials want but of highlighting what can actually be accomplished. For example, the National Children's Fund created important spaces that enabled practitioners to do creative work with children and families. But it didn't prevent social exclusion, which was its primary goal. (Marian Barnes)

As well as conducting government commissioned research and evaluation studies, academic participants were also often invited to offer informal responses to policy proposals or to attend government sponsored 'round tables'. Here, I return to my conversation with Liz Richardson and Catherine Durose, one focus of which was the ethical and normative dilemmas raised in such 'close encounters' with government:

> Recently we had an opportunity to talk to the new coalition government and me and a bunch of colleagues decided that we would. Other colleagues criticised us for doing that, and it does make you wonder whether to say, 'Oh well, it's better to be in than out', or whether you should just stand on the outside and criticize. (Liz Richardson)

I think that's a really interesting point because I think being in a [university] department that is increasingly going towards a critical perspective, there's an ethos of 'do not get your hands dirty' [by talking to government]. At the same time they really kind of look down on doing something, anything, that is kind of policy relevant. And I really struggle with that. (Catherine Durose)

These and other extracts raise questions about what sources of expertise such academics carry and the ordering of legitimacy attached to different sources of expertise. Such issues have been debated elsewhere:[5] much of the literature focuses on encounters between the relatively fixed institutional positions of government and university. However, what I think we can see happening is that the spaces of power that academics and other researchers mobilized shifted as both the academy and government itself were remade in accordance with 'modernizing' logics. The concerns of Helen, Catherine and Liz were not those of academics more securely placed in 'traditional' departments or in more 'critical' spaces (such as that occupied by Davina). The institutional field of policymaking had also become more complex and diverse, traversed by what I term 'policy entrepreneurs' and 'knowledge brokers' who worked across boundaries and who generated and mobilized new spaces of power. As well as creating knowledge through research they sought out knowledge from 'elsewhere', repackaged it, transformed it, translated it, publicized it and mobilized its use. Several participants engaged in such work were discussed earlier in the book: for example, Kate Oliver, Jane Foot and Tricia Zipfel, all of whom have had complex working lives in which 'knowledge brokering' became progressively more important. All had conducted research commissioned by government bodies and organizations such as the Joseph Rowntree Foundation; all had worked on major policy programmes; and some had gone on to work with think-tanks such as the Improvement and Development Agency (IDeA), Demos and the Young Foundation.

Lisa Harker, at the time of the interview, had just left her post as deputy director of the New Labour-oriented think-tank, the Institute for Public Policy Research, to take up a post at Demos. As noted earlier, she had earlier embarked on a PhD but:

I got more and more interested in how you change policy and how you change things quite quickly. I mean I very quickly learnt that I wasn't suited to academia because I was so impatient. I wanted to put my research findings on 'Women's Hour', and I wasn't really interested in academic journals. I wanted something that could be more immediate. (Lisa Harker)

Think-tanks and other spaces of knowledge brokerage were ambiguously positioned in the governance shifts of the 1990s that brought an increased focus on evidence-based policy. This brought academics into new contractual relationships with government, securing funds to research policy agendas and to evaluate policy programmes. Research Councils also began to fund a number of cross-disciplinary research centres (such as the centre led by Davina

Cooper discussed earlier) that might, it was hoped, generate innovation and inform policy and practice. Such developments generated a number of tensions. First, academics had to 'work the borders' with government, negotiating the objectives and terms of the contract in order to conduct credible research. Second, they had to face in (at least) two directions, both fulfilling the terms of contracts to deliver 'practice-oriented' recommendations and engaging in more theoretically driven and critical work that would enable them to publish the kinds of papers that would meet 'academic' criteria of success. Third, they had to manage the relationship between their own agendas – often highly critical of whatever the current ideology or policy might be – and those of government.

But academics and researchers also generated new spaces of influence and promoted new 'public conversations'. We saw in Chapter 4 how a number of academics (Hilary Land, Ruth Lister, Sue Himmelweit and others associated with the Women's Budget Group) and researchers (working in think-tanks and NGOs) sought to influence social, economic and development policy. But academics also worked on local policy agendas and local struggles. Jane Wills linked her work with London Citizens to her teaching role, developing an MA in Community Organizing and teaching research methods in ways that enable students to engage with community politics. She also offered an image of the university itself as a civic institution: *'We have become agents of the state, often becoming quite isolated from the communities in which we are located; and our academic labour has become so individualized.'* Instead, she offers an image of the university *'working in partnership with people in the production of knowledge'*; and on this basis, she argues, we *'may be able to renegotiate our relationship with the state'*.

A different conception of the public role of the university is represented in the formation of the Birmingham Policy Commission. Launched at the Conservative Party Conference in 2010, supported by Demos and led by Helen Sullivan, this brought together commissioners from the academy, policy and practice, and worked with young people from the National Youth Forum. The first commission focused on the coalition government's formal commitments to localism and the Big Society.

> *For me the point about doing a Policy Commission was that, yes, you had some academics but you principally had people from policy and practice. And one of the things that I tried to do was to get as many kinds of radical people into this process as possible, although it's harder than you might think. The aim was to find the questions that weren't being asked and what might be the consequences of not asking those questions, and how you bring them into debates about whether this or that policy is working or not. And I suppose that's what I've tried to do although not as successfully as I would like. Because very early on I realized, and this is just my naivety I suppose, but very early on I realized that I had a fundamental disagreement with the body of people, most of whom I respect enormously, that I had a fundamental disagreement with what they were advising, and that fundamental disagreement is ... and it's so difficult to write the report ... the fundamental disagreement I have is that they do not ... and*

this is people from both the private sector and the public sector, the voluntary sector, people who were politicians – the view they came to very quickly was that it doesn't matter who delivers public services, they could be delivered by the public, private or third sectors or some combination. What mattered was the outcome, what mattered was that there's accountability, what mattered was that there's value for money, but it did not matter whether services remained within the public sector or not. But it does matter to me. And the dilemma is that I had to write the report. When it comes to representing what it is they think they're doing, that's been my job, so the paths that I have trod or tried to tread have been very tricky. (Helen Sullivan; her emphasis)

Unlike other extracts I have here retained Helen's hesitancies about putting this experience into words, of pinning down the issue of which, at the time of the interview, she was still trying to make sense. The extract also hints at broader dilemmas about the independence of researchers operating in such ambiguous spaces of power, spaces that are cross-cut by competing rationalities and logics – but that have eventually to be at least temporarily resolved in a particular text (the report). It speaks to issues of political agency: is this concerned simply with bringing people together, of facilitating and enabling, or should academics have a view? And, if so, what is the basis of legitimacy for such a view? The contested nature of knowledge at stake in 'close encounters' was an issue developed in my conversation with Catherine and Liz, who discussed how far the evidence they presented to funders and policymakers should be experience-based; cumulative across years of study and engagement; or based on more 'objective' and experimental methods of research. Finally the Policy Commission raises issues of accountability: issues which have been debated in Helen's own work (Sullivan 2003). Interestingly, the Commission was supported by Demos, taking us back to the beginning of this section and raising questions about the different spaces of power in which knowledge-work is conducted and the possible tensions between them.

The spaces discussed in this section are specifically British. Different traditions of the role of the academy are represented in forms of 'engaged' or 'activist' anthropology, principally in the United States, in which research and political action are deeply entangled (see also Maskovsky 2011). Ida Susser is an excellent example of the possibilities opened up in such work. She is an anthropologist whose work is as informed by feminism, and which concentrates on the understanding of gender in relation to class inequalities, colonialism and empire since the 1970s. She sees her work as part of an overall political engagement and has been active in the past decade in helping to form and working with Athena: Advancing Gender Equity and Human Rights in the Global Response to HIV/AIDS. The embedding of research within and for activist communities is illustrated in her work on HIV prevention among homeless men and women in New York, in community mobilization around HIV in Puerto Rico and in South Africa. She also developed a training programme within South Africa attended by students, NGO workers, civil servants and academics, creating, like Jane, a new cadre of 'expert' activists. The spaces of power she generated and occupied, then, are both global and profoundly local; and they connect the broad roles of what she terms the 'public intellectual', opening debates and intervening in the wider public culture, with specific and embedded research-activism.

In and beyond the cultural turn

The shifting formations, sites and relations of knowledge-work were not only generated by institutional shifts (in the academy and government) and global/ local struggles but by theoretical and epistemological contestation. While the previous section highlighted the importance of experiential knowledge, the cultural, post-colonial and post-structuralist turns in social theory challenged the links between embodied experience, identity and agency (Brown 2005). The focus of many theorists turned to how subjects were formed through language and other forms of representation; experience, then, could no longer be viewed as the expression of a coherent and essential self (Haraway 1988; Scott 1991). And post-colonial scholars argued that stories grounded in experience were in any case problematic: 'experience is not a truth that precedes culturally given representations of experience but is actually mediated by those representations' (Stone-Mediatore 2000: 111). This created problems for feminism: if women could no longer be viewed as a common embodied category how might a feminist politics be pursued? The space for critique, Eisenstein argued, shrank as feminists turned to the theories of Foucault, Derrida and Lacan: 'I read declarations of the death of the subject with considerable suspicion, given that women had only just begun to declare their right to subjectivity and agency' (Eisenstein 2006: 52). In contrast Gibson-Graham offer a more positive reading of the political possibilities opened up by the cultural turn, arguing that post-structuralism 'enabled a turn away from the dominant focus on theorizing the unfolding of structuralist logics, and an enhanced focus on theorizing the contingency of social outcomes'. This, Gibson-Graham argue, 'gave us (and the world) more room to move, enlarging the space of the ethical and the possible' (Gibson-Graham 2008: 4; see also Laclau and Mouffe 1985).

I want to trace in this section some of the ways in which participants managed the tension between the deconstruction of 'woman' as an embodied category and the pursuit of politically informed research. Some were themselves agents of these transformations; but rather than being caught in Eisenstein's 'political paralysis' they saw new forms of theory as intrinsic to the activist struggles with which they were engaged:

> I still think of myself as a Black Marxist feminist, but I found that Marxist theory couldn't speak completely to the moment, couldn't do the race and gender politics of what I was looking at, couldn't unpick, make sense of it. So I turned

to post-structuralism through the feminist engagement with Foucault. It seemed to make sense, to give another kind of language that more happily aligned itself with the questions coming out of the political activisms I'd been involved with. Black feminist and anti-racist organizations were struggling to try to articulate the ways in which we understood the world, how to work with experience, how to engage beyond the old Marxist categories – you sort of can't. Then suddenly there is work that says you need to think of experience not as coming out of an essential self but as figured contextually and contingently in situated contexts. And this takes you beyond any essential characteristic of the subject; you realize that experience is subject to naming and framing practices. (Gail Lewis)

Gail acknowledge that post-structuralism was not necessarily a perspective that activist groups found useful, but that for her she could find a 'good enough fit' between notions of the de-essentialized subject and the idea of the subject as embodied, feeling and potentially political. She and other participants were engaged with inequality and difference, but through different theoretical frameworks. Avtar Brah, also coming out of Black feminist politics, talked of how she was:

Still sort of thinking through the implications of gendered inequality, anti-racism, ethnicity, identity, and the whole issue of what do we do about the questions we used to subsume under socialism – inequality, oppression, exploitation – how do we think about them today? These are the things that still preoccupy me. But the framing of the questions has changed in the sense that society has changed. For instance, I used to be involved in Feminist Review *and we used to call ourselves a socialist feminist journal. Now we don't specifically call ourselves that but we are still interested in issues of class inequality, and with issues we now call intersectionality, what we used to call difference. Feminism has changed obviously, people talk about post-feminism and all that – but some of the questions are still the same: questions of violence against women, employment issues, low wages.* (Avtar Brah)

I asked Avtar how she situated herself within this changed framework.

It led to new opportunities in what I was writing. I became engaged with new theories, such as theories of intersectionality, and also of globalization. At a personal level I became less active in political groups but through the 1990s I became much more involved in politics through my writing. (Avtar Brah)

'Politics through writing' was a means of speaking to key issues arising in the wider political-cultural shifts of recent decades. For Gail, this was conducted through pedagogic work at the Open University and in wider political and theoretical writings. And in her book Avtar reflects that her writing is: 'in part an inscription of the effects of my involvement with certain political projects. It writes them as much as is written by them. These projects – feminism, anti-racism, socialist envisaging of democratic politics – have had a critical bearing on the intellectual and political configurations of our times' (Brah 1996: 10).

The work of Gail and Avtar speaks to new formations of politics, culture and theory in the aftermath of the struggles against the exclusions of white, western, heterosexual feminism. P.G. Macioti (G4) reflected that:

If you want to fight for the self determination of people in the face of oppressive forms of power, then post-structuralism is helpful; it deconstructs the categories that keep people in fixed positions based on classed or racialized distinctions. Of course, I struggled with the tension between being able to say, 'This is the truth, this is why I am engaged in political struggle,' on the one hand and, on the other hand, to recognize that there is no truth. You have to say this is the best politics I can do; there is no single theory that you can work with, you just have to work from the experience of the people who are struggling with what they see as their truth. (P.G. Macioti)

Sarah Lamble's account drew attention to a different set of tensions. Her activism works across the politics of violence against women and prison abolition, in both of which she used the term 'social movements' to depict axes of political engagement. The term social movement is associated with forms of politics arising from the recognition of common axes of identity as the basis for struggle, a politics that is not readily configured within post-structuralist theory. But when questioned about her use of the term social movement, she went on to recount how:

The other part of my project is that I'm really interested in a kind of post-identity politics. So I'm interested in queer, trans and feminist organizing that doesn't organize around the banner of identity politics, but still takes questions of identity seriously. So that's why I wanted to focus on queer, trans and feminist activists who are doing work not only under the banner of a gay liberation movement or whatever but doing it under the banner of anti-prison work, or anti-border work, or anti-globalization. In my project they've clashed a bit, so it's not only people who are identifiers, queer or feminist, but people who take a kind of feminist or queer ethos to organizing the work that they do. And I'm also interested in forms of organizing that are very grassroots. I mean a lot of the projects that I'm interested in are very small, have very little visibility. People would attend marches and they would organize events but would be too small to get counted as a movement in the conventional sense. (Sarah Lamble)

These extracts suggests how Sarah, P.G. and many others I talked to worked effectively across what might be termed social or political movements and the more fluid and ephemeral political performances associated with 'post-identity' politics. In many interviews participants talked about being engaged in a 'practical politics' supporting particular groups – volunteering in women's refuges, supporting 'grassroots' community struggles – while at the same time deconstructing the very categories – women, community – on which it might be assumed such a politics depended. But rather than these being viewed as practices that were in tension with each other, they were spoken of as complementary; young researchers spoke of moving towards theoretical work in order to get deeper understandings of the very practices of violence, exclusion, oppression and injustice that they witnessed in their activism. This runs rather counter to claims that the post-structuralist turn, in deconstructing essentializing categories of identity and solidarity, has led to political paralysis. Sarah's extract also speaks to a discursive separation between feminism, gay liberation and other movements as a collective struggle based on an assumed common identity on the one hand and, on the other, the idea of feminist, queer and transgender as forms of political ethos or political performance (see Chapter 2). This puts 'experience' back into the political frame, but now from a position that acknowledges that the meaning of experience is subject, in Gail's terms, to processes of naming and framing rather than being an essential expression of an authentic self. What we can see in such work is, I think, a strategic use of categories such as class, race and ethnicity, and references to embodied women who are the subjects of domestic violence, at the same time that engagements with post-structuralism – integral to the project of rethinking difference through notions of intersectionality – deconstruct such categories.

The work of these and other academics can be viewed as exemplifying Gibson-Graham's call for scholars to constitute and perform 'other worlds' rather than being satisfied with critique and deconstruction:

> *Critical engagement – that very term – means a continuing attempt to unpack the kinds of internal logics of whatever the field of enquiry is, and what the implications might be. The generations who have come after are still doing this. They bring different understandings, and they certainly bring different technologies. But what I now feel – and this is because of the base [for intellectual work] becoming so narrowed to the extent that it is now deeply uncomfortable – is that critique is not enough. We also need to be able to construct. We need to be able to say this is what is wrong, these are its logics, these are the rationalities by which it works, these are the agendas that are being put forward and these are the ones that are being assimilated. So what is it that might make those very things different? And I think that is the question: how do we propose something that is different?* (Gail Lewis)

The attempt to *'propose something that is different'* can be traced across the accounts of this chapter, from the work on recognition to the engagements with policy to reframe knowledge itself:

> *I suppose what's remained continuous through the whole period is that the academic writing I've done has explored questions coming out of my political commitments. Initially this very much concerned what you can do with the state, and the radical potential and possibilities for those working within the state. And then I've gone on to think about how to re-theorize key political concepts: concepts like equality, power, the state, citizenship and so on; trying to find ways of thinking about these concepts that might open up other political possibilities. More recently, my work has moved towards other sites. The British state at the current moment doesn't feel like the site where much radical political mobilization is happening, so I've been looking elsewhere, to how people configure what I term 'everyday utopias' within the confines of the present.* (Davina Cooper)

Davina Cooper's current work on 'everyday utopias' (Cooper 2013; see also Cooper 2001) makes visible a range of alternative possible ways of living, working and performing politics, from women's bath houses to alternative economic exchange projects, in the process re-examining and reinflecting concepts that have been the primary currency of traditional disciplines: concepts such as the state, governance, and power. Davina's work, and Gail's comments about moving beyond critique and deconstruction to *make something different*, resonate with Sasha Roseneil's frustration at 'paranoid readings' of the present which left no space for action, for agency. She spoke about her interest in asking questions about social change:

> *That's what I've always been interested in, that's the theme that runs through everything ... trying to make social change happen and also understand process of social change. All my academic work is grappling with the question of social change, that's what I think sociology is about, but I think that there are those sociologists who kind of emphasize social stasis and continuity. That's very strong, I think, amongst feminists; there's a very strong tendency to kind of argue nothing's really changing, nothing much has changed, it's always as bad as it ever has been. My tendency has always been to look for the openings, look for the fissures, look for what is changing. And I think that you can kind of prise greater social change through finding the change that's already happening.* (Sasha Roseneil)

This analysis is informed by her reading of Rogoff (Rogoff 2003) and Sedgwick (Sedgwick 2003) on paranoid and reparative readings. Rogoff describes the limits of both criticism (leading to the allocation of blame) and post-structural forms of critique (which stop at deconstruction). Both of these, she suggests, leave no way out, no ground from which to act. The move to what she terms 'criticality', in contrast, focuses on the present and on how to both understand its flaws while actualizing some of its potential: 'We have that double occupation in which we are both fully armed with the knowledges of critique, able to analyse and unveil, while at the same time sharing and living out the very conditions which we are able to see through' (Rogoff 2003, cited in Roseneil 2011: 127).

Conclusion

The work of the women discussed in this chapter is not that of 'gaining' power but of challenging dominant hierarchies of knowledge and expertise in order to transform patterns of dominance and exclusion. Professional knowledges were challenged through a turn to experience, involvement and co-production. Academic hierarchies were challenged as women looked to new theoretical perspectives to understand the transformations of culture and identity they were witnessing. The chapter has also shown how participants opened up and engaged with theoretical developments that transformed much of the social sciences in the late twentieth century. The growth of women's studies, queer studies, post-colonial studies and cultural studies offered new disciplinary homes for many women within the academy (Ristock and Taylor 1998; Griffin and Braidotti 2002). New theoretical framings of power, subjectivity and belonging offered challenges to conventional understandings of how 'politics' might be understood and performed (Mohanty 2003; Narayan and Harding 2000; Butler 1999).

However, the chapter has also demonstrated the multiplicity of the institutional locations in which such work took place, and the diversity of the forms of intervention that were pursued. And, more importantly, it has shown that there was no common understanding of the politics that informed those interventions. The different critical and performative repertoires suggest at least two lines of tension that have run through the chapter. The first was between idea of knowledge as a route to empowerment and a more post-structuralist reading of expertise as a form of governmentality. The former looked back to Freirian notions of conscientization (see Chapter 2) in which knowledge of one's own condition was viewed as the first step to taking political action to address it. Knowledge here is viewed as a form of consciousness rather than a set of facts or data, but often leads to projects of wider enquiry about how particular conditions of oppression had been produced, and thus to the building of the kind of theory than could inform political action. This resonates with the Women's Liberation Movement process of consciousness raising through which women came to politics though collective engagement with personal experiences of oppression – of a particular group of women at a particular moment. Governmentality scholars would offer a rather different reading of such practices, noting how 'personal' and experiential forms of knowledge were integral to the constitution of new forms of self-governing and reflexive subjects. However, the tension between appeals to experience as the basis of political agency and more Foucauldian readings is not absolute. While Mohanty's post-colonial scholarship challenges appeals to experience that do not examine the cultural processes that shape experience, she also traces how subjects can be 'empowered' as knowledge producers (see discussion in Stone-Mediatore 2000). Theories of intersectionality offer new routes to how politics can be pursued (Brah and Phoenix 2004; Grabham, Cooper, Krishnadas and Herman 2009). And Gail Lewis and others cited in this chapter show how tensions can be reconciled in a 'good enough' way to enable common struggles to be forged across difference.

The second tension that has run across the chapter concerns the role of the academy. The work of Gibson-Graham both highlights the tension between a focus on critique and the idea of knowledge-work as performative and potentially generative of new worlds. Drawing on their work, Roseneil argues that: 'our understandings of the world are constitutive of it, and bring it into being.

At the simplest level this suggests that knowledge matters profoundly and that our models, theories, and analyses grant "performative force" ... to the systems and relations we describe' (Roseneil 2012: 18). This is situated in a wider literature on enactment and performativity (Butler 1999; Law and Urry 1994; Mol 2002; Sedgwick 2003; Strathern 1991) that points to the generative power of methods and other forms of knowledge work: their capacity to enact social worlds, to make realities through what Mol (Mol 1999) terms an 'ontological politics'.

Such a politics has implications for the analysis of the present conjuncture. Sasha Roseneil also draws on Sedgwick's contrast between paranoid and reparative readings of the present (Sedgwick 2003), the latter opening up space for hope, and the energies and potentials this brings:

> Reparative interpretations might not always be appropriate or possible, particularly as we enter a period of massive cuts to welfare states across Europe and an assault on collective provision of public services, with profound implications in terms of gendered, class and racialized inequalities. But if our research is conducted in a paranoid register our ability to analyse and oppose that which is new and normatively worse is greatly diminished. (Roseneil 2011: 129)

Rather than such paranoid readings, the chapter has shown how knowledge-work might open up, rather than close down, alternative spaces and rationalities. But how? Here I want to adapt Gibson-Graham's framework of reframing, rereading and creating (Gibson-Graham 2008) in ways that relate to the framework for analysing the generative labour of participants that I introduced in Chapter 1. This had three elements: 'making visible', 'fostering public conversations' and 'creative labour'. This chapter has traced different ways of using research to make visible that which is hidden: to bring it into public view and render it the object of political critique and action. Some of this labour concerns engaging with the experience of marginalized or silenced groups, including carers, front-line workers, sex workers, prisoners, asylum-seekers, and women subject to violence and abuse. But some concern tracing potentially forgotten histories of social movements, from Sasha Roseneil's work on Greenham (Roseneil 1995; Roseneil 2000) to Susan Pell's work on social movement archives. These are not simply 'academic' pieces of research but are important political interventions.

The work of participants has also been productive of new public conversations. The capacity of the women discussed in 'The politics of recognition' section of this chapter to bridge the academic/policy/practice boundaries has opened up new policy conversations but has also offered new discursive repertoires in which such conversations might take place. But it is not only policy shifts that are at stake. Across the chapter we can see how researchers and activists are opening up questions about current formations of politics and culture that are far reaching: the question of women in a culture increasingly characterized by religious fundamentalism (Sukhwant Dhaliwal), the value of friendship as a mode of sustaining care and welfare (Sasha Roseneil), the ethical as well as policy significance of care (Marian Barnes), and contested formations of citizenship and belonging (Alessandra Marino, Dana Rubin, P.G. Macioti).

This generative labour raises questions about the possible appropriations of innovative developments and new discursive repertoires. It also reopens a concern about the relationship between knowledge-work as a form of political practice and the policy shifts of the 1990s towards a focus on 'What works?' and evaluation studies. This was, of course, not simply driven by governments; as the chapter has shown, academics, professionals, knowledge brokers and others sought to find ways of influencing policy and speaking to 'practice' as forms of political engagement, while universities sought to 'modernize' in ways that brought them closer to governmental power. Together these shifts altered the spaces, sites and relations of knowledge-work. As in Chapter 4, the 'close encounters' that resulted were of different orders, but all raised questions about the proper relationship between theoretical development, personal politics and the generation of forms of knowledge that could be readily used by policymakers and practitioners. Each can be viewed as political; but across the chapter participants have given different kinds of accounts of how they sought to reconcile theoretical work and 'practical' politics.

But the possibility of finding (partial and ambiguous) resolutions was conditioned by shifts in the material conditions of those engaged in knowledge-work. Recent work on the modernization or 'neoliberalization' of the academy echoes these themes (Brown 2005; Clarke 2010b; Gill 2009). Clarke traces the progressive transformation of universities as corporate enterprises and the adaptive strategies that have followed, some of which he describes as a form of 'collective melancholia' that occludes questions about the relationship between professionalism, managerialism and politics. I asked Gail Lewis whether she thought that the space for political intervention had closed. After a long pause she replied:

> I never want to say that, but I think the space has contracted hugely. Now they [the government] are saying that we really do mean that we want a culture and rationality of competition. They want it to enter into the very ways in which the institution [the university] is structured, how it is governed, its cultural forms and so on. And although its [the university's] mission is still the same, the conditions in which it tries to fulfil that mission are hugely transformed, and we are all caught up in that. We are subject to its disciplinary rules, and that matters both individually and collectively. (Gail Lewis)

These transformations have consequences for the 'young' academics quoted in the first section of this chapter, and for the forms of politics they seek to pursue. Their position in the labour market is highly precarious. Many are also implicated in the tightening of national borders that squeeze the possibilities of more mobile forms of citizenship. Those students who had travelled to the United Kingdom to study, especially those from countries with oppressive political regimes, expressed considerable concerns about their futures. But even within the United Kingdom knowledge-work is taking place in more precarious labour market conditions, and for those that do have jobs the pressures are intensifying:

> It is a massive amount of work to do that kind of stuff [making material available to activist as well as academic audiences] and I do think it also requires a certain letting go, especially when … I mean, with all the pressures of impact and all that kind of stuff which I don't agree with. I mean, I do want my research to make an impact but certainly not the way the government envisions that impact, and so you do have to make choices. (Sarah Lamble)

This underscores the importance of the shifting institutional and material bases of knowledge-work. The academy is increasingly being subject to new performance regimes and new forms of contractual labour that circumscribe the so-called 'freedom' of the academic. But what is significant about the forms of knowledge-work discussed in this chapter is the refusal to be contained within a particular institutional location. Few of the participants have followed conventional career routes, whether inside or outside the academy. Rather, they have operated in the interstitial spaces between institutional locations, brokering and translating knowledge in ways that could be effectively used by policymakers, activists and those who were the subjects of research. They have themselves crossed institutional, sectoral, national and political boundaries, taking their experience, skills and networks with them. That is, they have engaged in different forms of 'border work', the focus of the next chapter.

7

Border Work: Generating Spaces of Power

Being an *'outsider'*, being *'close to the ground'*, being *'out there'*, *'on the other side'*, being *'inside-outside'*, *'meeting in the middle'*, *'shouting from the sidelines'*, *'working on the edge'*, being *'marginal'*, being *'in and against'* – the interviews were full of such images. As I read and reread the transcripts I began to wonder why this sense of being simultaneously inside and outside was so frequent. One possible reading would highlight women's marginal status in relation to established institutions. This may be due to the predominance of women in unpaid or low-paid work, in part-time jobs or on short-term contracts, or their marginality to the 'clubs' that dictate dominant institutional norms. But there is another reading that runs through participant accounts: that of holding commitments and allegiances that are grounded 'outside' while working in, or engaging with, 'insider' positions. That is, spatial metaphors were used to denote political identities and dilemmas.

This takes us to one of the central questions of the book: how women with commitments to working for social and political change can work the spaces of power within neoliberal ruling relations. As I noted in Chapter 1, such work is often viewed through a binary system of thought in which narratives celebrating individual agency are set against narratives of incorporation and professionalization. In subsequent chapters I have tried to offer a more nuanced account, drawing out contradictions and dilemmas and showing something of how these were negotiated by participants. Here, my focus is on teasing out how such negotiations are conducted through different forms of 'border work'. This is the substance of the first part of this chapter, while the second offers a number of different theoretical and conceptual resources for illuminating border work as generative – and gendered – labour.

Borders and crossings

The idea of border work produces different possible mappings of space and power. Sometimes place was used as key metaphors to express difference:

> You can't grow up in the West Highlands without being very aware of the social structure of the history of the clearances, of absentee landlords, and my family had ... certainly my grandparents were extremely poor and my mother, you know,

there were periods of time in which they were close to starving, so all of that ... there isn't any question that you would consider yourself, you know, on the other side. (Mary MacLeod; my emphasis)

My mother came from a poorer family – she left school at the age of thirteen to go and be an apprentice baker. But she made absolutely the most of her life bringing up her kids, feeding us on practically nothing, and helping us to progress and succeed. I feel as though I've had such a privileged life in comparison. I got a scholarship to a very posh school which was full of all the fee-paying girls, so I became very aware of class differences. I learned to sort of live with being me but also blending. So there was a duality I was aware of, of fitting in and also being the me who still lived with people I loved in that place [Bradford], who formed the basic me. And maybe a source of sensitivity to what are the informal rules of the game. If you really belong then you don't need to read those rules. If you don't belong then you do. (Sue Richards; my emphasis)

I am neither a South African nor a complete outsider to South Africa. I felt very aware of my own ambiguous national roots, or rights, but also an obligation to speak and write about the inequalities – especially the particular nature of gendered inequality – in many places, and the activisms this gives rise to. (Ida Susser; my emphasis)

Differences of place, history and class are overlaid in these extracts to express something of the 'selves' who later engaged with public policy, and to suggest something of the contradictory politics of belonging. Both Mary and Sue were highly successful actors in the policy world, but both attributed some of this success to bringing 'outsider' perspectives to their work, while Ida viewed her contribution to the politics of AIDS in South Africa to her ambiguous standing within the nation and her peripatetic experience.

Inside-outside metaphors were also used to depict political backgrounds and belongings. The next extracts are from women involved in equality work who brought 'outsider' identities into heavily circumscribed institutional spaces. Again, such outside perspectives could be productive:

Well, I think I was an outsider, *I mean I think there's no question, it's very hard to, particularly somebody like me, to be a real insider, and I think that was helpful.* (Angela Mason; my emphasis)

Pioneers of equality work – Angela Mason and Avtar Brah – brought strong political identities and a history of activism that enabled them to assert collective subject positions (Black, gay) in organizations that had hitherto not recognized them (see Chapter 4). They were outsiders not only because they were not acculturated to the Civil Service or local government 'ways of doing things', but also because of their political commitments and a sense that their very presence potentially threatened to rupture the taken-for-granted organizational silences on issues of race and sexuality. The work of both Angela (in central and local government, and in the Equality and Human Rights Commission) and Avtar Brah (in local government and higher education) was supported by strong external links that sustained equality work as a political, not just bureaucratic, project. Being an 'outsider' enabled Angela to offer her considerable political skills gained in other spaces to her work in government. But others, from later generations and social/cultural positions, faced considerable barriers. Munira Thobani came to the United Kingdom from Tanzania at the age of thirteen (see Chapter 2) and had a varied background before being appointed as a race equality advisor in a London borough in the 1980s. This was her first job after graduating:

> It was very interesting but very scary. I went in at a senior level, as part of the management team, working with white men who had been with social services man and boy and knew how things should be done. But there was also a group of Black women social workers – some of whom resented not having been appointed to the post. I was not part of this radical grouping. It was all very painful, and I felt scared of those who looked down on me since I didn't have the professional background, I wasn't really part of social work. But I managed to achieve what I did because of developing networks across the Council, gaining support from other colleagues and from some of the management team. (Munira Thobani; my emphasis)

There is a sense that Munira was appointed to her first post *because* of her outsider status: her youth, lack of experience and, indeed, her place outside politicized forms of Black social work. It shows how the experience of being inside yet outside the nation was carried through into ambiguous and difficult organizational spaces. But it also suggests multiple senses of being outside – of the profession, of Black politics and of white male 'management' – and the struggle to form organizational alliances. Munira later went on to work as a consultant within the Office of Public Management (co-founded by Sue Richards), retaining her focus on equality issues but as part of the proliferating array of training and development consultancies (see Chapters 3 and 5). Equality units offer a prime example of the tensions inherent in border work: the spaces of power tend to be highly contested, traversed by identity struggles within and surrounded by conflicting assumptions about agency and incorporation. It takes place in a 'liminal' unit connecting inside policy actors to outside networks, but both 'inside' and 'outside' are constantly shifting, rendering the border work a highly skilled but potentially destabilizing form of labour.

There are some resonances between this form of labour and that of other women who came 'inside' to challenge the integrity of existing norms and rationalities. 'Joined up government', promoted by Sue Richards, sought to develop forms of governance that challenged the integrity of inside spaces. For example, programmes such as Sure Start worked across government's strongly bounded departments around a common goal. But the 'joining up' was often strongly resisted by ministers and civil servants, creating a series of structural and cultural tensions that had to be managed. Naomi Eisenstadt, Director of

Sure Start, spoke of having to negotiate the conflicting agendas of central and local government, NGOs and professional communities:

> *I didn't set out to be innovative, but because I didn't know the rules, I was. It was very clear – they wanted me because I was different. They were looking for particular skills – and a real understanding of what it was like out there, of working with poor people, of knowing how it works on the ground.* (Naomi Eisenstadt; my emphasis)

Interestingly Naomi, Angela and Sue used similar terms to describe coming into the Civil Service as an *'outsider'*, and in the *'difference'* that the individual brought was viewed as an asset. Naomi's American accent confounded attempts to locate her in terms of her class position, and she also suggested that being a stranger to the strange workings of the Civil Service – of not knowing the system – helped her. Angela saw her outsider status as deriving from her radical past, but again she saw this difference as *'helpful'*. Both were sustained by strong external relationships with groups in which their commitments had been formed, and, for both, not knowing the rules enabled them to break them.

As Chapters 4 and 5 showed, the work of bridging between 'inside' and outside' was precarious, uneven and easily fractured as policy actors moved on or campaigns ran out of steam. And the governance shifts described in Chapter 4 – including 'joined up government', partnerships and participation initiatives – tended to render borders more porous and permeable, shifting the contours of spaces of power. In particular, the borders between academic research, feminist institutions and government were realigned through a double movement: the entry of feminist activists into the academy, the professions, the Civil Service and so on and the reaching out of policymakers to stakeholders previously excluded from policymaking circles. The experience of Julia Lowndes and Bec Bayliss, in positions with much less formal power than Naomi and Sue, suggests something of the increasing porosity of institutional and policy boundaries resulting from the turn to local partnerships: a shift that enabled agendas on domestic violence and the safety of urban gay populations to be pursued in public policy. We can extend this idea of a double movement to other areas of policy, including policies on children and families, care, disability, sexuality and local governance under New Labour.

But in these and other examples the work was also that of bridging the borders between policymakers and 'ordinary people' – the communities and citizens on whom policy was likely to have an impact. There were several examples of how the participants mobilized those living in poverty or experiencing disadvantage to 'speak to power':

> *We gave a lot of them [civil servants] the confidence to make the right decisions, actually, because we were close enough to the ground and very clear in the messages we were taking back. And we weren't operating as a political pressure*

group, that wasn't our role. We were on the inside and outside – *we* straddled *the Conservative government and a radical agenda.* (Tricia Zipfel; my emphasis)

This extract brings together two different forms of border work. The first is that of bringing the expertise and experience of those living on the ground – often those whom policy sought to address – into government. This is also key to Naomi Eisenstadt's comments about knowing what it was like *'out there'* and *'on the ground'* because of her previous experience in provision for young children and in the voluntary sector. The second offers a more political reading of border work, one which used the gaps in the Conservative housing policy of the time (based on the rights of tenants to buy council houses) to secure funding to pursue alternative, and radical, housing projects in the areas that were left behind. The 'straddling' metaphor speaks to the contradictions inherent in finding and using spaces of power in the context of a government pursuing policies antithetical to one's own politics (a metaphor that might speak to the present moment: see Chapter 9).

Many participants, like Tricia, were positioned in ambiguous organizational spaces. Working on the edge of an institution enables individuals and projects to face both ways, being neither inside (part of a major programme) nor outside. People and projects can, at any time, be moved further into the institution concerned, but can also 'fall off' (indeed the Priority Estates Programme that the extract from Tricia refers to was taken 'outside' by Tricia and a colleague who set up a company to do the work under contract to government: see Chapter 3). Again, 'edge-work' is less a spatial metaphor than a political one. Participants from generational cohort 2 often had a strong collective basis from which to work: there is a very clear sense of a 'we' as a position from which participants engaged with governmental projects. 'In and against the state' is a classic example here; this was a political position formed by a group of socialist feminist economists who, after the election of Thatcher, moved 'inside' the state as a conscious political strategy. Although they worked as individuals in a range of different spaces of power, they were sustained by a collective ethos (see the work of Jane Foot and Ursula Murray, Chapter 5). For later generations, however, edge-work was conducted in more vulnerable, less collective spaces. It nevertheless remained attractive for many:

I can't say that I have had a career plan ... but one of the things I knew I wanted to do was to work on the edges, to work in alternative places or spaces or organizations, i.e. in places that were not the norm. (Sonia Khan, G3; my emphasis)

I do want to work within institutions but I want to be able to critique them as well. Being outside is really difficult – it's beneficial to have a position inside. But if I am working outside I can do things quicker, I can invest time and energy in what I really believe in. (Cecilia Wee, G4; my emphasis)

My ideal is to remain on the edge of academia, working on projects that keep me thinking but that don't take my whole life. Knowledge-work is not the academy;

the kind of work I do is not really valued. It's not that I don't have the right language but that it's not the kind of language I want to use. But I don't know whether I can always stay marginal. (P.G. Macioti, G4; my emphasis)

Sonia Khan later moved into a strategic policy role in local government but spoke about how:

I am in the right job but there's that residual sense of not being a corporate person – I still want to be slightly on the edge. (Sonia Khan: my emphasis)

She also spoke about how her next job would probably be back in the not-for-profit sector. This ambivalence is reflected in the extracts from younger participants. There is sometimes a sense of what Katz (Katz 2005) terms the seductions of belonging – of having a simpler, more secure basis from which to work, and a more secure sense of how present and future might be connected. But there are also frustrations about working 'inside' and ambivalence about the belongings offered. The key feature of edge-work is that it is neither wholly inside nor outside; it faces both ways, enabling different rationalities, logics and political orientations to be brought together – though often in uncomfortable ways, producing considerable tension for the worker concerned. It is inherently unstable and tends to be short-lived. Over time it may be absorbed into mainstream posts; it may be incorporated as time-limited 'projects', subject to institutional logics of targets, management and audit; or it may be hived off into businesses sub-contracted to deliver defined services or form the basis for the growing consultancy industry.

This takes us to a different image of border work configured around 'interstitial' organizations, groups and individuals who serve as brokers and intermediaries between different entities. In the latter years of my study think-tanks and NGOs became more significant spaces in which this work was carried out. These were ambiguously placed in the polity and, as the interviews suggest, their power base was similarly drawn from the creation and management of relationships and their capacity to mobilize new discursive repertoires:

And so through all the career steps I took I became more interested and more adept at understanding the sort of face between campaigning for justice of one sort or another, and the reality of the public policy decision making, and how you meet in the middle. I sort of learnt – but I didn't want to be shouting from the sidelines all my life. I wanted to try and actually change things, and so I was drawn [to IPPR] for that reason. (Lisa Harker; my emphasis)

The think-tank in which Lisa worked had an independent status 'outside', but it could only function effectively because of its networks and links not only to 'insiders' (policymakers and government actors) but also to other places, people and ideas. The Office of Public Management, in which both Sue Richards and Munira Thobani worked, the consultancies of Sue Beardsmore, Marion Macalpine and Jan Etienne, even quasi-government bodies such as the

Family and Parenting Institute led by Mary MacLeod, operated as such brokers; their power was based on their role as hubs connecting diverse networks. But they did more than connect: they each had their own political, social or policy 'mission' that served as a prism through which policy ideas were bent or refracted (see also discussion of Compass in Chapter 9). As well as influence, such actors wielded considerable discursive power. Change was based on the success of actors in mobilizing new ideas and linguistic repertoires (children's rights, well-being, social exclusion, civil partnerships, joined up government and many others), and they had considerable success in constructing new public conversations.

Other participants chose to work in what they saw as more 'autonomous' spaces: in women's organizations (Carole Harte, Bec Bayliss, Hannah Berry), human rights legal practices (Camilla Warren), some NGOs (Kate Raworth), activist groups such as Southall Black Sisters (Avtar Brah, Sukhwant Dhaliwal) and those running specific campaigns (Sarah Lamble). Carole Harte saw herself as 'outside' the major NGOs whom she considered to be part of the machinery of the state. This enabled her to build an alternative space in which a collective, participative ethos could flourish, and resonates with Hannah Berry's efforts to create a cooperative base in which alternative enterprises could sustain each other (Chapter 2). Such spaces were traversed by the 'identity struggles' that focused attention on the borders between different claims for recognition and voice within and beyond feminism. And they were highly vulnerable to the withdrawal of funding and disciplined by the managerial logics of contracting. Campaigning work, in contrast, had to work the borders between those willing to engage with 'formal' politics and those wanting to remain detached in order to be able to retain and perform strong critiques. This takes us back to Angela Mason's work at Stonewall and Sasha Roseneil's analysis of the Greenham Common protest (see Chapters 2 and 6). And tensions also arose as participants sought to work across multiple struggles, as in Sarah Lamble's attempt to combine work in the prison abolition movement with interventions on domestic violence:

> *I think the prison abolition movement has historically not done enough to address issues around violence against women: it will talk a lot about how the number of really violent prisoners is much smaller than the number of people who are in for economic [poverty-related] offences. But that does nothing to deal with people's actual experience of sexual violence. On the flipside I feel like the anti-violence movement has very much got caught up in a kind of law and order agenda that equates justice with locking people up. And I see that actually as a failure within both movements. So part of my work is trying to bring those movements together, and think about how anti-violence work looks different if we said that prison and policing are part of the problem, particularly when we look at the use of sexual and gender violence by prison authorities and by police. And likewise how can we get anti-prison organizers to make the prevention of sexual and gender violence much more of a priority.* (Sarah Lamble)

Border work here, as elsewhere, required complex alliance-building between different struggles and movements; engagements between different scalar sites of governing in the constant search for funding; and difficult negotiations between what Carole described as an authentic space of agency grounded in grassroots experience, and the NGOs which she viewed as compromised by their 'insider' status. Of course, the degree of perceived autonomy varied; each had to present itself in ways that enabled it to secure funds, and each had to balance campaigning work with other activities.

What cannot adequately be conveyed in these different metaphors and images of border work is its dynamic quality, both institutionally and personally. The Family and Parenting Institute, for example (see Chapter 4), drew on each of the forms of border work depicted here: its ambiguous status within New Labour's policy programme meant that it served as partner and ally as well as broker and opponent. Being aware of the potential traps was crucial:

> *It became very clear what contested territory [family policy] was, and how complicated it was going to manage what we said publicly so that we didn't allow ourselves to be disregarded, marginalized, ridiculed, and any of the other things that comes up, and also how to manage relationships with government.*
> (Mary MacLeod)

Mary's role as Chief Executive had to align the relationship between the feminist-inflected politics of many who worked at FPI and the New Labour agenda. Like many of those working with government she too saw herself as an 'outsider'; indeed, her comment in one of the opening quotes to this chapter about coming from the 'other side' suggests a compounding of class, place and politics in her political formation. In her work with government she was at times an antagonist, referring to herself as a 'mole within' the policy process, and at times an 'insider' in the shaping of family policy.

Participants also worked the borders between early commitments (movements and struggles that were more securely positioned 'outside' or 'elsewhere') and later 'insider' roles. The skills participants had accumulated in community, voluntary and charitable work were reconfigured and elaborated as women moved into governmental or quasi-governmental programmes, and then back out again. Most participants engaged in different forms of border work over the course of their working lives. Jane Foot, Ursula Murray and other socialist women who had worked in 'autonomous' campaigns and groups (campaigning from the outside) later moved into local government work (see Chapter 5). Their decisions to do so were often provoked by funding crises in community or trade union resource centres, but were also the result of an awareness of how political struggles between local and central government had intensified, and how new legislation was likely to have an adverse effect on low-paid employees – especially women – as services were put out to tender to private-sector contractors. Avtar Brah took self-conscious choices about moving between the voluntary sector, local government and university work, seeing in each case where her work might bring greatest benefit. Angela Mason moved from being a radical activist 'outside' into the law, later heading up a campaigning organization, working within the Civil Service and taking up local authority political roles, bringing her commitments and skills with her and accruing new ones on the way. Tricia Zipfel, Lisa Harker, Mary MacLeod, Sonia Khan and others moved across multiple spaces in ambiguous inside/outside positions across their working lives. Overlaid on each of the metaphors of border work, then, are the zigzag patterns of individual trajectories that enabled skills and experiences to be accreted and networks progressively extended.

Border work as generative (and gendered) labour: conceptual resources

One of the arguments of this book is that the work of the participants generated new things: new pathways, new policies, new public conversations, new organizational practices, new governance foci, and new ways of understanding and practising politics. Previous chapters have hinted at some of the ways in which new things were created, drawing on notions of translation, relational labour, assemblage, knowledge-work and, here, border work. In this second half of the chapter I want to look a bit more systematically at the conceptual resources offered by different branches of the social sciences to an understanding of the generative features of border work. A concern with the analysis of borders and boundaries has proliferated across the social sciences in recent years, and I cannot hope to do justice to the wealth of conceptual and theoretical work that has taken place. My aim is not to cover each perspective in any depth but to hint at different understandings of how change can emerge from the new juxtapositions, alignments and performances traced earlier in the chapter.

Organizations, professions and sectors

The relationship between border work and organizational innovation is a difficult terrain, usually addressed indirectly rather than directly in the literatures on public and voluntary sectors. The dominant focus tends to be on contrasts between public and private sector innovative capacity (Cabinet Office 2003), on the management of innovation (Hartley, Donaldson, Skelcher and Wallace 2008) and on innovation for enhanced performance rather than for social benefit (Audit Commission 2007; National Audit Office 2006). Several early studies show how the public sector has taken up innovations developed in the not-for-profit sector (Osborne 1996; Osborne and Flynn 1997) but more recently the focus has been on the use of pilots, projects and experiments to generate innovation, on the innovative potential of devolution and decentralization, on the use of 'e-governance' to drive transformational change and on social, rather than organizational, innovation (Mulgan 2006). Mulgan has long campaigned against 'silo mentalities' (mentalities that derive from the strong internal boundaries of bureaucracies) and, closer to the spirit of this chapter, has also talked about the value of 'cultivating hinterlands' (Mulgan 2007: 26); but this receives only a brief mention. The dominant assumption is that innovation is driven by organization-wide corporate strategies.

Within organizational studies Kirton (Kirton 1976) points to the significance of links between boundary-crossing and innovation; the more boundaries that are to be crossed, the more innovative an individual has to be, and this was particularly the case where organizations were fluid and undergoing change. This offers one framework that suggests some of the conditions in which women were likely to be able to be effective change agents (Colgan and Ledwith 1996). Kirton also distinguished between change agents as 'adaptors' (who produce ideas that stretch and extend agreed definitions of a problem and its likely solutions) and 'innovators' (who tend to reconstruct the problem without regard for existing rules). The work of participants tended not to fall easily into one or other side of this binary formulation; however, the difficulties facing women who wanted to do things differently may help explain why some participants moved from 'inside' to 'outside' or 'in between' spaces that offered greater potential for innovation and creativity. More recent analyses of actors 'working across boundaries' in the context of new governance forms noted the rise of 'boundary spanners' and 'reticulists' and the multiple roles they play that enable inter-organizational collaboration (Sullivan and Skelcher 2002).

Professional change

While the organizational studies literature tends to focus on newly emerging boundary-spanning individuals, the literature on the professions highlights how contemporary shifts are challenging the bounded fields of action within which professional autonomy is exercised. The literature on boundary-crossing professionals is structured around two topics: the first traces how managerialism and market logics produced 'hybrid' professionals who combine professional, managerial and sometimes business roles (Ferlie, Pettigrew, Ashburner and Fitzgerald 1996; see also Clarke and Newman 1997); the second concerns the shifting borders between professionals and their clients produced through discourses of co-production, self-advocacy and consumerism (Clarke, Newman, Smith, Vidler and Westmarland 2007; Needham 2011). Both developments shift and reconstitute boundaries in ways that enable some professional workers to bring alternative rationalities and practices into the forefront, rather than the margins, of their work. We saw this in Chapter 5, where public librarians were depicted as shifting the borders between professionals and 'communities', constituting themselves as a new professional grouping – what, in terms of the mappings of this chapter, would be deemed as 'edge-workers' – a grouping that prefigured wider professional shifts. And in Chapter 6, Ann McPherson's work on bringing patient experience into policy development within the Department of Health might be viewed in terms of creating spaces (of like-minded professionals and policy actors) within a bureaucratic Civil Service and a hierarchical medical profession. The shifting borders between 'state' and 'society' or between 'welfare' and 'responsibility' are likely to bring these forms of edge-work closer to the centres of power. But new groupings are constantly emerging: Chapter 2 showed the emergence of 'community mobilizers' and Jane Wills spoke of her work helping constitute a new profession of community organizers through a masters programme, with highly committed students working the borders between academic and activist work. Each example supports Fournier's analysis of professional work and professional knowledge as performative and malleable rather than fixed and bounded (Fournier 2000), thus creating the possibility of change.

The cross-sector dance

Both organizational and professional literatures engage with the shifting relationship between 'sectors', and how this reconfigures work identities and practices. This is also a significant theme in the international development and voluntary sector literatures. D. Lewis's studies of those moving from voluntary to statutory sectors in both the UK and in Bangladesh (D. Lewis 2008) distinguish between boundary-spanners and boundary-crossers, with the primary emphasis on the latter. Milligan and Conradson (Milligan and Conradson 2006) talk about the 'cross sectoral dance' performed by volunteers as they move from being on the outside, 'knocking on walls', to taking up work within the system in order to exert influence from the inside. The biographical methods on which the studies by Lewis and by Milligan and Conradson draw fruitfully illuminate the processes of transition between outsider and insider identities as well as the processes of development and learning that take place over time. But while finding such literatures suggestive, I am concerned that they tend to replicate the policy discourse of 'sectors', and, like much of the organizational studies literature, suggest clear organizational boundaries. Crossings may be performed and partnerships created, but the containers themselves remain and are defined as much by the oppositions through which they are imagined as by their institutional characteristics.

I want, in contrast, to argue that the spatial metaphors used by participants cannot be understood through common binary oppositions: state and civil society, voluntary and statutory, public and private. Gupta (Gupta 2006) proposes an approach that re-examines the conventional distinction between 'state' and 'civil society' and views the state itself as discursively constituted. In his paper 'Blurred boundaries', he draws on post-colonial ethnography to show how the state is confronted as a series of discrete and fragmentary practices and performances. This is a helpful way of framing some of the different constructions of borders and boundaries in different political-cultural moments in the period covered by this research. In the 1970s we saw how activists constituted 'community' through its otherness to the state and institutional power, while in the 1980s we saw some participants using the metaphor 'in and against the state'. Both conceptualized the state as a strongly bounded entity that could be ignored, captured or reformed. But as governmental projects and programmes sought to reconfigure the state and to embark on programmes of 'governing the social' in the 1990s (Clarke 2006; Newman 2001; Newman 2005a; N. Rose 1999), so participants developed rather different constructions of the state and the borders with its others. Even being 'in and against' the state generated forms of labour that served to discursively and materially produce more flexible and distributed forms of state power – forms reliant less on coercion than on consent, and in which the state/market distinction was partially collapsed.

Liminal spaces

Rather than a focus on organizations and sectors, some forms of feminist scholarship point to how the liminal space between public and private can be used strategically by women to develop capacities and resources – for the benefit of self, community or other women – sheltered from the wider public gaze (Staeheli 1996; Ryan 1992; Jupp 2010; Fincher and Panelli 2001). Liminality here offers a particular gendering of politics, one in which women's agency connects the personal and political through a focus on the everyday, the local, the pragmatic. Many of the spaces of power with which I am concerned in this book are precisely those through which connections between the personal and political are made. Buckingham *et al.* note how debates about liminality as a spatial relationship emerged in feminist geography in the 1970s as a means of conceptualizing women's activity spheres, which were understood relationally rather than through the binary of public/private. They argue that liminal space is 'much more than an intermediary space between private and public – it is variously private, communal and public depending on the motivations of the women using it' (Buckingham, Marandet, Smith, Wainwright and Diosi 2006: 896).

We can situate the work of many of the 'community activists' discussed in Chapter 3, the policy entrepreneurs of Chapter 4, the organizational actors of Chapter 5 and the knowledge-workers of Chapter 6 in such liminal spaces, spaces that confound neat divisions between public, private and personal. Such spaces tend to be viewed as predominantly concerned with 'everyday' and informal forms of politics. But these examples also show how the work of participants was not just concerned with the 'here and now', the personal, the everyday, but was deeply engaged in generating what Rose terms 'fantatised futures' (N. Rose 1999: 280) – new ways of living, working and doing politics.

The idea of liminality has also been used to describe spaces 'on the edge', outside the norm and in which normal categories are disrupted (see Roseneil 2000 on Greenham Common). Currently it is also used to denote collective practices that transcend conventional definitions of public and private: attempts to create new 'commons' by the use of public land for collective garden and allotment projects, the creation of 'public' cultural artefacts and performances in privately owned property, or the generation of new temporary public facilities – from libraries to universities to deliberative events – within large-scale demonstrations or occupations on private land. But the predominant use of notions of liminality in feminist theory points to the entanglements between public, private and personal lives: 'The notion of liminality is therefore seen as a way of understanding the emancipatory potential of such spaces, with the suggestion that a fluidity between public and private might be empowering for women' (Jupp 2010: 77). However, Jupp goes on to suggest that liminality also marks a zone of intervention by governments into private or domestic settings, thereby drawing women into new formations of power. The liminality between public and private in community policy, programmes such as Sure Start or good parenting classes are a feature of such spaces of intervention. The notion of liminality, then, draws attention to particular gendered regimes of governance but does not tell us much about what actually happens within them. So rather than viewing spaces of power as the 'in between' spaces summoned up in some versions of liminality, I want to argue that they are formed relationally and are traversed by multiple forms of power. It is their (political) ambiguity rather than their (spatial) liminality that generates new spaces of possibility.

Strategic brokers

The process of reconfiguring of sectors, institutions and scales of governing generate conjuncturally specific spaces of possibility. Larner and Craig use the concept 'strategic brokers' to denote actors who work across sites, agencies, and scales in New Zealand and England (Larner and Craig 2005). Such brokers 'spend a great deal of time building and maintaining relationships because no policy or strategy is now complete or legitimate without evidence of consultation and/or collaboration'. They also work to 'avoid overlaps, sort out niches, and create wider platforms to legitimate the work of their organizations'. And 'they are geared towards *process* issues', facilitating, mediating and negotiating, nurturing networks and deploying cultural knowledge and local knowledge 'in ways that enable traditionally "silent" voices to be heard' (Larner and Craig 2005: 417–8; original emphasis). However, they are also vulnerable to being co-opted into newly professionalized roles in which, as pragmatic improvisers, they may 'unwittingly contribute to the hybrid, contested rolling out of neoliberalism' (Larner and Craig 2005: 405). They do so precisely because they were seeking to overcome the ravages resulting from previous phases of 'roll back' neoliberalism: 'In the wake of profound neoliberal fragmentation, the complexity of the re-joining task is such that these agents find themselves palpably stretched, often carrying personally the enormous costs of reintegration. In this regard, the new strategic brokers appear not just to be governmentalised in their professional functions, but in their personal and political commitments too' (Larner and Craig 2005: 406).

These are more than boundary-crossing actors: they are involved in reconstituting the categories of contemporary governance and generating new forms of agency. Interestingly, Larner and Craig note how the majority of the 'strategic brokers' in their studies of community activism and local partnership working in both the United Kingdom and New Zealand were women. They acknowledge Hochschild's work on emotional labour, but also locate the dominance of women in such roles in a twin process: the 'mobilisation of un- and underpaid labour, and the expansion of governmentalising ambits into feminised and domesticated realms' (Larner and Craig 2005: 419). An important feature of the work of Wendy Larner and her colleagues (e.g. Molloy and Larner 2010) is the way in which it links analyses of gendered labour markets with the analysis of the rise of new state forms – literatures that often do not speak to each other.

Wedel's work (Wedel 2009) on 'transactors' resonates with Larner's focus on changing spaces and scales of agency. She points to the role of NGOs in the ambiguous spaces of transnational consultancy work: actors who are able to deploy multiple identities in order to lever resources, 'playing the boundaries' (Wedel 2004: 167) between national and international, public and private, formal and informal, state and non-state. (I used the word transactor in a presentation at an event designed to promote learning on public participation between people from the global north and south. One woman came up to me at the end, very excited, saying, 'Yes, that describes me exactly – I have to face both ways, I'm a transactor.' She subsequently agreed to participate in this research.) Similarly Lendvai and Stubbs (Lendvai and Stubbs 2006; Lendvai and Stubbs 2007) note the significance of transnational consultants located in hybrid spaces 'in between scales, organizations, discursive practices, knowledge systems and geographies, as located in a kind of "liminality" characterized by a blurring and merging of distinctions' (Lendvai and Stubbs 2006: 8). This takes us back to the feminist geography discussed above, but again denotes not a 'space between' but a blurring and merging of distinctions. However, the blurring of inside and outside rationalities and commitments has implications for how activism can be sustained. This means turning to rather different literatures.

Emotion and affect

Border work can produce profound discomfort as different identifications – as insiders *and* outsiders, as both different *and* part of the dominant order – are lived and performed. Rather than attributing particular 'feelings' to participants, my aim here is to note how discursive reasoning is conducted through emotional registers. In Chapter 1, I suggested that the interview transcripts might be read in different ways, bringing into view cognitive, affective and reflexive understandings of the self. We can see each of these in the earlier extract from Munira Thobani, who spoke of her experience as *'interesting'* and offered explanations for what happened. This implies a cognitive self who, as other sections of the interview suggested, learned from that experience and took that learning to other places. She is reflexive, looking back on what she achieved with some pride. And she also hints at the emotions the experience surfaced: of being scared (repeated), of being resented, of being looked down on, of not being *'really part of'* social work. Other participants also highlighted such insider-outsider feelings. Being *'inside-outside'* – of the nation, the organization, the polity, activist networks, the academy – clearly brings feelings of both inclusion and exclusion. Participant accounts suggest other affective dimensions of border work: being *'shocked'* and finding it *'difficult'* (Mary MacLeod), taking risks and finding things *'bizarre'* or *'weird'* (Tricia Zipfel); being proud and *'fulfilled'* (Carole Harte); not being able to *'bear'* one sector while feeling *'stifled'* by another (Sukhwant Dhaliwal), of being viewed (and perhaps viewing the self) as selling out (Hannah Berry – see Chapter 2).

Paying attention to emotional registers of discursive reasoning brings other dimensions of 'self-work' into view. Participants spoke of the problems of sustaining working the borders, the exhaustion that can result and the need, eventually, to make compromises. But many also spoke of the excitement of looking back on what had been achieved:

> *Talking to other women about how we get into the positions of power that we get into, and then what we do with that power and how we use it ... particularly with women who come through a very activist, feminist route. So there are a number of people I come across who've come from similar backgrounds, in fact recognize me from, you know, twenty to thirty years ago, and we have those conversations which is how did we get here, and that we never thought we would be in these positions, and what do we do with them, and how do we come to terms with our kind of personal politics, but yet being in these positions of influence and power.*
> (Adi Cooper)

I have included this extract here since it shows how notions of inside and outside can be a collective subject position stretched over time. It brings into view a highly reflexive self and hints at the dialogic processes through which participants made sense of their lives. But it also underscores a theme running through this chapter: how border work links notions of 'personal politics' and 'public power' in complex ways. Participants draw discourses and repertoires from different worlds, forming new configurations of what 'work' means and how it is to be conducted. Indeed, it is this capacity to span different worlds and identities that generates the spaces of power with which I am concerned. The transcripts suggest multiple and partial positionings of the self: at the same time an activist and paid worker, as an insider and an outsider, as a stranger and professional, as an individual, making her own decisions and compromises, and as part of collective entities.

I want to suggest how this can be traced in four particular accounts. Carole Harte spoke of how:

I've been able to be a bit of a hybrid really. I'm a working-class woman who's been able to access an environment that isn't usually available to women like me. (Carole Harte)

Her self-proclaimed 'hybridity' linked her strong working class identity and the 'academics' and policy actors she engaged with. But she retained a sense of being an outsider of the process of policy formation and governance, challenging from the margins.

Sue Richards, in contrast, was a skilful 'insider', adept at negotiating change within government. She linked her skills to a tough upbringing that made her very aware of class differences and led her to try to find *'a way of being me while also blending'*. Later in her public career she continued to find ways of *'fitting in'* while still *'being the basic me'*. She described herself as *'always watching'* (holding herself apart) while also being *'heavily engaged'*. And it was this watching that enabled her to quickly assess the rules of the game in whatever context she worked.

The third is Jane Foot. I asked Jane what she had taken from her activist experiences into her working life in and beyond local government:

Networking – developing and sustaining them; lateral thinking; being at home with councillors, trade unions and officers and able to work across all these boundaries; empathy for the professionals delivering services that I knew were needed; values; soft power; and an identification first with users and communities rather than the organisation – though that got buried. (Jane Foot; my emphasis)

This hints at the 'self' work required to hold multiple allegiances and identifications together. Jane suggests that it was her activism, and the need to see how power works, where the contradictions might be, that has led her to try to *'knit things together'*. But her references to what *'got buried'* imply a sense of loss as issues faded from the agenda.

Finally, I want to return to the account of Ursula Murray in Chapter 5. Describing her role in managing CCT, she recalled how:

It was being a consultant but from the inside. This was hard. We were not insiders. People reacted against you, there were charges of selling out – and a feeling of trench warfare. One minute you were a hero, the next the enemy. But the bigger enemy enabled people to work together. (Ursula Murray)

Throughout the extracts in this chapter we can see hints at the emotion work (Hoschild 1979; see also Hoggett 2000; G. Lewis 2000) at stake as participants engaged with dominant rationalities while holding on to their personal and political commitments. We can also see how cognition and emotion are not easily distinguishable. But notions of affect take us further, drawing attention to non-cognitive, somatic responses to the world and raising questions of how 'experience' can be represented other than through language itself (though language is not dismissed: Wetherall 2011). The turn to psychosocial methods in studies of policy and governance (Froggett 2002; Hoggett 2000; Hunter 2012) offer rich resources for engaging with what Hunter terms 'impossible governance'. Such perspectives, drawing on Kleinian psychoanalytical concepts, would explore notions of being both 'inside' and 'outside', of 'fitting in' or 'bending' while also holding on to one's politics and values, of 'watching', 'holding oneself apart', while also being 'engaged', as suggesting a form of psychic 'splitting' that can result in melancholia. Psychic and organizational splittings may be dynamically connected, as in Ursula Murray's accounts of the rupturing of established teams in the client-contractor splits of CCT in Chapter 5, and the *'unfinished political business'* associated with the personal and organizational damage that resulted:

Tendering was a focus of horrendous projections, with the splitting between clients and contractors – the rupture of teams that had been together. So I got very interested in all of that. The last period [in local government management] I spent restructuring. What had been enacted was a defensive structure, not a structure for innovation. CCT did at least challenge entrenched ways of doing things. In the end we brought the clients and contractors together again.

There is unfinished political business about all this. There was a feeling of becoming the enemy within – part of the loony left – there was no legitimate language. We were not acknowledged as part of history. (Ursula Murray)

This goes beyond conventional views of emotion work to draw attention to the psychosocial dynamics of work and organization, and has formed a productive form of analysis, especially in theorizing equality work (Hunter 2012) and analyses of how 'difference' is embodied and lived (G. Lewis 2000).

Power and agency

Border work creates conjuncturally specific spaces of power. It challenges binary categories such as state/society, inside/outside, autonomous/incorporated, personal/political. Rather, it shows a multiplicity of spaces that intersect, and are sometimes in relationships of alignment and sometimes of antagonism. However, the blurring of distinctions, then, does not dissolve difference, contradiction and antagonism. Indeed, spaces of power are spaces in which difference is negotiated and in which working across difference can produce new ideas, energies and projects as well as potential antagonisms.

I want to develop the analysis by pointing to two very different ways of understanding power and agency. The first draws on notions of 'translation'. Translation appeared as a practical discourse in some of the interviews – a way in which women described what they did (see, for example, Chapter 3). The work of Carole, Tricia and others evokes the sense of translation as an active, agentive process, requiring the labour of summoning, mobilizing, assembling and then – most importantly – that of combining elements into new configurations. Translation thus forms a valuable counter to notions of the flow of ideas across boundaries; attention shifts to the local and particular settings in which ideas are received, translated, mediated and adapted into new practices (e.g. Czarniawska and Jeorges 1996; Czarniawska and Sevón 2005; Freeman 2009; Lendvai 2005; Salskov-Iversen, Hansen and Bislev 2000). The image of 'source' and 'recipient' is rejected in favour of chains of association in which difference produces the possibility of the transformation of both: 'translation involves creating convergences or homologues by relating things that were previously different' (Callon 1980: 211). It is such creative reframings that offer new possibilities of public action and forms of political agency. Rather than networks of people or flows of ideas, the focus is on associations between things – objects as well as people (Law 1999). Actants (humans, goods and services, skills, ideas, money, practices, technologies, institutions and other entities) are assembled in new ways. These new associations change the meanings or other properties of individual components drawn into interactive practices.

This is a helpful way of engaging with the 'border work' of participants: rather than viewing them simply as boundary-crossing actors, they can be seen as engaged in a creative process that opens up new potential pathways and that generates new emergent practices. It suggests how processes of translation, brokering and alignment may be *productive* of new forms of identity and agency, including the constitution of forms of political subjectivity. However, translation does not capture the ways in which dominant and subordinate forms of power may be reconciled – or not (see discussion in Chapter 3). Power is assumed to be everywhere (inscribed in an array of discourses, technologies, actors, texts, institutional norms, policies and projects); but its very multiplicity renders it somewhat elusive. Here, I want to turn to a second way of conceptualizing power and agency. The notion of 'contact zones' as elaborated in post-colonial theory suggests ways in which actors engage with dominant and subordinate formations of power and forms of subjectivity. Contact zones are described as 'social spaces where disparate cultures meet, clash and grapple with each other, often in highly asymmetrical relations of domination and subordination – like colonialism, slavery, or their aftermaths as they are lived out across the globe today' (Pratt 1992: 4). They are non-innocent settings in which power differences between colonizer and colonized are formed through historical patterns of racialized subordination and exploitation. As such, contemporary tracings of historically embedded forms of power and oppression may resonate through contemporary struggles (see also Askins and Pain 2011).

Applying this concept beyond post-colonial studies can weaken or distort it by subordinating issues of race and colonialism to other forms of oppression. However, it offers a valuable way of drawing attention to the legacies of historical forms of domination and subordination out of which new spaces – the community forum, the task force, the 'social inclusion' project, the participation initiative – arise. It suggests how such spaces continue to be traversed by formations of power, despite the discursive repertoires (for example, of partnership, empowerment, inclusion), which mask them. And it suggests the possibility of subordinate groups coming to view themselves through dominant discursive repertoires, as well as that of dominant groups being transformed through encounters with 'the other'. Returning to some of the different mappings with which this chapter began, we can understand the spaces of power as cross-cut by tracings of embedded orderings of rule that constituted participants as both 'the other' (the colonized subjects distant from centres of power) and the agents of reform (expected to transform colonial power, to modernize the centre itself).

Viewing border work in this way brings different insights into some of the mappings proposed earlier. Inside-outside spaces challenged institutional (colonial) power by learning its language and translating counter or oppositional voices in ways that could be seen to fit with dominant projects (see Chapter 3). Such spaces were also spaces in which dominant orders could be modernized and transformed through contact with the subordinate (the colonized). But this opens up questions about how to understand the dominant; rather than a single order of rule, it shows how it is constituted as multiple, with some would-be hegemonic political projects deliberately welcoming in counter projects in order to render them agents through which dominant orders could be transformed. The results are zones within which tracings of new hegemonic projects may emerge alongside residual orderings of power. They are zones in which participants sought to reconcile conflicting interests, build alliances, reconfigure relationships, align conflicting discourses, resignify existing symbols, retell old narratives and develop new ones. Their work was also that of managing – or not – the contradictions produced by the perverse alignments of different forces, an issue I return to in the next chapter.

Conclusion

I began the chapter by problematizing the idea of clear-cut distinction between an authentic space of politics 'outside' and 'insider' projects, a distinction central to theses of incorporation and professionalization. Inside and outside are categories that appear to be opposites that map neatly on to narratives of authentic political agency on the one hand and of incorporation or professionalization on the other. But this chapter has explored different ways of being both 'inside' *and* 'outside' and the complexity of working lives and identities this produces. Rather than a single border – between an authentic activist politics 'outside', in social movements and political struggle, and 'inside', in positions of power within dominant institutions – participants in this research tended to work across multiple borders: those between different political identities, between different sectors, between paid and unpaid work, between multiple institutional sites and practices, between different disciplines or professions, between 'community' and government and, of course, between personal and political. The borders were variously more or less porous, more or less clearly delineated, more or less the object of governmental concern, and were constantly reconfigured by the profound cultural and institutional transformations that took place between the mid-twentieth and early twenty-first centuries. Indeed, it was out of such reconfigurations that many new spaces of power could be mobilized.

My analysis of 'inside-outside' draws on notions of space as a 'relational construct' (Massey 1994; Massey 2005) that does not conform to – and indeed challenges – dualistic thinking. The focus on border work in this chapter, then, serves to challenge power/resistance models of politics, in which dominant formations of power are challenged from 'outside'. The languages of social movements, counter publics and civic action all tend to assume a clear distinction between entrenched formations of power and processes of political resistance and struggle. I do not want to denigrate the importance of oppositional politics nor of social movement activism; it is through such struggles that oppressive regimes may be challenged and sometimes overthrown, through which women's movements have secured rights and resources, through which trade unions have squeezed concessions from employers and through which the overreaching powers of the securitized state have been challenged – often at great cost to those engaged in dissent and disobedience. As I will show in Chapter 9 to this book, such struggles are by no means over, and new sites and practices of resistance are currently emerging to contest the politics of austerity and retrenchment. And as Chapter 2 showed, such struggles – and the institutions that sustained them – are crucial for the formation of activist identities. But they cannot be conceptualized as entirely 'free' spaces, untrammelled and untainted by dominant forms of power. With Böhm, I want to suggest that:

> Autonomy is itself (im)possible, as autonomous social movements are always embedded in specific social, economic, cultural and political rationalities that one cannot simply escape ... We do not see autonomy as a 'good outside' which allows an escape from politics into a pure space of self-determination, Rather, autonomy is an antagonistic political demand. (Böhm, Dinerstein and Spicer 2010: 28)

My aim here has been to trace how antagonistic political claims and demands were refracted through the 'border work' conducted by women working the spaces of power. Border work sometimes concerns performing crossings between different organizations, sectors, nations or institutions, but also changes the relationships between them to render borders more porous such that 'membership' becomes more diffuse. Across these accounts the notions of 'we' and 'them', of inside and outside, are rather slippery, and this slipperiness intensified as participants worked in ways that rendered boundaries more permeable in order to extend the influence of social and political movements on dominant ruling relations. But they also sought to stay in touch with the places where 'reality bites', to build bridges between policy actors and the 'grassroots', to link community based actors and those in poverty to resource streams, and to enlarge opportunities for 'voice'. Finally, as I argued earlier, border work has be understood as political rather than geographical: the 'inside', 'outside', 'edges', 'middles' and so on referred to by participants were less concerned with defined places as with political possibilities. They were spaces of agency, of power: but also spaces of ambiguity, discomfort and emotion work.

The chapter has offered a number of different conceptual resources for understanding the generative potential of such border work: its capacity to make new things and to prefigure new ways of living, working and performing politics. In the present, border work is shifting as a result of the realignments of state and society, economy and politics produced by current cycles of cuts and state retrenchment. This does not, as I will argue, foreclose the possibility of politics; but before assessing these possibilities I want, in the next chapter, to engage with broader arguments about the erasure of feminist-inflected activism in the face of the overwhelming power of neoliberalism.

8

Activism, Neoliberalism and Gendered Labour

This book is about change; about how different generations of women have worked to bring about fundamental shifts in politics, governance and culture. Their labour produced a succession of new laws, new policies and new institutional rationalities. It generated shifts in how 'politics' was understood and enacted, and how claims for social justice, recognition and voice were realized. But how can these transformations be situated in contemporary narratives of the rise of neoliberalism and the erasure of feminist politics?

In this, the first of two concluding chapters, I want to offer some response to the plethora of recent feminist work on the complicity of feminism, LGBT and other movements in the rollout of neoliberal economic strategies and ruling relations (though the work on feminism has been most prominent and thus drives my engagement with the debates). The first two sections engage with literatures on feminism and neoliberalism respectively and are largely theoretical. I then reflect on how the work of participants in this book can offer insights into political-cultural analyses of the present, revisiting previous chapters to show how neoliberalism works across the different 'landscapes of antagonism' traced in previous chapters. My aims are both theoretical and political. Theoretically, I want to puncture the seeming coherence of narratives of the incorporation and erasure of feminism by reintroducing questions of contradiction and ambivalence. Politically, I want to open up a space for a politics of the present; one that does not simply deny the possibilities of political agency by rolling its achievements into accounts of the progressive erasure of politics in the face of all consuming neoliberalism.

Feminism and neoliberalism

The coincidence between feminism and global capitalism has been a central concern of feminist scholarship. Such scholarship offers subtle arguments and well-developed theory to which I cannot hope to do justice here. But I want to draw out two interlinked narratives: first, on how processes of 'mainstreaming' served both to acknowledge and depoliticize feminist claims; and second, on how neoliberalism appropriated identity politics. These narratives rest on rather different conceptual and political assumptions. Mainstreaming (see Chapter 4) is particularly associated with Third Way politics that is viewed as having selectively incorporated feminist claims in ways that stripped them of their radicalism to produce a 'post-feminist' climate (Duggan 2003 and Genz 2006; see Squires 2005 and Walby 2009 for counter-arguments). McRobbie (McRobbie 2009) argues that the Third Way occluded and displaced the multiplicity of feminisms and substituted a version of feminism that was anti-male, strident and anti-pleasure, rendering it out of date so that it might be undone, stripped of its political force. Eisenstein (in a book tellingly titled *Feminism Seduced*) recounts how feminism became complicit in its own undoing, showing how, in the United States, 'the many and varied struggles of the 1970s have been selectively filtered into a hegemonic, mainstream feminism, of a kind that can be readily used by people whose motives are anything but women friendly' (Eisenstein 2009: ix). Her earlier intervention, on the fate of feminism in 1980s Australia, focused on the 'femocrats' whose 'brilliant political manoeuvring' enabled them to lever an alliance with the then Labour administration. She saw the advancement of women, through federally funded childcare, domestic violence and rape prevention, as 'compatible with the policies that simultaneously increased the gap between rich and poor and weakened the labour movement' (Eisenstein 2006: 49; see also Yeatman 1990 and Watson 1990 on the rise of 'femocrats'). Similarly United Nations activity around gender seemed to be victories for the women's cause; 'Yet the success of women in creating special agencies for women was not connected to any larger success in extending and strengthening welfare state provisions for the poorest part of the population', while structural adjustment programmes meant that 'the safety net around the world was being shredded simultaneously with the increasing visibility and activism of a global feminist movement' (Eisenstein 2006: 50). Entry was not unproblematic: in the United States under the Clinton administration women could be explicitly feminist 'as long as they practiced the tough love of the Clinton regime' (Eisenstein 2006: 55). But in the same period the Clinton administration 'was using mainstream feminism to assist in the project of selling neoliberal, free market capitalism to the world' (Eisenstein 2006: 55).

This implies that something more than the politics of mainstreaming might be at stake. Rather than imply that neoliberalism conceded to feminist demands, feminism is viewed, in some accounts, as generative of or complicit with the very rationalities and ideologies of neoliberalism. Such accounts tend to be located in the impersonal and elusive forces of 'neoliberalism' or 'globalizing capitalism' that appropriated second-wave feminism for its own purposes – expanding consumerism (McRobbie 2009) and smoothing the way for a post-Fordist, disorganized, transnational capitalism (see discussion of Boltanski and Chiapello in Chapter 5). Nancy Fraser draws on Boltanski and Chiapello to highlight what she terms the 'elective affinity' between feminism and neoliberalism (Fraser 2009). In a carefully argued paper she points to how feminist critiques of patriarchy ('anti-androcentrism') that opened the way for new forms of capitalist exploitation in which women's emancipation was tied to the engine of capitalist accumulation. At the same time, second-wave feminism's critique of welfare state paternalism slid easily into Thatcher's critique of the nanny state and welfare protection; and the feminist critique of bureaucratic paternalism was recuperated by neoliberalism. Similar debates have opened up in reflections on the achievements of LGBT politics. Smith (M. Smith 2005) shows how lesbian and gay organizing at both federal and local levels in Canada can be understood in terms of both resisting and reinforcing neoliberalism, while Richardson (Richardson 2004; Richardson 2005) argues that new citizenship claims, including those for same sex marriage, are complicit with neoliberal strategies. She writes of the professionalization of sexual politics and of a 'neoliberal politics of normalisation' in which sexual politics is influential in the development of neoliberal policies: not only through the constitution of consumer citizens but also integral to broader shifts towards social governance (Richardson 2005).

Much of this is convincing, but I am concerned about three features of such accounts. The first is the problem of explanation. There is a tension about how far feminism is viewed as the agent of its own demise, selling out its politics in exchange for welfare and other benefits (the mainstreaming narrative), or whether neoliberalism or capitalism – the language shifts between accounts – has appropriated feminist claims and aspirations in its own interests. There is also a troubling confusion around how far the focus is on the neoliberal economy (seeking new forms of exploitable labour in the face of the decline of manufacturing in the western heartlands); the neoliberal state (doing deals with women to promote projects of modernization); or on neoliberal cultural forms (new patterns of consumption that, in McRobbie's analysis, displaced feminist politics and substituted a stripped down, impoverished version of female empowerment). Each of these explanations is plausible, but the relationship between them – and thus the relationship between 'culture', 'economy' and 'state' – is not explored. Implicitly such accounts tend to collapse the social, political and cultural into the economic, reproducing forms of determinism that feminism, together with Gramscian, Althusserian and other engagements with Marxist theory, rejected decades ago. This takes me back to the arguments of Gibson-Graham and Roseneil on the problem of 'paranoid readings' of the present in Chapter 6. Gibson-Graham, responding to Eisenstein and others in a special issue of *Women's Studies Quarterly* in 2006, suggest that such thinking betrays a 'paranoid sensibility' that was all too common in leftist or radical thinking. They go on to ask:

> What is the image of power that underlines such an interpretation of events? It seems to be one in which power is predominantly distributed to capital ... Surely the building of an immense apparatus of integrated and implicated parts produces a veritable 'Christmas effect' (Sedgwick 1993) in which women's rights,

femocrats, changed life chances for women, shoring up of capitalist globalization, enclosures of land and sea, informalisation of the labor markets, increased exploitation, ransacked state services, a shredded welfare system, and the war on terror all sing to the same tune. (Gibson-Graham 2006a: 74)

This conflation of 'effects' raises significant problems of explanation. 'Strong theory ... affords the pleasures of recognition, of capture, of intellectually subduing that one last thing, [but] it offers no relief or exit to a place beyond' (Gibson-Graham 2006b: 4). That is, it erases the possibility of spaces of agency and of politics.

My second concern about the complicity of feminism in neoliberalism centres on what might be termed a politics of blame. Feminism's demise is attributed to the actions of white, middle-class feminists who sought equality, doing deals with the neoliberal devil and abandoning their own radicalism in the process. But blaming feminism for its own undoing too easily slides into the continued demonization of feminism and its achievements by the conservative right, fed by the popular press. It also chimes with the rise of an anti-liberal and anti-feminist political culture following the financial crisis of 2008 and, in the United Kingdom, the election of a coalition government committed to deep cuts in benefits and public services. The Women's Budget Group's response to the 2010 budget elicited a stream of vitriol; bloggers on the *Guardian* website responded, in colourful and abusive language, that women's claims of the past had discriminated against men and should now be silenced. And David Willetts, at the time Minister of State for Universities and Science, controversially claimed that feminism was to blame for the lack of social mobility in Britain, and hinted that high-earning women had contributed to the rise in house prices that had precipitated the banking crisis (Newman 2011b).

It is not only a question of blame; sometimes women are viewed as willing dupes of processes of political and cultural change that were not in their interests. McRobbie's emphasis on the cooption of feminist claims for choice and freedom in the developing consumer culture are relevant here. However Weeks offers a strong response to claims that the focus on identity politics helped generate a cult of individualism that was readily taken up in new forms of consumption-based citizenship. He argues that:

> The problem with such arguments is that they all assume that the individual is forced to live with the illusion of freedom while actually being wrapped in the gilded cords of late capitalism ... A related argument ... is the proposal that ideas of individual autonomy and self responsibilization are not so much illusory or deceptive as the very forms of regulation which can be most effectively articulated with the current form of capitalist, and by extension social and cultural, organization: neoliberalism. (Weeks 2007: 129–30)

This takes me to the third, and most troubling, problem: that of the relationship between the 'undoing' of feminism and the rise of neoliberalism. As I noted in Chapter 5, McRobbie traces the emergence of a 'gender aware govermentality' supported by the thesis of reflexive modernization (Beck *et al.* 1994; Beck and Beck-Gernscheim 2001). This, she argues, 'contributes to the eclipsing of feminism as a valid force for social and political change' and has provided 'a rationale for the rise of neoliberalism and the shift to the right in British politics' (McRobbie 2009: 46). She shows how women were losers in this emphasis on reflexivity, becoming disembedded from old institutions (e.g. an equal opportunity-based public sector) and set free to take their place in the post-Fordist flexible economy. For Nancy Fraser it was feminism's emphasis on culture (in a politics of recognition rather than redistribution) that was aligned with the demands of a new phase of post-Fordist, transnational and disorganized capitalism. Her 2009 paper 'Feminism, capitalism and the cunning of history' centred on how far feminism had 'unwittingly' supplied the key ingredients of the 'new spirit of capitalism' described by Boltanski and Chiapello:

> Was it mere coincidence that second wave feminism and neoliberalism prospered in tandem? Or was there some perverse, subterranean elective affinity between them? That second possibility is heretical, to be sure, but we fail to investigate it at our peril. Certainly the rise of neoliberalism dramatically changed the terrain on which second wave feminism operated. The effect, I shall argue, was to resignify feminist ideals. Aspirations that had a clear emancipatory thrust in the context of state organised capitalism assumed a far more ambiguous meaning in the neo-liberal era. (Fraser 2009: 107)

Feminist anti-economism, Fraser argues, collapsed into a politics of recognition that privileged identity politics over claims for redistribution and economic justice. 'Feminism absolutised the critique of culture at precisely the moment when circumstances required redoubled attention to the critique of political economy' (Fraser 2009: 109). She underscores the feminist challenge to traditional authority and its value for the emergence of a new form of post-Fordist capitalism based on horizontal teams, flexible network and management processes oriented towards releasing individual creativity:

> Disorganised capitalism turns a sow's ear into a silk purse by elaborating a new romance of female advancement and gender justice. Disturbing as it may sound, I am suggesting that second-wave feminism provided a key ingredient of the new spirit of neo-liberalism. Our critique of the family wage now supplies a good part of the romance that inflects flexible capitalism with a higher meaning and moral point. Endowing their daily struggles with an ethical meaning, the feminist romance attracts women at both ends of the social spectrum ... At both ends, the dream of women's emancipation is harnessed to the engine of capitalist accumulation. (Fraser 2009: 109–110)

We might, in passing, point to the binary opposition here between feminism as 'romance' and the economy as 'machine' in this extract. However, I want to draw attention to how Fraser avoids the politics of blame and victimhood by using the language of an 'elective affinity' between feminism and a new phase of capitalism. She also offers a more disaggregated conception of both feminism and neoliberalism, showing how different feminist critiques and claims generated multiple points of alignment with emerging capitalist logics. Her concept of 'resignification' suggests a less deterministic and more ambiguous reading of the shifts she describes. Resignification, which I introduced in Chapter 2, is a form of cultural practice in which chains of signifiers are disrupted in order for a concept to take on a new meaning. For example, if the chain that links feminism, justice and equality is ruptured, feminism can be resignified as outdated, anti-male and, indeed, the cause of women's oppression (see, for example, the vilification of the 'superwoman' syndrome of the 1980s). The same rupturing enables particular concepts in the chain – for example, justice and equity – to become sutured into other chains of equivalence: equity and choice; justice and a post-welfare concept of fairness. These new couplings fundamentally change the meaning of (i.e. resignify) the concepts and render them compatible with projects of depoliticization and welfare reform.

The processes of articulation, disarticulation and resignification are helpful ways of framing both the relationship between different varieties of activism and the accommodations between activist claims and governance shifts that I have traced in previous chapters of this book. I do not want to suggest that politicized forms of feminism were not subject to exclusion, marginalization and demonization. But there is little regard in many of the accounts for political agency, and for how contradictions are lived, managed and potentially produce lines of fracture. The agency of capitalism or neoliberalism itself is unquestioned, whether it is depicted as an entity into which social movements are incorporated and assimilated, or whether it is a dynamic force which requires the agency of others – including activists – to generate productive mutations and flexings. And while the treatment of feminism is nuanced and subtle, neoliberalism tends to be regarded as an unproblematic category: it is feminism that has to flex, not neoliberalism itself. This opens up some puzzles about how neoliberalism itself might be understood, and how questions of contradiction, antagonism and instability might offer rather different narratives of change.

Neoliberalism in question

In much of the critical literature neoliberalism itself is treated as a given; as a self-evident phenomenon that needs little discussion. It is depicted as a global and globalizing phenomenon that rolls over all before it, operating at a different scale from and thus subsuming 'local' and 'particular' struggles. Whatever happens in the spaces of power I have been concerned with in this book, it follows, neoliberalism will emerge triumphant. But what is neoliberalism? It is a highly contested concept (Brown 2005; Ward and England 2007) and has become what Clarke (Clarke 2008) regards as a 'promiscuous' term that is widely overused and notoriously difficult to pin down. One difficulty is that it is more likely to be a term used by critics than by its advocates; and this, Ferguson argues, leaves us 'with a politics largely defined by negation and disdain' (Ferguson 2010: 166). Within political economy, which tends to dominate the field of critical scholarship, David Harvey (Harvey 2005) views neoliberalism as a class-based political project of creating new means of capital accumulation, while Jessop (Jessop 2002) and Peck (Peck 2004) place more emphasis on the role of the state in securing political and ideological reform in order to enable the expansion of the scope and reach of corporate capital. In contrast Foucauldian inspired theories of governmentality (Brown 2005; Ong 2007; N. Rose 1999) view neoliberalism in terms of technologies for governing populations by installing 'economic' logics of calculation (constituted through discourses of markets, efficiency, managerialism, consumer choice and individual autonomy) and strategies for promoting 'self-governing' subjects.

Clarke (Clarke 2008) and Larner (Larner 2000), coming respectively from cultural studies and feminist geography, draw on such perspectives but carefully distinguish between neoliberalism as an ideology, as a set of political projects and policies, and as techniques of governing. Such distinctions are important, opening out questions about the coherence of neoliberalism as the singular source of 'all bad things' – an image that potentially undermines the possibility of contestation. As Larner suggests, 'this delineation of different interpretations of neoliberalism is not simply an academic exercise: our understanding of this phenomenon shape our readings of the scope and content of possible political interventions' (Larner 2000: 5).

This is an important point, which resonates with the analysis of the constitutive power of theory itself (Chapter 6): its capacity to make more solid that which is the object of critique, and to displace attention from experiments and examples which do not neatly fit. This is a point made strongly in my discussion with Sasha Roseneil:

> I got just really, really fed up with how everything gets understood in certain circles of academia as being about neoliberalism, and the lack of nuance in the overarching account of it's all neoliberal. There's a similar move gone on in queer work. This shows a lack of ability to be properly historical, I would say, to actually see the changes that have been brought about and the way in which those changes – both political, legal, policy and cultural – have been brought about by political activism, and the way those politics have been suffusing everyday life. A lot of my work has been about trying to trace processes of social change. But I think there's a kind of whole tendency to flatten out social change, to ignore it. There's a much greater comfort with the kind of pessimism that says it's all neoliberal and it's all unstoppable than there is with really kind of grappling with what might we do with our power. This goes back to my kind of anarchist politics which has always said 'you have power, I have power and we have to use our power'. You know we're not just kind of victims of anything, of patriarchal or neoliberalism, or any kind of set of macro forces. And there's a kind of pyschodynamic and post-structuralist take on that which is about the way in which we can continually reconstitute things by speaking them, so the more we say it's all neoliberalism, it's all impossible, the more we make it so. (Sasha Roseneil)

As Sasha and others have argued, theories of neoliberalism seem to fall too often into a form of 'epochal analysis' that reads all particularities as instances of a general phenomenon. In contrast, others have pointed to its variability:

> New political configurations are more multi-vocal than we might previously have understood. Most immediately, we are alerted to the possibility that there are different configurations of neoliberalism, and that close inspection of particular neo-liberal political projects is more likely to reveal a complex and hybrid political imaginary, rather than the straightforward implementation of a unified and coherent political philosophy. (Larner 2000: 12)

The analysis of coexisting and divergent political projects in New Zealand (Larner, Le Heron and Lewis 2007) and of contradictory governance regimes within the UK Third Way (Newman 2001) each demonstrates the significance of multiplicity, antagonism and contradiction. None of this denies the significance of the hegemonic project of neoliberalization and its disastrous implications for women and the resulting intensification of poverty and new global patterns of exploitation and inequality. But I do want to argue that viewing neoliberalism as a singular and all-encompassing force squeezes the capacity both for analysis and for agency. Across the chapters of this volume it is possible to trace multiple projects of neoliberalization and to suggest some of the different problematics that neoliberal governance might seek to address, from creating more flexible, educated workers to constituting community as a governmental terrain; from generating innovation to fostering new policy logics. These require different kinds of agents, operate at different temporalities and spatialities, and may not always be coherent. Rather than general questions (Is this neoliberal or not? What kind or phase of neoliberalism is this?), the focus of analysis shifts to how multiple projects coexist and how contradictions between them are resolved in *particular* sites at *specific* moments, and what forms of labour are at stake. Such questions are, I want to suggest, empirical as well as theoretical.

Spaces of power

Rather than just confronting neoliberalism, then, I want to open up space for thinking about what happens as activist projects confront neoliberal rationalities in the series of the 'perverse alignments', 'close encounters', 'modernizing moments' and 'critical engagements' discussed in this book, and to offer something more than Ferguson's politics of negation and disdain.

Issues of community (Chapter 3) have been integral to analyses of neoliberalism, but have been understood – and gendered – in rather different ways. The international development literature points to the centrality of women in economic development programmes in the global south, highlighting new patterns of exploitation and appropriation but also women's role in cultural and political change (Cornwall, Harrison and Whitehead 2007; Gaventa and McGee 2010; Gaventa and Tandon 2010; Gibson-Graham 2006b; Mohanty 2003; Sharma 2008). The literature on participation in the nations of Latin America and on Latina migrants in the United States highlights the problem of politics as strong and autonomous social movements confront globalizing neoliberal ruling relations (Coll 2010; Dagnino 2005; Dagnino 2007; Pearce 2010). The governmentality literature – especially in the global north – tends to centre on the constitution of new citizen subjects (the active citizen, the empowered citizen, the responsible citizen) situated in community as an ambiguous terrain that has taken on new significance in advanced neoliberal governance (N. Rose 1999).

Some feminist literatures point to community as the 'human face' of capitalism: 'Community is posited as particular where capitalism is abstract. Posited as its other, its opposite, community is often presented as a complement to capitalism, balancing and humanising it, even in fact, enabling it' (Joseph 2002: 1). Joseph notes how the discourse of community positions women as the defining other of modernity, of capitalism. Her idea of community as 'excess' that, because of its separateness from capitalist logics, can grow innovations on which capitalism can subsequently draw, is helpful. Indeed, this chapter has shown how women's labour on collective and cooperative projects served to generate commitments, resources and skills that were later utilised in governmental projects of inclusion, participation and empowerment. Such projects prefigured significant policy shifts and reconfigured sectoral and organizational boundaries, transforming public and professional labour and containing dissent.

But this is only part of the story. Even in the United Kingdom, as Chapter 3 suggested, women's engagements with community cannot be collapsed into a singular conception of neoliberal governmentality seeking to produce responsibilized citizen-subjects. But nor do they suggest a conception of the state in which it surrenders power to the 'empowered' community. Rather, Chapter 3 used the term 'perverse alignments' to suggest the relationship between multiple governmental projects and the resources generated through gendered labour. Such labour can be viewed as generating sources of power – or mobilizing community 'assets' – on which neoliberalism might draw, and/or of smoothing the edges of the conflicts resulting from the exacerbation of poverty, inequality and injustice. But it also generates images of potential alternatives that drew on – but failed to be subsumed by – governmentalities of community. In the UK context the conceptual and political hybridity of community enabled activist struggles to be resignified by government, but this did not mean that the original meaning was erased. 'Community' remains, in Britain and beyond, an intense focus of ideological and political struggles as welfare states seek to devolve responsibilities for care and welfare to 'local', personal, familial and faith-based actors, and as activists mobilize to define and pursue their own struggles, often drawing on public resources.

Chapter 4 highlighted the multiple projects that connected feminist-inflected activism, social policy and the regendering of governance. The selective incorporation of gender agendas in what has been termed the social investment state can be viewed as a triumph of neoliberal forms of appropriation of feminist politics. But in the same period concerns about parenting, family stability and care became amplified. These projects addressed women as citizen-subjects in different ways, the first calling on women to participate in the economy as full, adult-worker citizens; the second summoning them as carers, parents and responsible citizens. One might, rather crudely, depict feminism as functional to neoliberalism in two different and contradictory ways. In the first, the expanded role of female labour – more flexible, less unionized and more suited to the service economy – is viewed as constitutive of a new economic order of flexible accumulation. In the second, women are viewed as integral to advanced neoliberal strategies of governing the social and sustaining the informal economy that reproduces the conditions of capital accumulation. The contradictions between these projects, and between the subject positions women are expected to adopt, open out global patterns of migration (to meet care needs) but also intensify tensions between paid and unpaid work that can only be resolved by what development economists term the greater elasticity of women's labour (Elson 1995).

Such functionalist readings, however, offer limited purchase on the contradictions at stake in the regendering of the economy and of the social. In each case neoliberal projects were themselves transformed – in part – through their encounters with feminist and other activist claims. Employers came to bear the 'costs' of equality governance, parental leave and more complex patterns of work demanded by women's entry as full worker citizens. Welfare states, while looking to curb benefits paid to 'dependent' women, had to invest in development, empowerment and training and to launch a multiplicity of 'social' programmes in order to enable women both to contribute to the economy and to manage care work, however flawed and partial such programmes proved to be. It is not the case, then, that women were included in policy and economy in ways that left the social order unchanged (Brodie 2008): neoliberalism had itself to adapt and flex to take account of feminist projects. However, there is no doubt that feminist politics (especially the claim that 'the personal is political') laid the basis for the emergence of new governmentalities of the self and personal lives. Notions of active citizenship, for example, drew extensively on social movement (especially feminist) claims and practices, reinflecting and resignifying them in line with hegemonic political projects (Newman and Tonkens 2011). The development of what Pykett terms the 'maternal state' (Pykett 2012), with its emphasis on 'soft paternalism' as a form of rule, reworked feminist vocabularies of the emotions and the body into new strategies of behaviour change and social control. Conceptions of neoliberalism as 'policy' and as 'governmentality' thus offer different readings of the regendering of governance.

Chapter 5 traced multiple modernizing logics, showing that 'modernization' was not a singular ethos but a rationale for a range of disparate projects. The 'challenges to tradition' in the 1960s can be viewed as both good for women and post-colonial citizen-subjects (symbolically, if not materially, freeing them from subordinate and dependent status), and good for capitalism (opening up access to new productive workforces and new products that were at the 'leading edge' of an economy to come, drawing on 'wasted talent' and introducing new production systems: ones that, in the case of F-International, 'fitted' with women's lives). But they also opened up spaces that women could seize, occupy and subvert. Some decades later some women who had previously worked in socialist and community based projects entered local government to head up the process of competitive tendering (CCT). We might understand this as local authorities appropriating the experiences, politics and skills of socialist feminists and reworking them to extend market rationalities. But we might also see women appropriating local authority spaces to work new articulations between trade union discourses, feminist discourses and professional/managerial discourses within the local authority. This work of articulation was done 'from below' rather than by dominant actors, subverting – at least for a while – the rationalities of contracting in order to enhance the employment status of women and the value placed on women's labour. This was a collective project – participants worked with women in the cleaning, catering and other services, with some local authority councillors and some trade unionists to generate new practices and service logics. And this government-imposed modernization, which can be understood as the state creating the conditions for the neoliberal logics to come, opened up spaces for 'other projects': catering services were modernized in ways that led to better school meals services, and contracts had equality provisions built into them. Both of these were, of course, temporary gains. But CCT also brought low-paid women's work in cleaning and catering to the fore of local political agendas, leading to a partial modernization of trade unions around issues of gender and race, and prefiguring the 'equal value' legislation of later years.

A rather different modernization, becoming more evident through the 1990s, was characterized by the rise of managerialism (Clarke and Newman 1997). This superimposed economic forms of calculation on to embedded social, professional and public rationalities and was fundamental to the new 'spirit of capitalism' discussed by Boltanski and Chiapello (Boltanski and Chiapello 2005) on which Fraser drew (Fraser 2009). Managerialism privileged constant organizational change in the search for flexibility, performance and innovation. The 'management of change' was the key managerial skill sought out by employers through the 1990s, and who better to help them than those who understood the significance of the personal in organizational life and who could work with the emotional as well as the structural dynamics of change?

Women entering management can thus be viewed as doing important work in softening and humanizing organizations in ways that made them fit for service-based rather than industrial, Fordist processes of capital accumulation. The feminization of management not only highlighted the role of women as change agents but also heralded the valorization of flexibility and reflexivity, both needed for the expansion of new capitalist logics. These qualities were promoted by a range of policy entrepreneurs, educators and consultants, and by those engaged in 'partnership' work. As the chapter showed, such actors helped to generate a new discursive organizational repertoire of culture, values, development, empowerment, quality, customer focus, missions, visions and participative leadership and so on that, although readily appropriated by modernizing logics, provided ample spaces for 'other projects'.

Chapter 6 showed how participants helped constitute the reflexive and educated subjects required by the 'information society' or 'knowledge economy', both integral to new logics of capital accumulation and central to national projects of global competitiveness. The turn to 'experiential knowledge' can be linked with the forms of reflexive modernization required by neoliberalism. It also enabled the production of new governmentalities of the self: the empowered citizen, the responsible citizen, the active citizen, the participating citizen and the citizen consumer. Each, as previous chapters have shown, was integral to neoliberal projects of state retrenchment. Each made more of the 'self' available for new governmental projects of coproduction, partnership and responsibilization; but also generated more critical and potentially politicized actors. Such paradoxes ran through a number of different forms of knowledge-work discussed in the chapter. For example, the professional shifts that sought to enhance citizen's knowledge of their own needs and conditions can be viewed as integral to their role as consumers of services in a disaggregated and marketized welfare state. Yet Ann McPherson, who was a pioneer of opening up peer-based systems of enhancing access to such knowledge, was adamant in her opposition to the UK choice agenda in health services.

Chapter 6 also showed how some participants engaged in a series of 'close encounters' with the policy process, using both the knowledge elicited through research and their own activist agendas to influence, inform and evaluate policy initiatives. This led to a series of dilemmas – dilemmas concerning the proper relationship between research and policy, about the methods and ethical consequences of different approaches, about the value and utility of their work to practitioners, activists and those who were the subjects of the research. The role of activists in knowledge-work, then, opens up many of the same paradoxes as other forms of work: participants may have their work appropriated for purposes other than those which were intended; they may unintentionally be complicit with the elaboration of political projects that they do not support; and they may find their words being 'stolen' and resignified by actors promoting projects of exploitation rather than empowerment. Yet knowledge remains a locus of power, and participants all brought important political framings of the work in which they were engaged: making visible unrecognized patterns of exploitation and bringing silenced subjects to voice; opening up public conversations and influencing decision-makers; and generating new practices and objects through forms of creative labour.

Chapter 7 looked across these substantive chapters in order to assess the 'border work' of participants as they attempted to work between activist projects and dominant ruling relations. It showed how, in doing so, they frequently occupied positions on the edge of mainstream institutions, acting as brokers, transactors and translators between 'inside' and 'outside' networks, organizations and sources of power. Much of their work was concerned with partnering, joining up and reconciling difference. One of the perspectives on which I drew for understanding this work was that offered by Larner and Craig's analysis of the role of 'strategic brokers' whose skills and knowledges were put to use in minimizing the fallout of an earlier phase of neoliberalism, softening its edges and addressing the fragmentations that had resulted. They were thus complicit in the turn to more 'social' governance strategies associated with the Third Way and the move from 'roll-back' neoliberalism with a 'roll-out' form in which the state played a more significant role in constituting neoliberal subjects (Peck and Tickell 2002). However, there may be tensions between the social and economic goals of neoliberalism, which could be exploited by those working its borders.

This brief chapter review demonstrates something of the multiplicity of neoliberalism. But how is this multiplicity to be understood? Ong (Ong 2007) treats neoliberalism as a 'mobile assemblage' comprising technologies, techniques and practices that are appropriated selectively as they come into contact with 'local' politics and cultures. They are mobile and connective rather than a 'tidal wave' that rolls out from dominant centres of power. There is a need, then, to distinguish between grand ideological projects and their uneven and fractured enactments at local level. From a governmentality perspective Li (Li 2007a) argues that most of the political work of neoliberalism involves practices of de- and re-articulation of existing elements into new configurations, assemblages or constellations. These are each perspectives that I have found productive in trying to analyse the 'spaces of power' discussed in previous chapters. As activist struggles and neoliberal projects encounter each other, rather than the former being erased, they are *selectively* appropriated into mobile configurations or assemblages that are always incomplete. The spaces of power that participants generated and occupied, then, were not 'spaces of exception' in a field of power dominated by neoliberalism; they were formed in a *dynamic* field marked by contradictions, strains, antagonisms and ambivalences.

Landscapes of antagonism

The previous section highlighted some of the sites in which feminist-inflected agency was selectively – and contradictorily – appropriated in new ruling relations. It suggested how feminist activism prefigured new governmentalities of empowerment and community; how women's involvement in policymaking supported the emergence of new forms of governing based on partnership and participation; how feminism was ambiguously aligned with new organizational and leadership practices; and how the emphasis on experience-based forms of knowledge and research could be appropriated. These were, I want to emphasize, different political projects associated with multiple negotiations of new forms of rule. In highlighting multiplicity, however, I do not want to suggest that all projects carried equal weight, nor that each was a site in which neoliberal appropriations and erasures were successful. Rather, neoliberal projects and feminist politics encountered each other in differently constituted 'landscapes of antagonism'. To explore these I draw on two different analytical frameworks. The first is that of Raymond Williams, who, in contesting what he termed 'epochal' forms of analysis, argued that:

> We have certainly still to speak of the 'dominant; and the 'effective', and in these senses of the hegemonic. But we find that we also have to speak, and indeed with further differentiation of each, of the 'residual' and the 'emergent', which in any real process, and at any moment in the process, are significant both in themselves and in what they reveal about the character of the 'dominant'. (Williams 1977: 121–2)

Feminism, I want to suggest, was the source of emergent forms of politics and practice which in turn opened up what I term 'prefigurative pathways', some of which were articulated into would-be hegemonic forms of rule to become a new 'dominant' formation. But in the process neoliberalism itself had to adapt and flex to take account of feminism: its claims and demands, and the cultural and politics shifts it had generated. Other pathways were configured with traces of 'residual' formations that continued as effective forces into the present in ways that disrupt readings of 'epochal' change.

This form of analysis problematizes concepts of 'after' and 'post' neoliberalism developed in some feminist literature (see discussion in Simon-Kumar 2011). But the argument I want to develop here is rather different and takes me to the second analytical framing: one that points to how new orderings of the 'dominant' emerge in conditions where counter projects and movements have formed a 'perverse alignment' with neoliberal logics. This concept, introduced in Chapter 3, is inspired by the work of the Brazilian scholar Evelina Dagnino who traced a 'perverse confluence' between popular participatory projects (represented in the success of struggles against the military dictatorship in Brazil) and the neoliberal conception of a minimal state. The perversity is located in the fact that despite 'pointing in opposite and even antagonistic directions, both projects require an active, proactive civil society' (Dagnino 2007: 335; see also Newman and Clarke 2009: 139). This offers a different, but sympathetic, reading of the 'elective affinities' between feminism and neoliberalism referred to by Fraser. I want to use it here to suggest the significance of the different 'perversities' generated in the multiple spaces of power traced in the previous section.

Chapter 3 traced the emergence of particular governmental concerns with 'community' in the United Kingdom in the 1970s in the Community Development Programmes that sought to contain and manage particularly 'deprived', and therefore potentially disruptive, communities. This opened new spaces of power that fostered emergent forms of anti-state and anti-capitalist activism that flourished through the 1980s. Under the Blair governments, while antagonisms continued, the socialist-inflected and anti-racist community activisms that had been supported – and often funded – by local governments were displaced, in part, in the attempt to forge a new hegemonic settlement based on ideas of social inclusion and community cohesion. As in the Dagnino example, both political 'resistance' and neoliberal governmentality required a strong and active civil society: for community activists, this represented new configurations of resistance within, rather than outside, dominant projects; for neoliberalism, a strong and active civil society was a source of potential forms of innovation that could be appropriated by capitalism in the search for new sources of profit (as in Joseph's conception of community as 'excess') as well as potentially displacing some forms of state expenditure.

This hegemonic settlement, I want to emphasize, was a project rather than an accomplishment. State expenditure in this period tended to grow rather than diminish, and activism flourished in 'emergent' spaces at the same time as older – more residual – activist projects became subject to processes of professionalization. Both contribute to the dominant projects of cuts and retrenchment in the present. In the United Kingdom, civil society is being recast, ideologically, as an alternative to public services and state welfare; the hoped for Big Society of David Cameron was explicitly depicted as an alternative to the (overgrown, dependency inducing, paternalistic) Big State. Emergent civil society forms generated by the opportunities of 'competition' and 'choice' in previous decades are becoming more mainstream, creating important shifts in the cultural and political landscape. However, these emergent (neoliberal) ideological forces are neither equivalent to actual (neoliberal) policies and projects, nor do they signal a coherent new (neoliberal) governmentality. In the United Kingdom, the policy agenda associated with the Big Society was weakened and had, to say the least, uneven political purchase, either within government, the Civil Service or popular consciousness. And its associated governmentalities – of self-reliance and mutuality – were, as we will see, in tension with other neoliberal logics. However, there is no doubt that the ideological project of vilifying the state and all its works and privileging the local community as a locus of moral and ethical values has been particularly successful.

This is, in part, due to its appropriation of residual and emergent vocabularies, sensibilities and practices. The Big Society and other policies on local devolution and active citizenship did not emerge fully formed from the pens of politicians and policymakers; they were prefigured by emerging critiques of New Labour's hyper rational-instrumentalist mode of politics (Jordan 2010);

by residual attachments to moral, ethical and relational norms and values, including those of care and mutual responsibility espoused by many women; and by the emerging role of 'faith actors' in the marketplace for schools, care homes and other formerly 'public' services. This marks 'the local' as a field in which different forces and interests are played out. And its gendering is paradoxical: women are positioned as the vilified agents of state expansion and state paternalism of the (residual) past, and as the potential mobilizers of a more ethical and moral society characterized by mutual care and responsibility. However, women are already being profoundly disadvantaged by these new ideological framings and their consequences, not least the cuts to state services and the possibilities of state-funded employment.

The policy shifts traced in Chapter 4 suggest a different 'perverse alignment' in which both capital and the state sought to mobilize women as reflexive, educated worker citizens as well as cheap and flexible labour. In the affluent West, the dynamics of change privileged the former, using the possibilities of global migration or outsourcing to the global south to secure access to cheap labour. This mobilization is a critical point of alignment with second-wave feminist claims for economic and political independence. Emergent forces in that period prefigured the phenomena of gender mainstreaming, together with the (partial and conditional) recognition of issues of gender, race and sexuality in public policy, the professions and organizational practice.

Throughout the 1980s and 1990s these emergent forces helped reconfigure the dominant orthodoxies of policy, management and business, such that 'diversity' was ideologically and discursively valorized as a source of innovation and a drive to enhanced performance. This can be read as a form of neoliberal 'flexing' to take account of unresolved contradictions, but the reframing of individualism and choice around notions of diversity and equality can be viewed as its attempt to smooth increasingly problematic antagonisms. In the process, as McRobbie argued, the political dimensions of feminist and other claims became residual; but they did not disappear. They continued as effective forces, persisting precisely because neoliberalism had not flexed sufficiently, had not erased the possibility of a feminist politics. Indeed, just as neoliberalism 'stole' some of the discursive repertoires of feminism and other struggles, so feminist actors sought to appropriate neoliberal repertoires (for example, those of efficiency and investment). Politics continued through alternative new vocabularies of action (LGBT rather than gay, human rights rather than recognition, migration and asylum rather than race). But older vocabularies that had been the focus of co-option – such as equality and fairness – remained as effective forces into the present; indeed, they came back into prominence in feminist institutions such as the Fawcett Society and Women's Budget Group, as the disenchantment of women to Conservative-led coalition policies on cuts and state retrenchment became increasingly vocal (the Fawcett Society was backed by a coalition of charities, trade unions and academics – much in the style of the policy entrepreneurship described in Chapter 4). The residual, perhaps, can bite back: though how sharp its teeth can be in the present political conjuncture is as yet uncertain.

Many of the 'modernizing' projects evident in the next set of mappings can also be read as points of potential perverse alignment between feminist claims and capitalist logics. Both feminism and neoliberalism privilege reflexive, flexible forms of subjectivity and 'empowered', information-rich actors. This produced what appears to be a new dominant formation characterized by post-Fordist organizational forms, 'soft' management skills, person-centred leadership and high levels of investment in the training and development of workforces. But this dominant formation generated new spaces that women could take up: as project workers, consultants, entrepreneurs, trainers, partners and leaders, many of whom levered or bent the dominant in ways that took account of very different projects (Newman 2005c). Post-Fordism also opened up space for the reframing of equality. The bureaucratic systems through which equal opportunities had become inscribed became threatened as bureaucracy itself became discredited. But this very process of de-bureaucratization created new spaces of power in which activists could bend the new logics, taking equality rationales into service provision by resignifying 'quality', inscribing equality into audit and performance management measures, linking 'diversity' to the expansion of participative technologies and so on (Brietenbach, Brown, Mackay and Webb 2002). At the same time bureaucracy, rather than being eradicated in the neoliberal search for mobile and flexible ways of organizing, was supplanted by new global imperatives of 'good governance' (see publications of the World Bank, International Labour Organization, World Health Organization and other transnational institutions). These became the focus of contestation (what was to be included), inscription (of feminist and other claims, especially those of 'presence'), and indeed expansion (to accommodate new social justice claims that expanded feminist politics beyond the limits of the nation state). The power and capacity of 'good governance' to exert control over capitalist enterprises is of course extremely limited. The banking crisis of 2008 and beyond, and the failure of governments to extend control through regulation and other governance devices, demonstrates these limits in stark terms. However, 'good governance' is by no means a residual discourse, and remains the locus of antagonistic mobilizations and contested rationalities.

In Chapter 6 we can trace the contours of a perverse alignment in which both activist projects and neoliberal governmentalities seek to constitute more reflexive, knowledgeable actors. This has offered up multiple spaces of power that could be mobilized by activists, and in which the meanings and practices of new subjectivities could be negotiated. The evidence of this book, and of other research, is that subjects do not readily take on the subject positions offered to them; they may not 'hear' the summons or may use new forms of knowledge and power for 'other' purposes (Barnes and Prior 2009: Barnett,

Cloke, Clark and Malpass 2011; Clarke *et al.* 2007). They may hold on to older (supposedly residual) identifications as rights-bearing citizens, or may become part of emergent formations of connectivity and agency based on ethical, environmental or social justice claims that are not easily reconciled with governmental projects. In assessing the pattern of dominant, residual and emergent forces what seems to be significant is how knowledge is inscribed in particular assemblages. The wok of Tania Li (Li 2007a; Li 2007b) is helpful here. She shows how the work of assemblage involves six practices: those of 'forging alignments'; 'rendering technical'; 'authorizing knowledge'; 'managing failures and contradictions'; 'depoliticization'; and 'reassembling'. In terms of the forms of knowledge-work described in Chapter 6, we saw how new alignments were forged between policymakers and academics, as well as between 'experts' and 'ordinary people'. But experiential knowledge had to be 'rendered technical' – stripped of nuance and complexity – in order to be packaged for policymaking or policy evaluation. The accounts also show how some forms of knowledge became authorized, and how contradictions between experiential and more objective knowledge had to be managed. 'Dominant' and 'residual' forms of knowledge and knowledge-work are not, then, absolute categories but are aligned in different ways. However Li's final two practices are of particular importance, returning to the processes of professionalization referred to in Chapters 3, 4 and 7. The process of 'rendering technical' serves to depoliticize the field from which knowledge is derived; expertise, this implies, becomes removed from the activism that brought individuals and groups into 'close encounters' with dominant ruling relations. Political questions of equality and justice tended to be reposed as matters of technique and transposed through the filtering devices of action plans, monitoring, auditing and so on. In a similar way the political question of the marginalization and exclusion of particular population groups came to be addressed through technologies of 'public participation' that privilege certain forms of knowledge and render others illegitimate (Barnes *et al.* 2007; Mahony 2008). But the book has also shown the significance of 'reassembling'; how participants resignified existing discourses, deployed new capacities and resources, and combined existing elements in ways that serve to repoliticize a field of action.

This analysis has offered a way of reframing narratives of the decline or erasure of feminism through its inscription in policy and in organizational systems. It points to the multiple ways in which feminist politics and neoliberal projects encounter each other and to the contradictions – for both feminism and neoliberalism – that result. It shows how feminism, as well as neoliberalism, has the capacity to adapt and flex. Jain and Elson (Jain and Elson 2011) show how feminism continues to inflect development projects in China, India, Japan, Cuba, Africa and other nations, and how feminist knowledge can help shape public policy for a 'post crisis' world. But in neoliberal times, as Dagnino argued, politics becomes both more difficult and potentially dangerous: there is greater likelihood that one's very words will be stolen, that the language through which politics was conducted will be appropriated, potentially leaving political movements 'lost for words'. Indeed, in Chapter 3 I quoted Jane Foot speaking angrily about how *'New Labour have stolen our language'*, while Carole Harte, who had been promoting active citizenship through women's empowerment projects, spoke of her shock when Cameron began using the same language, and her feelings at how here words were coming back and *'biting me on the bum'*.

I do not, then, want to propose an optimistic image of agency in place of the pessimistic image of neoliberal triumph. In the face of processes of appropriation, displacement and co-option, it is difficult to delineate a common political project and to pursue it in the kinds of spaces of power I have traced in this book. But I do want to highlight the importance of readings of change that allow for continued points of conflict, disruption and antagonism. This takes me back to the work of Sasha Roseneil (quoted earlier in this chapter). The narrative of neoliberalism and the erasure of feminism offers a way of understanding dominant trends and tendencies, but overlooks both 'residual' and 'emergent' forms. It overlooks the continued existence of strong feminist institutions and orientations formed in an earlier political-cultural moment that are still effective in the present – and which can continue to 'speak to power'. It also overlooks emergent ways of reframing feminist struggle: ways that do not necessarily speak the language of 'equality' but which address issues that were on the margins of older feminist campaigns – on care work, migration, sex work, environmental issues, global social justice and so on. The study thus challenges narratives of feminist complicity with neoliberalism, showing how both are multiple formations that became aligned in particular ways in particular places at particular political-cultural moments. Mapping these as temporary and conditional alignments in landscapes of antagonism that are always in motion does not foreclose the possibility of politics.

Conclusion

What has been the value of this analysis for readings of the present political-cultural moment? In Chapter 1, I set out the theoretical and political goals of this research. Theoretically, this chapter has challenged a conception of both feminism and neoliberalism as singular entities that can be aligned – stitched together – in an overarching and epochal account of the present. Each 'mapping' generated from the research shows the coexistence of multiple neoliberal rationalities and intersecting activist projects, and suggests ways in which the antagonisms are worked, contained or reconfigured, in part, through gendered labour (see also Newman 2012a; Newman 2012c; Newman 2013).

Each also illuminates the current political moment through an understanding of the changes that have taken place over the previous sixty years. The spaces of power that participants in the research generated and occupied, then, were not 'spaces of exception' in a field of power dominated by neoliberalism; they were formed in a *dynamic* field marked by contradictions, strains, antagonisms and ambivalences. However, spaces of power, I argued in Chapter 7, are spaces of strain and discomfort; as 'contact zones' traversed by competing forms of power and authority they are spaces that call on essentially political, rather than professional or managerial, skills.

Politically, the chapter has reviewed how the term 'spaces of power' opens up the possibility of contingent and temporary forms of intervention through which activist projects can be pursued. The research on which this book draws shows how women have generated such spaces by working the contradictions inherent in neoliberal projects, and have used them to lever resources and other forms of power in order to pursue activist goals. They have worked with multiple understandings of politics, and have performed that politics in very different ways, often changing their performance over a life-course. Their successes may be partial or temporary, but their work attests to the importance of finding alternatives to Ferguson's politics of 'negation and disdain' in which narratives of neoliberal incorporation foreclose the possibility of political agency. The women on whose accounts I have drawn often themselves challenged feminism's own accounts of incorporation and complicity:

> Some of what's happening might be subsumed under neoliberalism, but not all of it. There are still women working in public sectors who bring feminist and class-based agendas into their work. But then we had those same debates in the 1970s where we had debates between liberal and socialist feminism – we didn't call it neoliberalism in the 1970 but we were debating those same questions. Nowadays neoliberal policies have become more hegemonic than before, but there are still lots of women who are struggling with these issues. But it is disappointing when there is some big name who says she now rejects feminism, or that it's no longer relevant. It's very disappointing when that happens. (Avtar Brah)

This extract shows the importance of bringing a historical perspective to political debates about liberalizing economic reforms. It warns against assumptions about the erasure of some of the forms of activism described in preceding chapters. But it also expresses a sense of disappointment about the rejection of earlier forms of political commitment and action on the part of 'big names'. This, she argued, not only gave succour to an anti-feminist politics of the right, but also sent out harmful signals to younger women, the potential activists of the present and future. As younger women generate new ways of performing feminist politics there is a need for better narratives of the fate of those who came before.

9

Postscript: Speaking to the Present

The research on which this book draws is incomplete; I am still meeting active and activist women and trying to capture how they are making sense of their lives and work in a period of cuts, austerity and political reversals. What, then, has been the value of this book? Is it a historical narrative of times past or might it offer some small hope for the future? In this Postscript I want to look both backwards and forwards, revisiting the analysis and assessing its capacity to illuminate some features of the present political conjuncture. This has been the hardest thing to write: trying to hold on to a sense of political possibility while seeing, every day, a new manifestation of austerity politics and its consequences, not least in the reversal or erasure of many of the changes for which the women in this book fought.

All to whom I spoke in the later stages of the research viewed the conditions of the present with anger, concern and dismay:

> *I think that's the way that British society is developing in light of the cuts and everything that's happening; it's really, really worrying and I just really kind of despair about what this country is going to look like, and the increasing divide between rich and poor, and where I position myself in that.* (Cecilia Wee)

Many viewed the present as heralding a form of hyper-neoliberalism in which global capitalism reigns supreme, unfettered by state regulation and untrammelled by concessions to 'old-fashioned' notions of welfare and equality. They worried about the effects of the public sector cuts, the withdrawal of benefits for many categories of people and the impact of high levels of unemployment. These each have a disproportionate impact on women (Women's Budget Group 2010; Fawcett Society 2011) but those I spoke to were equally concerned about the classed and racialized dynamics of recession and the spatial unevenness of its effects. They also spoke of the personal consequences: in parts of Britain the cuts to public services, the reductions in funding for childcare and elder care, the transformations of the NHS and growing material inequalities were making managing the balance between personal and public/political lives more difficult. Many of those I interviewed had been made redundant, had their funding cut or were juggling multiple jobs to try to make ends meet. Some were themselves having to 'rip up' organizations they had helped shape and to cut services they knew would have awful consequences for those most in need – the very people to whom participants were politically committed. The younger women I spoke to were finding new ways of enacting politics but often in parlous financial circumstances and, for some, with problematic citizenship status.

One way of reading the present, then, is through images of loss and reversal: the undoing of much of what the work of the women in this book had produced. For example, support for the work of community-based and voluntary-sector organizations (see Chapter 3) was being severely reduced as the cuts bit, and many of the policy reforms secured by feminist activists (see Chapter 4) were being reversed. As I write, Naomi Eisenstadt was drawing attention to the increase in child poverty likely to result from the closure of many Sure Start Centres and the Fawcett Society was calling for the restoration of government support for childcare costs, the ring-fencing of funding to childcare centres and for government to prevent local authorities viewing domestic violence services as a 'soft touch' for cuts (Fawcett Society 2011). Others were campaigning against welfare cuts and reforms that were likely to restore a 'male breadwinner' model that earlier feminist campaigns had successfully fought against (see Chapter 4). These specific reversals were set in a wider ideological framing of the relationships between politics and economy, state and society. Such framings were not new, but had been hugely amplified in the orchestration of responses to the banking crisis and subsequent economic recession such that the 'naturalness' of markets was constituted as the new common sense (Newman and Clarke 2009; Massey 2011). The discursive framing of the market as 'outside' and beyond the reach of politics, its presence as an invisible but potent and demanding force, served to justify attempts to appease it through programmes of debt reduction, austerity and cuts. It also served to subject populations to economic logics – we must all change the ways we live and work according to an economic calculus of debt reduction and financial stringency. Poverty, cuts, austerity and hardship were depicted within a masculine discourse of toughness and rugged resilience, displacing – in part – more feminine and feminist discourses of interdependence and ethical concerns (for intimate others, for future generations, for the environment, and for distant populations as well as members of 'local' communities).

But ideologies are never complete; they form crucial components of hegemonic projects, but such projects are always in the making rather than 'won'. And here the arguments of this book have much to offer. Analytically, the book has drawn attention to processes through which hegemonic projects seek to incorporate alternative capacities and resources, but has also depicted these processes as dynamic, taking place in landscapes of antagonism characterized by multiple political forces (see Chapter 8). Politically, it has shown how feminism and other social movements constituted lines of fracture and antagonism that challenged the hegemonic political settlement of the late twentieth and early twenty-first centuries in Britain. The legacies of such movements were highly visible in the policy programmes of New Labour and other Third Way governments, not only in terms of specific policies (civil partnerships, welfare provision, the focus on children and the brief flowering of 'multiculturalism'), but also in terms of a wider attention to the social and its governance, and the associated reframing of both 'personal' and 'political'. Feminism and other movements also created a discursive repertoire and political resource that continually challenged the status quo (Williams's 'dominant'; Williams 1977) and which generated alternatives, preventing the settlement from becoming settled. 'Race' continued to be a troubling presence that refused to be accommodated in strategies of cohesion and inclusion. 'Gender' was partly silenced in the dominant discursive repertoires of families, parenting and responsible citizenship, but young women continued to assert new feminist agendas and to disrupt taken-for-granted assumptions about the power of a 'gender aware' governmentality to satisfy women's demands for equality and justice, both for themselves and their children.

Writing about the present is more problematic; the specifics of British political culture are rather marginal in contemporary global realignments of power, inequality and access to social and economic justice. And even within Britain, events are so fast-moving that it is difficult to distinguish between temporary blips and more sustained conjunctural movements. But, in early 2012, it appeared that the extent to which the naturalness of markets and the prioritization of supposedly apolitical strategies to appease them were uneven; responses to the effect of budget cuts and austerity packages suggested that support for the idea that 'There Is No Alternative'[1] was far from universal. Trade unions, financial commentators, journalists and organizations on the left were becoming more vocal in their critique of economic policy – not least since it was manifestly failing to stimulate growth. Disquiet about the loss of political support for the coalition government among women voters as a result of cuts to crucial benefits and services had led to some tactical repositioning and a few symbolic (rather than substantive) nods towards the female electorate. And the government's desire to constitute citizens as workers rather than welfare claimants, as volunteers (in the Big Society) rather than activists (on the street), also seemed to have little traction: connections between people and government appeared to be characterized by 'disaffected consent' (Gilbert 2010) rather than positive engagement, coupled with the explosion of new (and old) forms of activism.

However, an analysis that posits neoliberal ideology on the one hand and new forms of resistance on the other replicates the paradox (of simultaneous dismay and a sense of possibility) that I referred to earlier, and does not take us very far. In trying to understand how the work of this book might speak to the present and future I want to revisit four of its key concepts: 'political formation', 'border work', 'spaces of power' and 'generative labour'.

Political formation

Chapter 2 showed something of how individuals come to politics; how social movements created spaces for activism and how the intersections between different political spaces – community action, political parties, social movements, environmental movements, trade unions – opened up particularly productive possibilities. It also suggested how political struggles and key events produced fractures in earlier political, economic and social settlements: the emergence of the New Left, the civil rights movement and second-wave feminism all shifted political discourses and practices. And it showed how events symbolized the redrawing of the political landscape: the miners' strike and more adversarial politics of Thatcherism; the conflicts between police and Black populations and the rise of anti-racist struggles; Greenham Common and the 'queering' of feminism; the struggles over local government as an oppositional space; the rise of environmental and social justice movements; the explosion of anti-capitalist activism and the associated turn to 'post-identity' forms of creative, performative politics. Each of these arose in response to would-be hegemonic projects (colonialism, Thatcherism, the managerial and military state, the Third Way, consumerism and, of course, capitalism itself). And each generated lines of contradiction and antagonism that were 'worked' by participants to generate social, cultural and political change. It is already evident that political work in the present and future will be very different but will be shaped by the same double process – new forms of politicization and the generation of new spaces of power wrought from fissures and fractures in dominant ruling relations.

As I wrote the final draft of this book, something new appeared to be stirring. People were mobilizing in Greece, Spain and Italy against austerity programmes, and emergent groupings were transforming traditional forms of protest – the demonstration, the petition, the campaign – through web-based social media and imaginative political performances. All of this was taking place against a backcloth of images of a new style of politics in Egypt, Tunisia and Libya and other nations in which 'people power' appeared – for a while – to be able to topple dictatorial regimes, albeit with considerable bloodshed. The Occupy movement was particularly significant. Originating in Spain with the Los Indignados protests, it was taken up in New York and spread to more than 900 cities across the globe. It echoed earlier anti-capitalist protests in Seattle, Genoa, London and other cities, and more recent student led anti-cuts demonstrations, but responses from establishment media and institutions were rather different. The slogan 'We are the 99 per cent' and the explicit targeting of the banks and financial institutions captured the imagination not only of the young and disenfranchised, but of a wider public. The movement thus created some elite anxiety, not least because of sympathetic reporting in leading media (including the *New York Times* and

Financial Times). This anxiety was evident in responses from Barack Obama in the United States and Ed Miliband in the United Kingdom, both of whom offered affirming if qualified responses, and in conflicts within the Church of England about how to respond to the Occupy encampment at St Paul's Cathedral in London. Even though specific protest encampments were subject to enforced closures by police and bailiffs, the impact of the movement may not be so easily contained.

These forms of political mobilization appeared fresh and new. They were less based on single-identity politics and were enabled in part – but only in part – by new social media such as Twitter, Facebook and YouTube. They combine a focus on education and collective practice with that of political protest and dissent. However, they confronted issues and raised questions that resonated with earlier movements. The dilemmas for the Occupy movement – of how to maintain an open and ethical, spontaneous and performative, non-hierarchical and leaderless movement – resonated with many earlier protests, and, in particular, with the dilemmas lived at Greenham Common (Roseneil 2000).[2] And the struggles at Greenham also suggested something of the dilemmas for the securitized state in dealing with non-violent protest and dissent. Such resonances are significant. New movements, like older ones, emerge from putting together new alliances and building new networks. But should the aim be to build loose alliances across multiple movements or to try to build a common base? To run a tight and effective campaign that might lead to policy change or to hold on to the value of more spontaneous, open and non-hierarchical models of organizing? To put back what is being lost or to develop new models and practices? These dilemmas, and different responses to them, are threaded through this book.

But resonances between past and present are not a matter of history repeating itself: they are refracted through intergenerational and political differences. Many younger participants pointed to the exhaustion of traditional forms of politics, while those from older generations sometimes bewailed the lack of young women willing to contribute to campaigns to defend services and benefits that their generation had won. Talking about this research to a group of socialist women, they were generally sympathetic but one asked, tellingly:

Ah, but what comes after the performance? Who is going to keep the issues alive and try to influence those with the power to deliver?

Others I spoke to in the final stages of the research expressed concern about the erasure of the discursive repertoires of feminism, anti-racism and queer politics in the search for common cause. Such tensions were often presented as intergenerational, but they also speak to well-worn lines of fracture between socialist and more anarchist, embodied styles of politics; between attention to a politics of identity and a 'post-identity' form of struggle. The borders between first- and second-wave feminism, between gay liberation and LGBT struggles, between a politics of 'race' and a politics shaped by notions of intersectionality had become the focus of important forms of intergenerational border work. But such work confronted a series of myths (for example, younger women viewing second-wave feminism as liberal and compromised, or older women viewing third-wave feminism as performative and pleasure-seeking, ready to sacrifice – and often ignorant of – the gains made by the second wave). Such intergenerational myths reconfigure narratives of 'inside' and 'outside' in uncomfortable ways (Chapter 7), and inform wider narratives of the fate of feminism and other forms of activism in neoliberal times (Chapter 8).

Border work

Participants I interviewed towards the end of the project faced difficult choices of where and how to be political, and of what politics might mean:

> *Other people [previous activist comrades] have made different choices, been more committed. I still join in campaigns and so on and have contact with people – for example, activists living outside the economy, in squatted households with illegal migrants, eating from skips, intervening in politics through direct action. They are not implicated in any way in the system – and, of course, don't have a voice in the system either, or at least their ideas don't reach the majority of the population to have a chance of making waves. But not everyone can do that. I want to know what choices I am making and why. It doesn't feel that getting paid by [name of organization] to do little projects is part of the revolution. But on the other hand ...*
>
> *[Janet: So what's on the other hand?]*
>
> *I'm trying to get to grips with what I am doing, what I am buying into – the whole neoliberal stuff. OK, inequality's a given, capitalism's a given, but within it you can still enable people to have a voice.* (Hannah Berry)

At stake in this extract is the tension around how far to remain 'outside', in oppositional and alternative spaces, and how far to engage with what Hannah called *'the system'*. Chapter 7 showed something of the discomfort and ambiguity associated with being in 'inside-outside' spaces, but also highlighted the generative potential of those engaged in such border work. However, borders and boundaries had become the focus of governmental projects of state retrenchment. There was less talk, at least in the United Kingdom, of partnerships and interdisciplinary working. Units and projects that had previously been 'on the edge', such as that in which Hannah worked, had been either cut or cast adrift, made to fend for themselves in an increasingly competitive funding and business environment. The worsening job market meant that many women had become less able to move between sectors or to span boundaries. Agencies and projects that supported 'community' and 'civil society' had been squeezed of funding or abolished in state-driven strategies of 'disintermediation'. The boundary between 'state' and 'society' that was partly blurred in the governance shift of the 1990s was hardening, even as society (in the United Kingdom in the shape of an imagined series of 'local communities') took centre stage in political discourse. The assumption was that if the state retreated, community action and social entrepreneurship would grow to fill the empty space. But the mediators, translators, transactors and brokers who worked across this boundary (Chapter 5, 7) were finding their spaces of agency squeezed, leaving communities and civil society actors adrift.

However, this is too general a picture. Some forms of border work had also become amplified as a stripped down centre attempted to find allies with which to work in developing new strategies for 'governing the social'. Community-mobilizers had become the focus of training and empowerment work; and groups bidding to take over formerly public 'assets' or to run local public services found themselves working across multiple borders even as those borders were being configured. New kinds of consultants and entrepreneurs had emerged to do some of the 'joining up' between a hollowed out state, malfunctioning market and impoverished civil society. And faith groups had taken on new significance, both in the developing market for schools and other formerly public services, and in projects of moral renewal and civic action.

Border work, then, was continuing, and in some cases offered new kinds of opportunity for activists to mobilize spaces of power. The spatial dynamics of this work were complex. Governments within and beyond the United Kingdom were seeking to extend the strategies of governing through community discussed in Chapter 3, opening up new landscapes of inequality that differ from those generated by earlier community programmes because of the scale of cuts and their impact on human and material 'assets' in different regions and places. Some participants were themselves taking on multiple jobs (paid and unpaid) in an increasingly unfavourable economic climate. The intensification of 'precarious labour' (Chapter 5) was opening up new freedoms but also new forms of economic and political vulnerability. This has implications for how far individuals are able to mobilize spaces of power.

Spaces of power

One of the contributions of this book has been to illuminate something of the plurality of spaces of power from which protest and dissent are conducted and new possibilities are enacted. Spaces of power are not, as previous chapters have shown, simply associated with formal political or governmental power, nor with status and seniority; they emerge as contradictions in would-be dominant political projects are worked and fissures opened up in hegemonic ruling relations. Those working them have the capacity to disrupt taken-for-granted ideas, and to challenge ideological assumptions of what is natural and normal. They mobilize resources, texts and people, bringing them into new relationships and networks. They work to resignify the meanings of policy discourses and projects. And they perform activist commitments in a multiplicity of 'contact zones' traversed by dominant, emergent and residual formations of power.

So what of the future? I want to trace here the threads of three rather different spaces of power: those of campaigning and protest; of building new political institutions; and of working in practical, grounded ways. Each offers a rather different space of power or possibility. The examples I focus on are not intended as templates for the future – each, as I show, has been the object of critique – but as indicators of the plural landscape on which new and old antagonisms were being played out.

The explosion of new forms of protest discussed earlier took place against a backcloth of challenges produced by less visible but more focused campaigning work. The Women's Budget Group, the Fawcett Society and other feminist groups orchestrated campaigns against the cuts, with a particular focus on the consequences for women. Others participated in campaigns to defend cherished institutions, from the BBC World Service (threatened with cuts) to the woodlands (threatened with losing the protection of public ownership) and, of course, the NHS. Their success was variable: many well-orchestrated campaigns to save public libraries failed, while the early promise of challenges to the NHS reforms by clinicians and by members of the House of Lords was not realized. But such campaigns helped to challenge would-be dominant ideologies and to mobilize new 'inside-outside' alliances. This resonates with campaigns discussed in earlier chapters: those that successfully challenged policy and legislation (Chapter 4) and that worked both with and against 'modernizing' logics (chapter 5). Such examples show both the potential – and the problems – of campaigns that sought to defend threatened institutions while also, at the same time, seeking to change them.

This tension between defence and transformation was a recurrent theme in the responses of those I spoke to about the present. The welfare state of the 1970s and 1980s, some suggested, was not wholly beneficial and there was some ambiguity about the taken-for-grantedness of state provision of services:

> *Being a socialist, a 1960s socialist, I think the state has a role, the state has a role in distribution. But this can lead you to defend the indefensible. And I wonder – whether public services have contributed to alienation, whether I should have been more supportive of co-ops, more sympathetic to self-help. The paradox is, when we said we didn't want the welfare state or council housing in their present forms, we didn't mean they should be taken away.* (Jane Foot)

> *When I was younger we did a lot of work, it's all being undone, and so now it's got to be all done again. I mean we've got to defend what we can but also write a new political script.* (Angela Mason)

Both extracts underscore the tension between defending what is being threatened and the work of writing new political scripts or performing new worlds. Protesting against cuts, then, was only part of the agenda. Many participants were engaged in trying to write a *'new political script'*, and I want here to briefly trace three very different examples: those of UNISON, London Citizens and Compass. When I spoke to Heather Wakefield (G3) at UNISON she was heavily involved in the struggle to defend public sector workers against proposed changes to their pension entitlements, but also spoke of a broader project of renewal:

> *We had a three-pronged strategy. The first,* getting technical, *was an attempt to get to grips with local government finance so we could challenge the need for cuts. Some cuts are necessary, but many are not, and we had been confronting a game of smoke and mirrors in the rationales we were given for cuts to services as well as jobs. So we developed more technical skills, doing things like impact assessment – especially on equality issues – so we could talk back effectively. And we have been going out to branches doing training on how to understand local government finances so we would be better armed for negotiations with employers.*
>
> *The second thing was about* getting political, *trying to get people to re-engage at local level. Of course, bad situations – like the present – always tend to lead to new revivals, especially among trade unionists, but we have lost many of our old activists and need to work with the new ones coming through. Morale at present is low, people are scared of redundancies so are sometimes reluctant to come forward. But while the short term is bleak, we are trying to develop our capacity for the future.*
>
> *And the third thing is about* getting organized – *trying to strengthen the ways we organize, helping people with how to talk to employers, deal with the media, do press releases and so on – a lot of this is in handbooks we have put on the web.*
> (Heather Wakefield; her emphasis)

The three components of this strategy speak to issues raised in earlier chapters: for example, 'getting technical' refers to what in Chapter 5 was termed monitory power, the 'development' activities to forms of knowledge-work in Chapter 6, 'getting organized' to the campaigning work of Chapter 4 and shifts in political struggles to some of the material in Chapter 2. But there was a sense of strain, in her account, between these capacity-building activities for the longer term and the immediate demands of the campaign against proposed changes to public sector pensions. This tension pervaded other accounts where participants were trying to combine taking action against immediate threats with thinking about how to write new political scripts and 'perform new worlds'.

I will return to this later, but first want to point to a very different form of 'getting organized' in what Jane Wills described as the revival of community organizing. This, of course, was not new but was taking new forms in a number of broad-based community alliances modelled on the success of

London Citizens: for example, in its work to secure the London Living Wage and in the formation of a Community Land Trust. As Chapter 3 described, the alliances were formed out of what Jane termed *'islands of social capital'*, and the work generated new kinds of public relationships and political action. London Citizens has understandably been very attractive to politicians, but at the same time the alliance had considerable success in holding politicians and other decision-makers to account for the pledges they made. This is the terrain of what in Chapter 3 I termed the 'perverse alignments' between activist projects and governmental programmes, mediated here through the discourses of faith, responsibility and active citizenship. Those working in organizations such as Southall Black Sisters have suggested that inter-faith alliances were tending to reinforce hardline positions on gender and sexuality, abortion and reproduction: where there was conflict, more 'liberal' positions were sacrificed in the interests of alliance-building, including alliances on projects of civil renewal that were much favoured by the Conservative-led coalition government (Patel 2011). However, as I argued in Chapter 3, the possibility of perverse alignments does not erase the capacity of activists to inflect discourses, policies and resources to more 'progressive' political ends.

A rather different engagement with rewriting the political script centred on attempts to renew the political left in Britain. Ruth Lister described her associations with Compass as generating new forms of democratic public politics:

> *It takes positions I feel comfortable with, and I like the way it works – it tries to be democratic. It tries to bring different strands of politics (green, left, social democratic) together, it offers a pluralist politics and it is open-minded – it operates in a good way. It is also future-oriented, trying to articulate the kind of vision that Labour failed to do.* (Ruth Lister)

The work of Compass has some resonances with my discussion of the political work associated with linking 'inside' actors (in this case mainstream politicians) with academics, campaigners and social movements (see Chapters 4, 6, 7). Again it has attracted critics; its closeness to 'mainstream' politics, especially some strands of the Labour Party, made it an uncomfortable place for those disenchanted with the workings of party politics in general and New Labour in particular; and its attempt to work across different constituencies in a democratic way tended to produce reports that some view as lacking in substance. But it also did sharp campaigning work (for example, on the politics of debt), and the publication of 'Plan B', an alternative economic strategy for Britain produced by a group of leading left economists, was widely welcomed. Its earlier (and continuing) work on delineating a vision of the Good Society offered a challenge to the Conservative project of the Big Society while drawing on many of the strands of creative thinking and action that the Conservative Party had sought to appropriate.

However, these attempts to renew and reinvigorate democratic politics do not speak strongly to earlier formations of feminism, anti-racism, or LGBT politics. Many participants spoke of their concern about both the reversal of what had been achieved – the kinds of inscription of feminism in social policy discussed in Chapter 4 – and the loss of an explicitly feminist activism. This relates to the erasure of feminist politics in the face of Third Way and neoliberal strategies discussed by Angela McRobbie, which I analysed in Chapter 8. However, feminist bodies such as the Fawcett Society, the Women's Budget Group and Southall Black Sisters, together with a multitude of local groups, were continuing to raise issues of gender inequality, and to campaign for change and against cuts (Fawcett Society 2011). And feminist issues were threaded through other mobilizations: the Living Wage campaign of London Citizens took up issues of low-paid women's work; the Good Society of Compass drew on feminist agendas and perspectives; UNISON was strengthening its use of equality impact studies to challenge employer-led changes; and feminist performative repertoires were integral to many of the new forms of street protest and occupation.

Many of the younger participants were involved in new feminist debates and actions: in local, grassroots forms of feminist politics, in anti-pornography and street-harassment campaigns, in protests against the opening of new lap-dancing venues, in work on rape and domestic violence, and so on (see Banyard 2010; Redfern and Aune 2010). These campaigns resonate with those of the 1970s in the way they summon a politics of identity, but were taking place in a landscape in which Kurdish women, Palestinian women, Sikh women, Black women and other groups were shaping and speaking diverse forms of feminist politics, and in which feminism had a much stronger engagement with transnational and global struggles against injustice. Debates within the academy were engaged with how to combine scholarship and activism in these times (see, for example, Maskovsky 2011 on the possibility of an activist anthropology, and the Autonomous Geographies Collective 2010, on 'scholar activism'). But there was some ambivalence about how to conduct feminist politics in these times. The following is taken from a discussion with three young women at a workshop in 2011 at which I spoke about the research leading up to this book:

> Participant A: I can see women getting angry again, and that is wonderful. They told us feminism was over, but it's not.
>
> Participant B: Yes, but I am uneasy about how not to just replicate the politics of the past. This is not 1968, and we can't recapture that moment; we have to find our own way.
>
> [Janet: So what is your own way?]
>
> Participant B: It's working on issues that affect the women we meet and work with. Enabling them to have a voice.

Participant C: And it's about finding new ways of doing politics that link us more into global agendas – the big ones, like the environment, anti-capitalism, social justice, but also supporting individual women in oppressive regimes, working for peace, in prison, awaiting deportation. That's where my main energy is.

Participant B: But don't you think we have to work first where we are, to practise it in our own lives and try to link in to other women around us?

[Pause]

Participant A: But I think it's much harder now. We have to make harder choices about how to make a living while we are doing all this, and whether making a living is possible anymore. I'm just not sure what the future holds.

This discussion exemplifies many of the tensions faced by young women I met in the course of this research but also speaks to the difficulty of finding coherent definitions of what a feminist politics might be in these times and how it might be conducted. Protests, campaigns and new political mobilizations were only part of the story. Many participants were continuing to work through what they termed a more 'practical' politics, using what spaces of power and influence were available to them:

Sometimes I try not to think about the big picture, however awful it is. I just try to do what I can in my own corner. (Ruth Lister)

Her corner was, she admitted, one of relative privilege. Now a baroness with a seat in the House of Lords, Ruth continued to bring a gender perspective into her writing and her political work in Compass, and into debates on welfare reform. She noted how most of the Labour benches of the Grand Committee of which she was a member, apart from the chair of that group, were women (what had been termed 'a battery of baronesses'), challenging ministers on the detail of proposed legislation as the 2011 Welfare Reform Bill was being debated.

Here and elsewhere participants were struggling to make policy 'less bad than it might have been', but also to use it to generate positive forms of change. Adi Cooper, at the time still working in a senior local government role, was exploring the potential, as well as the dangers, of current policies on localization from the vantage point of a senior local government manager:

I think there's a vacuum that opens that allows potential ... I actually think there's a potential here for ... I'm trying to avoid the ... Big Society rubbish rhetoric, sorry, but there is something about if the state is shrinking then it opens up opportunities to renegotiate the social contract for communities to reclaim some of that, but unfortunately it often comes out of negatives. Resistance movements and activism and politics are often in response to negative stuff aren't they? It comes out of what you can't have or you don't have or you're prevented from having. But there is an opportunity in that kind of shrinking [of the state] for a different way of community to develop. The danger is that it only develops in that kind of space where people are in positions of privilege and power, and those who are dispossessed and disadvantaged aren't able to, and there's always that risk, isn't there? (Adi Cooper)

There was cynicism here (*'Big Society rubbish'*) and scepticism (*'the danger is …'*). But there was also hope – about potential, about what was being opened up. At the start she was struggling for words that were not complicit with the government's own discourse (*'trying to avoid the rhetoric'*). She, like others, viewed the Big Society and proposed localization policies (including the Localism Bill, 2011) as ripe for critique, but also saw them as attractive in that they placed more emphasis on ways of living together, on the local and on ethical practices of everyday life.

Others warned that such mobilizations were likely to be spatially uneven and to open up different contradictory alignments between a gendered politics of place and identity on the one hand and other political projects of resistance and regeneration:

It's about how you see politics – as party politics or informed by opposition to some monolithic neoliberalism or as more complex and which engages with where people are on the ground. There is still a need for a politics informed by a gender perspective but what is different now from the 1980s is that gender on its own isn't enough – but that form of politics based on identity and locality still has a place. So the way I see the Big Society is to see it as contradictory (an assemblage if you like) which will be played out differently in different places. In some communities and on some issues there will be opportunities to pursue different rationalities and different outcomes, liminal spaces will be opened up. But they are likely to be limited and circumscribed. (Sue Brownill)

Sue looked back to her early days of activism and saw current policy as offering a continuation of the kind of community programmes through which neighbourhoods were funded, governed and incorporated in the past. She worried that the initiatives in which she was (positively) involved were just *'exceptions in a sea of cuts'* (taking us back to the point about spatial differences highlighted earlier). She also wondered whether, by engaging with the possibilities opened up by policy, this provided legitimation for the cuts themselves:

As ever with community work there are these dilemmas and I think women are more prepared to make these compromises and negotiate the contradictions. (Sue Brownill)

This is the essence of 'working the spaces of power'. Rather than celebrating political agency or assuming the all-consuming power of neoliberalism, I have tried, in this book, to illuminate the ways in which different rationalities and commitments were (unevenly) aligned through gendered labour. And I have shown how such labour has been generative of new possibilities in how we might live and work.

Each of the kinds of spaces of power I have discussed here is likely to be temporary, fragile, and traversed by ambiguity and contradiction. This is not, then, a platform for the future. My aim, rather, has been to show how currents and threads within the present political and ideological project echo earlier struggles and surface some of the same dilemmas. While many young activists currently engaged in dramatic, radical and disruptive performances have an image of older movements as rather dour, boring and conventional, it is possible to map echoes and resonances: between, for example, the dramatic occupation of Greenham Common, with its innovative communication channels and its theatrical and symbolic queering of a military installation, and the activities of UK Uncut in 2011 as it occupied banks and shops, and installed crèches, libraries and other public facilities; between the Free University projects of the 1970s, the housing squats of the 1980s and Occupy's take-over of a building owned by Swiss bank UBS and its launch of a 'Bank of Ideas' in London in November 2011; or between the older Reclaim the Streets marches and the recent Slut Walks. This is not to say that the *politics* is the same; but that there are resonances in the political performances across different times. Each is a site of antagonism, negotiation and alliance building. Each has to deal with questions of difference. Each builds on the profound shifts in political culture produced by the impact of feminism and other social movements, whether implicitly or explicitly. Each is the site of intense 'border work' through which new possibilities are realized. And each is constituted through the forms of generative labour discussed in earlier chapters.

Generative (and gendered) labour

One of the aims of this book has been to show the significance of the generative labour through which new possibilities and practices emerge. In this final section I want to explore present and future possibilities, returning to the three dimensions of generative labour introduced in Chapter 1: those of 'making visible', 'creative labour' and 'public conversations'.

Making visible

One way of 'making visible' is through embodied protest – on the streets, in demonstrations and actions that testify to collective anger, distrust, unease and disaffection from dominant ideologies and political groups. But the work of making visible is analytical as well as performative. It involves drawing attention to the changing patterns of inequality, exclusion, hardship and ill-health and also articulating that which is silent and hidden from view (Hilary Land, Sue Himmelweit and Ruth Lister's work on gender; P.G. Macioti's engagement with the politics of sex work and migration; Sukhwant Dhaliwal's concerns about the silencing of issues of sexuality in faith based activism; the fate of LGBT prisoners in Sarah Lamble's work). It involves highlighting the gendered and racialized impact of cuts and austerity politics: how informal care work is intensifying, how racial abuse and police harassment are increasing, how responsibilities for filling gaps in health, education and welfare services are being devolved to 'families' and 'communities', both highly gendered entities; and how pressures generated by inequalities of money, time, care and work are exacerbating mental and physical ill-health.

There is already plenty of evidence about the effects of austerity on different population groups and places across the global north and south. There are signs of a new journalism of poverty, updating the black-and-white photos of inner-city slums in Charles Booth's studies of the late nineteenth century for an ever-hungry media which both brings to attention and exploits personal narratives of hardship (constituting what Chouliaraki terms a 'spectatorship of suffering'; Chouliaraki 2006). But participants did not just seek to bring those living with hardship and poverty to public attention; they sought to bring them to collective voice and to action. Programmes of development and empowerment (Chapter 3) may have been double-edged but they nevertheless had profound impacts on the discursive repertoires through which negotiations with power were conducted and on the people who conducted them. Chapters 4, 5 and 6 traced how such repertoires informed practices of 'making visible' through a combination of research, action and policy intervention. There are difficult challenges for academics and other researchers trying to use creative ways of framing research in order to secure funding for the investigation of new patterns of exploitation, hardship and disaffection in a climate in which such agendas are unlikely to attract research funding. But nevertheless many were engaging with current policy agendas, making visible the impact of budgetary and policy changes or bringing alternative economic and social experiments to public attention.

There are, of course, dangers inherent in allowing such experiments to be taken up by government; the landscape is already littered with green papers and policy briefings profusely illustrated with vignettes of projects, pilots and 'vanguard' initiatives. These both flatten complexity, removing particular projects from the contexts that generated them, and also announce that all is well, that critics and analysts are wrong since the policy concerned is already successful. One of the lessons of this book, then, is that 'evidence' and 'publicity' alone are insufficient: action depends on alliances between researchers, policy actors, think-tanks, journalists, political parties and social movements, coupled with the performative work of campaigners and activists. The work of making visible is both analytical and political, and is most powerful when these come together, creating the capacity for new 'public conversations' to emerge.

Public conversations

Earlier chapters of this book have traced how the work of 'making visible' inequalities and exclusions and the creative labour of doing new things was framed by a series of public conversations that shifted the discursive repertoires of government and of the wider public culture. Such conversations succeeded in challenging ideologies that rendered then dominant ideas and practices natural and inevitable. They challenged normative ideologies of the 'naturalness' of the nuclear family founded on heterosexual marriage; of the inevitable superiority of men as leaders and managers; of class as the fundamental line of division and identity in Britain; of the subordinations of race embedded in the legacies of Britain as a colonial power; of women's dependence on male breadwinners and subordinate contributions to the economy, and so on. And each of the policy shifts traced in previous chapters rested on the success of building a public conversation about the particular issue concerned, whether of women's full citizenship within the welfare system, the needs and rights of children, workplace discrimination, pay inequality, domestic violence, the exploitation of migrant workers in global production and care chains and many other issues.

These conversations not only reshaped public culture but also enabled the remaking of public institutions: the state, local government, public policies, the professions, the public sector. The paradox of the present, however, is that the space for such conversations, supported by a public sector and public institutions, has become impoverished precisely at the moment when we face ideological framings that seek to naturalize a new common sense of the pre-eminence of 'the market'. One task, then, is to find new spaces and actions of publicness: the constitution of a new commons. In other work (Mahony, Newman and Barnett 2010; Newman 2011), myself and colleagues have drawn attention to processes of 'public-making': of constituting public actors, of framing issues as public issues and of articulating an explicitly public discourse.[3] We have also argued that notions of publicness have to be recovered from their inscription in particular institutional forms, from their associations with a common people circumscribed by the boundaries of the nation state and from the privileging of rational, dispassionate styles of communication (Newman 2007; Newman and Clarke 2009). The work of some participants has stretched notions of a collective commons to encompass transnational and global agendas (through NGOs, legal practices specializing in human rights work and activist groups using 'monitory' power – see Chapter 4). Others sought to bring traditional public values – equality, openness, justice – into the managerialized and marketized spaces of public service delivery (see Chapter 5). Those working on environmental issues sought to redefine the meanings of publicness to encompass ethical agendas and global notions of responsibility, not only for the present but for future populations. And this postscript has suggested processes through which new publics might be constituted: the capacity-building work of UNISON, the alliances formed out of community mobilizations and the participative ethos of Compass through to the 'We are the 99 per cent' slogan of the Occupy movement.

The work of participants has also shown the significance of discourse: the words through which issues are framed and the meanings that are generated. The idea of the Big Society re-inflected publicness through the prism of locality and ethical conduct, displacing wider interdependencies and issues of resource (re)distribution. The idea of a 'Big Society' may have been short-lived, but the emphasis on localization continues both within and beyond Britain. The question, then, is how to retrieve ethical concerns as necessary features of *public* life, rather than as foreclosed by bounded conceptions of 'family', 'community' and 'faith'. This could open up the possibility of a more political framing of the social; one that reposes moral questions about care, welfare and responsibility as public, rather than simply personal, questions. As this book has shown, public conversations do important work to reframe dominant discourses and offer alternative political repertoires and social imaginaries.

Creative labour

The work of public-making is creative labour, stitching together new alliances and finding new ways of performing and enacting politics. As I have shown, the creative professions often seek to elicit emotional as well as cognitive responses to political issues. For example, Chapter 2 described the work of Cecilia Wee, whose *'spectacles of resistance'* challenged the sponsorship of cultural institutions by the oil industry, and whose wider work mobilizes actions and events connecting art and politics. She, and many of the artists she works with, saw their creativity as a means of expressing their politics:

> Lots of you [academics] are involved in policy, you can influence things directly. For me there is no alternative, this is the only voice I have. (Cecilia Wee)

At the same time creative forms of performing politics were at the heart of many of the new movements and protests, including anti-globalization, UK Uncut, Occupy, and new forms of feminist and queer politics. Much of this links back to the 'transgressive' enactments of politics discussed in Chapter 2:

> Traditional leftist politics can be very analytical and dour. But queer politics is often more playful and creative. You are doing politics by making connections and creating alternatives. People can really grab on to that. I always look to the success of Reclaim the Streets: people always want to come to a party. (Sarah Lamble)

But the creative labour with which I am concerned was not only transgressive; it was also that of stitching together or weaving new possibilities. I want here to go back to one of the quotes from in Chapter 2 because it captures the creative work out of which new things – discourses, actors, movements, projects, experiments – were generated:

> *I think what I bring is lateral thinking: I am a very good lateral thinker, I like making connections. I think quite a lot of women do that but [laughs] I also think that being a socialist feminist – endlessly having to knit things together, to see how things are connected and to make the connections and to see where to make the connections and how to exploit the connections and work with the contradictions. I am not sure whether you learn those things from being an activist or whether you become an activist because you have got that kind of brain.* (Jane Foot)

These are precisely the skills and capacities that are integral to the work of women struggling to find and mobilize spaces of power in the present, and to the work of participants in public services having to implement massive cuts. In early 2012 Sonia Khan spoke of how, in her local authority, she was engaged in the creative labour of integrating services both to make savings and to make them more outward facing, with the aim of supporting the most vulnerable as inequalities worsened. Others, as I showed earlier, are using governmental discourses of localization and the Big Society in creative ways.

Creative labour is, as the extract from Jane implies, relational labour. It is out of such labour that new political entities – new publics, new forms of protest, new ways of practising politics – are generated. And such labour rests on what Jane sees as a political mentality: one of making conceptual connections as well as knitting together disparate entities. This is the 'border work' of Chapter 7, in which participants mobilized spaces of power at the interface between 'inside' and 'outside' rationalities, doing the work of assembling, translating, stitching, threading, brokering and working the contradictions. These attributes were not, of course, confined to women, but they tend to be created in or amplified by the fractured and diverse working lives of the women concerned, enabling skills and capacities to be carried between different sites. In particular, the experience of being simultaneously 'inside' and 'outside' enabled many women to bring activism into their working lives, brokering and translating between different rationalities in order to bring about extensive policy and institutional shifts. But it is uncomfortable work that raised some key dilemmas: where to put your energy; how to sustain multiple and often competing loyalties and commitments; how to make a living while living your politics; how to combine working for an imagined future while living, prefiguring that future in the here and now.

This takes us back to the analysis in Chapter 6 of the work of Gibson-Graham and Roseneil who argued that dissent should not stop short at critique but should try to enact new imagined worlds within the present. This is perhaps the long-lasting contribution of feminism, queer, anti-racist and other forms of what were, and often remain, transgressive political movements. As well as critiquing dominant formations of power, they performed new styles of politics, often based on non-hierarchical and non-violent ways of organizing. They also combined critiques of the welfare state and professional power with the creation of new forms of provision. Many of the current forms of protest and dissent noted earlier carry into the present these ways of combining critique and creativity, generating new forms of democratic practice, offering alternative forms of education, care and welfare, and tracing the contours of new repertoires of public-political engagement. These offer alternative imaginaries of how we might live and work together, not in a fantasized future (when the financial crisis is over) but in the grimly real present.

In the past many women talked of how they tried to live the future in the present, modelling the kind of society they wanted, and we can see such creative labour continuing in some of the spaces of protest that embody new forms of democratic practice and global interconnectedness. But as Sue Brownill suggested:

> As academics and activists there is a difficult act of not closing off the positive but also not over-celebrating what can be achieved. We also need to keep re-politicizing the debates, but through a politics that is inclusive and grounded, and which itself does not similarly close the spaces for action. It is a dilemma that has always been there, between community politics and class politics, if you like, a dilemma that feminism has always straddled. And therefore there is much to learn from the past, but it needs to be placed within a dramatically changed context. If we can pull that off, through small-scale projects and through maintaining different rationalities, visions about what is to be done, there could be some small grounds for optimism. (Sue Brownill)

Final reflection

One reader of this postscript noted how the writing of this book has itself exemplified the framework I have offered here. The book has tried to make visible some forgotten histories: of how benefits and services were won, how legal changes were secured, how women used spaces within Thatcherism, managerialism and the Third Way to work for progressive forms of change. It has brought missing voices into public conversations about the fate of feminism and other forms of activism in neoliberal times, and challenged some of the stereotypical distinctions between activist outsides and incorporated insides. It has raised important questions about the generative relationship between individual action and collective practice. And it has opened up public conversations between some of the participants through which narratives of the present and future could emerge across lines of difference. Finally, writing the book has been (admittedly a narrow) form of creative labour in which I have tried to stitch together multiple accounts into a series of narratives, drawing out differences rather than trying to construct a coherent whole (in the spirit of the institutional ethnography described in Chapter 1).

As such, it is very different from other books I have written, not least because it has tried to make sense of the times I lived through but also because it is, at heart, a collective product. I want, then, to end by acknowledging the importance of the conversations I have had, both with the individual women who participated and with those others who gave me intellectual and material forms of support (Wendy Larner, John Clarke, Lin Clark, Peggotty Graham, Esther Saraga, Marian Barnes, Sasha Roseneil, Shona Hunter and Clive Newman, at whose party this all began). I also want to thank those who contributed to collective processes of sense-making: the panel at the CASCA conference in 2009 (Catherine Kingfisher, Jeff Maskovsky, Dana-Ain Davis) at which the first paper was presented; the Feminist Reading Group at the Open University; contributors to Economic and Social Research Council seminars at Bristol, Newcastle and the Open University; and those who tolerated me trying to work things out at many invited seminars. Without their engagement and excitement, support and critique, this book would never have been written.

Appendix

Conducting the Research – Ethics, Methods and Modes of Analysis

As I argue in Chapter 6, the idea that knowledge and ways of knowing are co-produced tends to conceal inequalities of power between researcher and researched. This raised a series of ethical questions for this research, questions that are widely debated in feminist literature (Hesse-Biber and Leavy 2007; Letherby 2003; Roberts 1981; Stanley 1997). One was how far to define the field in advance of conducting the research. As I noted in Chapter 1, the 'institutional ethnography' approach I followed allowed the field to be shaped and reshaped during the process of the research. So the interview style was such that the person I was speaking to could pose different questions from those with which I began or could take the interview in a new direction; this served to enrich the field of study.

A second ethical concern was about the naming of participants. The usual convention of anonymizing quotations was not available to me because many of the participants were readily identifiable: there was only one founder of Stonewall, one director of Sure Start, one leader of a particular local authority in a given period and so on. All agreed to be named but I invited participants to indicate where specific parts of the interview should not be made public. I also gave an assurance that people they talked about in the interview – collaborators, opponents, sources of inspiration or frustration – would not be referred to by name. Nevertheless, the decision to use real names has both political and ethical consequences (Guenther 2009). For example, it had repercussions for the process of selecting and framing extracts from the interviews. I took care to enable participants not only to check quotes I was using for accuracy, but also to clarify their meaning and to check the contexts in which their extracts appeared. So I made draft chapters available on the internet (password protected) and sent everyone copies of the chapters in which they appeared, with a request to change, adapt, disagree with, object to or delete quotes I had attributed to them. This often provided an opportunity to continue our conversations, whether by phone, email or second meetings. Where changes were proposed, new versions were sent out in an iterative process of framing and reframing the material. This was, on reflection, an important source of feedback for me, with participants taking care to refine what they had said but also often responding with enthusiasm to drafts.

The interviews themselves combined political biography (Mulinari and Räthzel 2007) with accounts of working lives. The first questions explored political commitments and allegiances and how these shaped patterns of life and work. As we moved into accounts of working lives I encouraged the person I was interviewing to focus on key moments and decisions – episodes and encounters – that stood out, rather than trying to recount a series of jobs and roles. We also explored how they found spaces of power and influence that had not necessarily been anticipated: perhaps a chance to move across sectors; new kinds of funding being made available; or spotting an opportunity to move on or to do something different. A set of questions focused on the skills, capabilities, orientations and networks that the participant brought into her work; and how she had draw on them. But we also explored the contradictions she experienced as activist-inspired programmes became managerialized or as policies failed to deliver the promised reforms. Questions explored how working lives were crafted to combine paid and unpaid work, sustained through governmental shifts, coped with the exigencies of funding streams and contractual relations, and managed the stresses and strains of what were often marginal, low-paid, precarious forms of labour. Each of the accounts linked individual experience to the changing social/political context of the times through which participants lived and the changing governmental practices that they encountered – and sometimes shaped – in their work.

In analysing the transcripts I drew on a range of theories within and beyond the 'post-structuralist' turn. The stuff of interview is language, which cannot be regarded as representing a fixed and objective reality but which is socially produced, not only in the interaction between interviewer and respondent but in the discursive repertoires, narratives and cultural scripts on which each draws. My focus, then, was not only on the 'facts' of what happened but also on how encounters are performed and understood, and on how individuals 'storied' their lives. Such stories are open to multiple readings. One centred on the construction of narratives – and as I show in Chapter 7, the narrative form differed considerably across generations. A second was emotional – how it felt to be in a particular role at a particular time in a particular place. Another reading explored reflections – how experiences were interpreted and understood from the vantage point of the present. This is a cognitive rather than affective self, one who struggles to construct meaning and make sense. It is also a dialogic self: participants were constructing stories and narratives through interactions both with embodied others (peers, colleagues and me as interviewer) but also with socially circulating theories, narratives and a wider sense of a collective history (Holland and Lave 2001).

These multiple readings hinted at ways in which the self is performed – relationally and materially – at different ages and in different circumstances, and how that self goes about constructing coherence out of changing and often conflicting experiences. I paid particular attention to the accounts of conflicts and contradictions that had to be managed, of struggles that had to be overcome and, conversely, of how new energies were generated and mobilized. I also focused on break points and fractures: how and in what ways the outsider found herself on the inside, how and why the participant fled a particular place or job, how someone decided to shift from being an employee to trying their hand at being an entrepreneur, consultant or researcher and so on. I was not concerned with trying to reveal the selves that participants might choose to keep hidden. But I was interested in the accounts of contradictions and points of fracture for what they say about the changing material circumstances of work and the shifting spaces of power at particular cultural and political moments. This means that as well as paying attention to how the self was performed I also brought a more material interest in how, in both their political and working lives, participants confronted hard, objective realities, and in how their knowledge about and experience of such realities – racism, inequality, poverty, exclusion – shaped their politics.

Notes

Chapter 1 Introduction: Research as Mapmaking

1 This approach is developed in theories of 'intersectionality': see Brah and
   Phoenix 2004; Collins 1986; Collins 2000; Crenshaw 1991; Grabham, Cooper,
   Krishnadas and Herman 2009; Siltanen and Doucet 2008; and further analysis
   in Chapter 6.

Chapter 2 Talking Politics

1 A BBC documentary style drama shown in 1966, which brought the plight of
   homeless families to public attention.
2 Gender auditing is a technique used to monitor the effectiveness of equality
   policies; see Chapter 4 on 'monitory power'.
3 Paulo Freire was a Brazilian educator known for his radical approach to
   overcoming poverty through pedagogy. He is associated with the radical theology
   movement and is known for his work on education as conscientization, in which
   'the oppressed' can regain their humanity and overcome oppression through
   liberatory forms of education (Friere 1970; Friere 2005).
4 At the time apprenticeship schemes and technical colleges mainly catered for boys
   and young men.
5 The Women's Peace Camp (1981–2000) established to protest at the siting of
   nuclear missiles at a US army base in the UK.

Chapter 3 Perverse Alignments: Women's Activism and the
   Governmentalization of Community

1 CDF (Community Development Foundation) is a charity and public body
   (now also described, on its website, as a 'social enterprise') that was founded in
   the 1970s to support community development activity.
2 The Greater London Council was established in 1963, as part of local government
   reorganization. Although its powers were limited, its strategic role and the power
   of its elected mayor gave it considerable prominence in the political landscape,
   especially during the Thatcher years when it formed an important base and
   resource stream for oppositional policies. This led to its abolition by Margaret
   Thatcher in 1985.
3 Communitarianism is a political philosophy associated with concerns about
   the 'loss' of social cohesion and social capital (Etzioni 1993; Putnam 2000).
   Some have argued that it informed the community policies of New Labour –an
   approach that Driver and Martell view as characterized by conformity, conditionality
   and moral prescriptions (Driver and Martell 1998; see also Dwyer 2000; Mooney and
   Neal 2009; and discussion in the introduction to Craig, Mayo, Popple, Shaw
   and Taylor 2011).
4 I lived through such tensions in Small Heath, an inner-city area of Birmingham, at the
   time of the racial disturbances in the early 1980s. The school and community centre

in which I worked began its life with open doors and weak boundaries between school, leisure centre, library and community/adult education activities. Its senior managers – of whom I was one – failed to agree on how far young black youth should have access to the centre, how to deal with complaints from the traditional white community and how far the school and its pupils should be defended from adult use of the centre. The four departments of the city council, and the elected councillors they reported to, tended to hinder rather than aid our negotiations, despite the formal ethos of partnership out of which the centre had been formed.

5 Community Development Programmes ran from 1968 to 1978 as action research projects, initially in twelve areas of local deprivation; the Inner Area Studies of the 1970s also linked research and intervention in projects in Liverpool, Lambeth and Birmingham; the Priority Estates Programme was established in 1979 to experiment with introducing localized housing management on rundown and hard-to-let social housing estates; the New Deal for Communities ran from 1998 in thirty-nine 'neighbourhoods' in England, but was displaced by projects under the National Strategy for Neighbourhood Renewal, which focused on eighty-six 'deprived' local authority districts.

6 2001 saw the launch of the Active Communities Unit with substantial funding to support and promote voluntary activity. This was followed by the Civil Renewal Unit, with a wider remit to promote citizenship and community action, and the Active Communities Directorate within the Home Office. These New Labour initiatives were followed by David Cameron's Conservative notion of the role of citizens in contributing to the 'Big Society' and by legislation aimed to devolve power to localities.

7 The turn to the local as a site of communitarian inflected participation and partnership initiatives is, as I have argued elsewhere, antithetical to feminist and anti-racist projects (Barnes *et al.* 2007; Newman and Clarke 2009).

8 This refers to a 1979 pamphlet produced by 'The London Edinburgh Weekend Return Group', a working group of the Conference of Socialist Economists. *In and Against the State* combined a critique of state practice with a concern to defend state services (see London Edinburgh Weekend Return Group 1979; London Edinburgh Weekend Return Group 2011).

Chapter 4 Close Encounters: Feminism, Policy and the Remaking of Governance

1 Section 28 of the Local Government Bill 1988 banned local authorities from teaching the acceptability of homosexuality in schools or its depiction as a 'pretended family relationship'. This was not repealed until 2000 in Scotland and 2003 in the rest of the United Kingdom.

2 This refers to the small group and non-hierarchical form of political practice associated with the second-wave women's movement, a form of politics that sought to be transformative of political practice.

3 ESRC Centre at Leeds University from 1999–2004, which explored changes in parenting and partnering and the implications for the future of welfare: http://www.leeds.ac.uk.CAVA.

4 *The Macpherson Report* on police investigative failures following the murder of a young black teenager in London in 1993 had charged the police with institutional racism.

Chapter 5 Modernizing Moments: Work, Organizations and the Entrepreneurial Self

1 Radical librarianship continues in surprising places; Alice Corble, in 2011 a PhD candidate at Goldsmiths, told me how she travels the world with a mobile poetry library, setting it up in different locations in exchange for basic food and shelter, eliciting new networks, friendships and contributions to the collection. I return to the fate of public libraries in the present in Chapter 9.

2 See Marsh, S. (2008), *The Feminine in Management Consulting: Power, Emotion and Values in Consulting Interactions*, Basingstoke: Palgrave.

Chapter 6 Critical Engagements: Knowledge-work as Political Practice

1 The collective name of Julie Graham and Katherine Gibson.

2 In 2010 Ann, who herself was suffering from terminal cancer, led 'Healthcare Professionals for Change' which sought to challenge the British Medical Association's position on assisted death: *Observer* (2011), 3 October: 3; and see Ann's obituary in the *Guardian* (2011), 31 May: 33.

3 See Marsh and Macalpine 2008; Macalpine and Marsh 2005.

4 Shona Hunter, who was one of the readers for this chapter, argued for bringing teaching more into the discussion and spoke about both the attractions of experienced-based methods and also the problems raised for students who have to perform in particular ways in the neoliberalized academy. But she also saw it as a form of political activism through which those likely to hold positions of power in the future had some of their assumptions troubled.

5 See, for example the special issue, *Ideas into Policy: Rethinking Governance and Governmentality* (2011), *Policy and Politics*, 39, 4, which included contributions from Helen Sullivan, Liz Richardson and myself.

Chapter 9 Postscript: Speaking to the Present

1 TINA (There Is No Alternative) is a phrase that resonates strongly with the political rhetoric of Margaret Thatcher.

2 Such resonances were picked up by established media, including the *Guardian* (with several pieces in the final week of October 2011) and in an interview with a Greenham woman on the BBC 6 p.m. news on 2 November 2011.

3 See also http://www.open.ac.uk/ccig/emergentpublics.

Bibliography

Aapola, S., Gonick, M. and Harris, A. (2005), *Young Femininity: Girlhood, Power and Social Change*, Basingstoke: Palgrave Macmillan.

Amit, V. and Rapport, N. (2002), *The Trouble with Community*, London: Pluto.

Annesley, C. (2010), 'Gendering politics and policy', *Policy and Politics*, 38, 3: 333–6.

Annesley, C., Gains, F. and Rummery, K. (2010), 'Engendering politics and policy: the legacy of New Labour'. *Politics and Policy* 38, 3: 389–406.

Anning, A. and Ball, M. (2008), *Improving Services for Young Children: From Sure Start to Children's Centres*, London: Sage.

Askins, K. and Pain, R. (2011), 'Contact zones: participation, materiality and the messiness of interaction', *Environment and Planning D: Society and Space*, 29: 803–821.

Audit Commission (2007), *Innovation in Local Government*, London: Audit Commission.

Autonomous Geographies Collective (2010), 'Beyond scholar activism: making strategic interventions inside and outside the neoliberal university', *ACME: an International E-Journal for Critical Geographies*, 9, 2, http://www.acme-journal.org.

Baggueley, P. (2002), 'Contemporary British feminism: a social movement in abeyance', *Social Movement Studies: Journal of Social, Cultural and Political Protest*, 1, 2: 169–85.

Baker, J. (2008), 'The ideology of choice: overstating progress and hiding injustice in the lives of young women; findings from a study in Queensland, Australia', *Women's Studies International Forum*, 31: 53–64.

Banyard, K. (2010), *The Equality Illusion*, London: Faber and Faber.

Barnes, M. and Prior, D. (eds) (2009), *Subversive Citizens: Power, Agency and Resistance in Public Service*, Bristol: Policy Press.

Barnes, M., Newman, J. and Sullivan, H. (2007), *Power, Participation and Political Renewal*, Bristol: Policy Press.

Barnett, C. (2003), *Culture and Democracy: Media, Space and Representation*, Edinburgh: Edinburgh University Press.

Barnett, C. (2005), 'The consolations of neoliberalism', *Geoforum*, 36: 7–12.

Barnett, C., Cloke, P., Clark, N. and Malpass, A. (2011), *Globalizing Responsibility: The Politic al Rationalities of Ethical Consumption*, Chichester: Wiley-Blackwell.

Barry, J., Dent, M. and O'Neill, M. (2003), *Gender and the Public Sector: Professionals and Managerial Change*, London: Routledge.

Beck, U (1999), *The Reinvention of Politics; Rethinking Modernity in the Global Social Order*, Cambridge: Polity.

Beck, U. and Beck-Gernsheim, E. (2001), *Individualization*, London: Sage.

Beck, U., Giddens, A. and Lash, S. (1994), *Reflexive Modernization: Politics, Tradition and Aesthetics in the Modern Social Order*, Cambridge: Polity.

Belsky, J., Melhuish, E. and Barnes, M. (2007), *The National Evaluation of Sure Start: Does Area Based Intervention Work?*, Bristol: Policy Press.

Benhabib, S. (ed.) (1996), *Democracy and Difference: Contesting the Boundaries of the Political*, Princeton, NJ: Princeton University Press.

Bevir, M. (2010), *Democratic Governance*, Princeton, NJ: Princeton University Press.

Blond, P. (2010), *Red Tory: How Left and Right Have Broken Britain and How We Can Fix It*, London: Faber.

Böhm, S., Dinerstein, A. and Spicer, A. (2010), '(Im)possibility of autonomy: social movements in and beyond capital, the state and development', *Social Movement Studies*, 9, 1: 17–32.

Boltanski, L. and Chiapello, E. (2005), *The New Spirit of Capitalism*, London: Verso.

Bondi, L. and Laurie, N. (2005), 'Introduction', in N. Laurie and L. Bondi (eds), *Working the Spaces of Neoliberalism*, Oxford: Blackwell.

Bondi, L., Carr, D., Clarke, C. and Clegg, C. (2011), *Towards Professional Wisdom: Practical Deliberation in the People Professions*, Farnham: Ashgate.

Braig, M. and Wölte, S. (eds) (2002), *Common Ground or Mutual Exclusion? Women's movements and international relations*, London: Zed Books.

Brah, A. (1996), *Cartographies of Diaspora: Contesting Identities*, London: Routledge.

Brah, A. and Phoenix, A. (2004), 'Ain't I a woman? Revisiting intersectionality', *Journal of Women's Studies*, 5, 3: 75–86.

Breitenbach, E., Brown, A., Mackay, F. and Webb, J. (eds) (2002). *The Changing Politics of Gender Equality in Britain*, Basingstoke: Palgrave Macmillan.

Brodie, J. (2008), '"We are all equal now": contemporary gender politics in Canada', *Feminist Theory*, 9, 2: 145–64.

Brown, W. (1995), *States of Injury: Power and Freedom in Late Modernity*, Princeton, NJ: Princeton University Press.

Brown, W. (2005), *Edgework: Critical Essays on Knowledge and Politics*, Princeton, NJ: Princeton University Press.

Buckingham, S., Marandet, E., Smith, E., Wainwright, E. and Diosi, M. (2006), 'The liminality of training spaces: places of public/private transitions', *Geoforum*, 37, 6: 895–905.

Butler, J. (1999), *Gender Trouble: Feminism and the Subversion of Identity*, New York: Routledge.

Butler, J. and Scott, W. (eds) (1992), *Feminists Theorise the Political*, New York: Routledge.

Cabinet Office (2003), *Innovation in the Public Sector*, London: Cabinet Office.

Callon, M. (1980), 'Struggles and negotiations to define what is problematic and what is not: the socio-logic of translation', in K.D. Knorr, R. Kron and R. Whitley (eds), *The Social Process of Scientific Investigation: Sociology of Sciences, vol. IV*, Dordrecht, Netherlands: Reidel.

Cannan, J. and Shumar, W. (eds) (2008), *Structure and Agency in the Neoliberal University*, London: Routledge.

Castells, M. (2000), *The Rise of the Network Society. The Information Age: Economy, Society and Culture. Volume 1*, Malden: Blackwell

Charles, N. (2000), *Feminism, the State and Social Policy*, Basingstoke: Macmillan.

Chouliaraki, L. (2006), *Spectatorship of Suffering*, London: Sage.

Clarke, J. (2006), 'Introduction: governing the social', *Cultural Studies*, 21, 6: 837–46

Clarke, J. (2008), 'Living with/in and without neo-liberalism', *Focaal – European Journal of Anthropology*, 51: 135–47.

Clarke, J. (2010a), 'Enrolling ordinary people: governmental strategies and the avoidance of politics?', *Citizenship Studies*, 14, 6: 637–60.

Clarke, J. (2010b), 'Of crises and conjunctures: the problem of the present', *Journal of Communication Enquiry*, 34, 4: 337–55.

Clarke, J. (2010c), 'So many strategies, so little time … making universities modern', *Learning and Teaching in Social Sciences*, 3, 3: 91–116.

Clarke, J. and Newman, J. (1997), *The Managerial State: Power, Politics and Ideology in the Remaking of Social Welfare*, London: Sage.

Clarke, J. and Newman, J. (2010), 'Summoning spectres: crises and their constructions', *Journal of Education Policy*, 25, 6: 709–715.

Clarke, J., Newman, J., Smith, N., Vidler, E. and Westmarland, L. (2007), *Creating Citizen-Consumers: changing publics and changing public services*, London: Sage.

Clegg, S. (1990), *Modern Organizations: Organizational Studies in the Postmodern World*, London: Sage.

Clegg, S., Harris, M. and Höpfl, H. (2011), *Managing Modernity: Beyond Bureaucracy?*, Oxford: Oxford University Press.

Cockburn, C. (1991), *In the Way of Women: Men's Resistance to Sex Equality in Organizations*, Basingstoke: Macmillan.

Cohen, A. (1987), *The Symbolic Construction of Community*, London: Sage.

Colgan, F. and Ledwith, S. (1996), 'Women as organizational change agents', in S. Ledwith and F. Colgan, *Women in Organisations: Challenging Gender Politics*, Basingstoke: Macmillan.

Coll, C. (2010), *Remaking Citizenship*, Stanford, CA: Stanford University Press.

Collins, J. (2003), *Threads: Gender, Labour and Power*, Chicago, IL: University of Chicago Press.

Collins, P.H. (1986), 'Learning from the outsider within: the sociological significance of black feminist thought', *Social Problems*, 33, 6: S14–S32.

Collins, P.H. (2000), 'Gender, Black Feminism, and Black Political Economy', *Annals of the American Academy of Political and Social Science*, 568: 41–53.

Commission on Poverty, Participation and Power (2000), *Listen Hear: The Right to be Heard*, Bristol: Policy Press 2000.

Cooper, D. (1994), *Sexing the City: Lesbian and Gay Politics within the Activist State*, London: Rivers Oram Press.

Cooper, D. (2001), 'Against the current: social pathways and the pursuit of enduring change', *Feminist Legal Studies*, 9, 2: 119–48.

Cooper, D. (2013), *Everyday Utopias*, Durham, NC: Duke University Press.

Cornwall, A., Harrison, E. and Whitehead, A. (eds) (2007), *Feminisms in Development: Contradictions, Contestations and Challenges*, London: Zed Books.

Coyle, A. and Skinner, J. (eds) (1988), *Women and Work: Positive Action for Change*, Basingstoke: Macmillan.

Craig, G., Mayo, M., Popple, K., Shaw, M. and Taylor, M. (2011), *The Community Development Reader*, Bristol: Policy Press.

Creed, G.W. (ed.) (2006), *The Seductions of Community: Emancipations, Oppressions, Quandries*, Santa Fe, NM: School of American Research Press.

Crenshaw, K.W. (1991), 'Mapping the margins: intersectionality, identity politics, and violence against women of color', *Stanford Law Review*, 43, 6: 1241–99.

Cresswell, T. (2010), 'Mobilities 1', *Progress in Human Geography*, 35, 4: 550–58.

Cruikshank, B. (1999), *The Will to Empower*, Ithaca, NY: Cornell University Press.

Czarniawska, B. and Jeorges, B. (1996), 'Travel of ideas', in B. Czarniawska and G. Sevón (eds), *Translating Organizational Change*, Berlin: de Gruyter, 13–48.

Czarniawska, B. and Sevón, G (eds) (2005), *Global Ideas: How Ideas, Objects and Practices Travel in the Global Economy*, Malmö, Sweden: Liber.

Dagnino, E. (2005), '"We all have rights but ...' Contesting concepts of citizenship in Brazil', in N. Kabeer (ed.), *Inclusive citizenship: Meanings and Expressions*, London: Zed Books.

Dagnino, E. (2007), 'Participation, citizenship and democracy: perverse consequences and displacement of meanings', in C. Neveu (ed.), *Cultures et Practiques Participative: Perspectives Comparatives*, Paris: L'Harmattan.

Della Porta, D. and Diani, M. (1999), *Social Movements: An Introduction*, Oxford: Blackwell.

De Long, D. (1989), *Steve Shirley* (Harvard Business School Case Studies 9-490-004), Boston, MA: Harvard Business School.

Dent, M. and Whitehead, S. (eds) (2002), *Managing Professional Identities: Knowledge, Performativity and the 'New' Professional*, London: Routledge.

Department for Communities and Local Government (2011), *The Localism Bill*, London: Department for Communities and Local Government.

Downs, L. (2004), *Writing Gender History*, London: Bloomsbury Academic.

Driver, S. and Martell, L. (1998), *New Labour: Politics after Thatcherism*, Cambridge: Polity Press.

Duggan, L. (2003), *The Twilight of Equality: Neoliberalism, Cultural Politics and the Attack on Democracy*, Boston, MA, Beacon Press.

Dwyer, P. (2000), *Welfare Rights and Responsibilities*, Bristol: Policy Press.

Easen, P., Atkins, M. and Dyson, A. (2000), 'Inter-professional collaboration and conceptualisations of practice', *Children and Society*, 14: 355–67.

Edwards, R. and Mauthner, M. (2002), *Ethics and Feminist Research*, London: Sage.

Eisenstadt, N. (2011), *Discovering Sure Start: How Government Discovered Early Childhood Intervention*, Bristol: Policy Press.

Eisenstein, H. (2006), 'Scouting parties and bold detachments: towards a post-capitalist feminism', *Women's Studies Quarterly*, 34, 1–2: 40–61.

Eisenstein, H. (2009), *Feminism Seduced: How Global Elites Use Women's Labour to Exploit the World*, Boulder, CO: Paradigm.

Elson, D. (1995), *Male Bias in the Development Process*, Manchester: Manchester University Press.

Engestrom, Y., Engestrom, R. and Vahaaho, T. (1999), 'When the centre does not hold: the importance of knotworking', in S. Chaiklin, M. Hedegaard and U. Jensen (eds), *Activity Theory and Social Practice*, Aarhus, Denmark: Aarhus University Press.

England, K. and Ward, K. (eds) (2007), *Neoliberalization: States, Network, People*, Oxford: Blackwell.

Esping-Andersen, G. (2009), *The Incomplete Revolution: Adapting to Women's New Roles*, Cambridge: Polity.

Etzioni, A. (1993), *The Spirit of Community: Rights, Responsibilities and the Communitarian Agenda*, New York: Crown.

Faludi, S. (1991), *Backlash: The Undeclared War Against Women*, London: Chatto and Windus.

Fantone, L. (2007), 'Precarious changes: gender and generational politics in contemporary Italy', *Feminist Review*, 87: 5–20.

Fawcett Society (2011), *A Life-raft for Women's Equality*, London: Fawcett Society.

Ferguson, J. (2010), 'The uses of neoliberalism', *Antipode*, 41, January: 166–84.

Ferlie, E., Pettigrew, A., Ashburner, L. and Fitzgerald, L. (1996), *The New Public Management in Action*, Oxford, Oxford University Press.

Fincher, R. and Panelli, R. (2001), 'Making space: women's urban and rural activism and the Australian state', *Gender, Place and Culture*, 8, 2: 129–48.

Fink, J. and Lundqvist, Å. (eds) (2010), *Changing Relations of Welfare*, Farnham: Ashgate.

Fournier, V. (2000), 'Boundary work and the (un)making of the professions', in N. Malin (ed.), *Professionals, Boundaries and the Workplace*, London: Routledge.

Fraser, E. (1999), *The Problem with Communitarian Politics*, Oxford: Oxford University Press.

Fraser, N. (1990), 'Rethinking the public sphere: a contribution to the critique of actual existing democracy', *Social Text*, 25, 26: 56–80.

Fraser, N. (1997), *Justice Interruptus: Critical Reflections on the 'Postsocialist' Condition*, London: Routledge.

Fraser, N. (2009), 'Feminism, capitalism and the cunning of history', *New Left Review*, 56: 97–117.

Freeman, R. (2009) 'What is translation?', *Evidence and Policy*, 5, 4: 429–47.

Freire, P. (1970), *Pedagogy of the Oppressed*, New York: Continuum.

Freire, P. (2005), *Education for Critical Consciousness*, New York: Continuum.

Froggett, L. (2002), *Love, Hate, Welfare: Psychosocial Approaches to Policy and Practice*, Bristol: Policy Press.

Fukayama, F. (1999), *The Great Disruption: Human Nature and the Reconstitution of Social Order*, London: Profile.

Gabay, C. (2010), 'Denaming the beast: the Global Call to Action against Poverty and its multiple forms of publicness', in N. Mahony, J. Newman and C. Barnett, *Rethinking the Public*, Bristol: Policy Press.

Gaventa, J. and McGee, R. (eds) (2010), *Citizen Action and National Policy Reform*, London: Zed Books.

Gaventa, J. and Tandon, R. (eds) (2010), *Globalizing Citizens: New Dynamics of Inclusion and Exclusion*, London: Zed Books.

Genz, S. (2006), 'Third way/ve: the politics of post-feminism', *Feminist Theory*, 7, 3: 333–53.

Gibson-Graham, J.K. (2006a), 'Imagining and enacting a post-capitalist feminist economic politics', *Women's Studies Quarterly*, 34,1–2: 72–8.

Gibson-Graham, J.K. (2006b), *A Post-capitalist Politics*, Minneapolis, MN: University of Minnesota Press.

Gibson-Graham, J.K. (2008) 'Diverse economies: performative practices for "other worlds"', *Progress in Human Geography*, 32, 5: 613–32.

Gilbert, J. (2010), 'The desire for participation', contribution to round table 'Crisis of Participation, Participation in Crisis', Centre for Citizenship, Identities and Governance, the Open University, April.

Gill, R. (2009), 'Secrets, silence and toxic shame in the neo-liberal university', in R. Ryan-Flood and R. Gill (eds), *Secrets and Silence in the Research Process*, London: Routledge: 253–64.

Gill, R. and Pratt, A. (2008), 'In the social factory: immaterial labour, precariousness and cultural work', *Theory, Culture and Society*, 25, 7–8: 1–30.

Gill, R. and Scharff, V. (2011), *New Femininities: Postfeminism, Neoliberalism and Subjectivity*, Basingstoke, Palgrave.

Gonick, M. (2006), 'Between "Girl Power" and "Reviving Ophelia"; constituting the neoliberal girl subject', *Feminist Formations*, 18: 1–23.

Gordon, L. (1990), *Women, the State and Welfare*, Madison, WI: University of Wisconsin.

Grabham, E., Cooper, D., Krishnadas, J. and Herman, D. (eds) (2009), *Intersectionality and Beyond: Law, Power and the Politics of Location*, Abingdon: Routledge-Cavendish.

Griffin, G. and Braidotti, R. (eds) (2002), *Thinking Differently: A Reader in European Women's Studies*, London: Zed Books.

Guenther, K.M. (2009), 'The politics of names: rethinking the methodological and ethical significance of naming people, organizations and places', *Qualitative Research*, 9, 4: 411–21.

Gupta, A. (2006), 'Blurred boundaries: the discourse of corruption, the culture of politics and the imagined state', in A. Sharma and A. Gupta (eds), *The Anthropology of the State*, Oxford: Blackwell.

Guy, D. (2009), *Women Build the Welfare State: Performing Charity and Creating Rights in Argentina, 1880–1955*, Durham, NC: Duke University Press.

Handy, C. (1989), *The Age of Unreason*, London: Business Books.

Haraway, D. (1988) 'Situated knowledge: the science question in feminism and the privilege of partial perspective', *Feminist Studies*, 14: 575–99.

Hartley, J., Donaldson, C., Skelcher, C. and Wallace, M. (2008), *Managing to Improve Public Services*, Cambridge: Cambridge University Press.

Harvey, D. (2005), *A Brief History of Neoliberalism*, Oxford: Oxford University Press.

Hesse-Biber, S. and Leavy, P. (eds) (2007), *Feminist Research Practice*, London: Sage.

Hochschild, A. (1983), *The Managed Heart*, Berkeley, CA: University of California Press.

Hoff, J. (1994), 'Gender as a postmodern category of paralysis', *Women's History Review*, 3, 2: 149–62.

Hoggett, P. (2000), *Emotional Life and the Politics of Welfare*, Basingstoke: Macmillan.

Holland, D. and Lave, J. (eds) (2001), *History in Person: Enduring Struggles, Contentious Practice, Intimate Identities*, Oxford: James Currey.

Hollway, W. and Jefferson, T. (2000), *Doing Qualitative Research Differently*, London: Sage.

Höpfl, H. (1992), 'The making of the corporate acolyte', *Journal of Management Studies*, 29, 13: 23–34.

Hoschild, A. (1979), 'Emotion work, feeling rules and social structure', *American Journal of Sociology*, 85, 3: 551–75.

Hunter, S. (2012), *Power, Politics, Emotions: Impossible Governance?*, London: Routledge.

Hunter, S. and Swan, E. (2007), 'Interview: Angela Mason on trips to Skegness, Maoists and briefings with the minister: a life in equalities work', *Equal Opportunities International*, 26, 5: 482–96.

Isin, E. and Nielsen, G. (eds) (2006), *Acts of Citizenship*, London: Zed Books.

Itzin, C. and Newman, J. (eds) (1995), *Gender, Culture and Organizational Change*, London: Routledge.

Jain, D. and Elson, D. (eds) (2011), *Harvesting Feminist Knowledge for Public Policy: Repackaging Progress*, London: Sage.

Jessop, B. (2002), *The Future of the Capitalist State*, Cambridge: Polity Press.

Jordan, B. (2010), *Why the Third Way Failed: Economics, Morality and the Origins of the Big Society*, Bristol: Policy Press.

Joseph, M. (2002), *Against the Romance of Community*, Minneapolis, MN: University of Minnesota Press.

Jupp, E. (2010), 'Private and public on the housing estate: small community groups, activism and local officials', in N. Mahony, J. Newman and C. Barnett, *Rethinking the Public*, Bristol: Policy Press.

Katz, C. (2005), 'Partners in crime? Neoliberalism and the production of new political subjectivities', in N. Laurie and L. Bondi (eds), *Working the Spaces of Neoliberalism*, Oxford: Blackwell.

Keane, J. (2009), *The Life and Death of Democracy*, London: Simon and Schuster.

Kerfoot, D. and Knight, D. (2004), *Management, Organizations and Masculinity*, London: Paul Chapman.

Kirton, M. (1976), 'Adaptors and innovators: a description and measure', *Journal of Applied Psychology*, 61, 5: 622–9.

Laclau, E. and Mouffe, C. (1985), *Hegemony and Socialist Strategy*, London: Verso.

Larner, W. (2000), 'Neoliberalism: policy, ideology, governmentality', *Studies in Political Economy*, 63: 5–25.

Larner, W. and Craig, D. (2005), 'After neo-liberalism? Community activism and local partnership in Aotearoa New Zealand', *Antipode*, 37, 3: 420–24.

Larner, W., Le Heron, R. and Lewis, N. (2007), 'Co-constituting "After neoliberalism": globalizing governmentalities and political projects in Aotearoa New Zealand', in K. England and K. Ward (eds), *Neoliberalization: States, Networks, People*, Oxford: Blackwell.

Lash, S. and Urry, J. (1987), *The End of Organised Capitalism*, Cambridge: Polity.

Lather, P. (1991), *Getting Smart: Feminist Research and Pedagogy with/in the Postmodern*, London: Routledge.

Latour, B. (1986) 'The powers of association', in J. Law (ed.), *Power, Action and Belief: A New Sociology of Knowledge?*, London: Routledge.

Latour, B. (2005), *Reassembling the Social: An Introduction to Actor-Network Theory*, Oxford: Oxford University Press.

Laurie, N. and Bondi, L. (eds) (2005), *Working the Spaces of Neo-Liberalism*, Oxford: Blackwell.

Lavalette, M. (ed.) (2011), *Radical Social Work Today*, Bristol: Policy Press.

Law, J. (1999), 'After ANT: complexity, naming and topography', in J. Law and J. Hassard (eds), *Actor Network Theory and After*, Oxford: Blackwell/The Sociological Review.

Law, J. and Urry, J. (1994), 'Enacting the social', *Economy and Society*, 33, 4: 390–410.

Leadbeater, C. (1996), *The Rise of the Social Entrepreneur*, London: Demos.

Lendvai, N. (2005), 'Remaking European governance: transition, accession and integration', in J. Newman (ed.), *Remaking Governance: Peoples, Politics and the Public Sphere*, Bristol: Policy Press.

Lendvai, N. and Stubbs, P. (2006), 'Translation, intermediaries and welfare reforms in south eastern Europe', paper to the '4th ESPANET Conference', Bremen, August.

Lendvai, N. and Stubbs, P. (2007), 'Policies as translation', in S. Hodgson and Z. Irving (eds), *Policy Reconsidered: Meanings, Politics and Practices*, Bristol: Policy Press.

Letherby, G. (2003), *Feminist Research in Theory and Practice*, Buckingham: Open University Press.

Lewis, D. (2008), 'Using life histories in social policy research: the case of third sector/public sector boundary crossing', *Journal of Social Policy*, 37, 4: 559–78.

Lewis, G. (2000), '*Race*', *Gender, Welfare: Encounters in a Postcolonial Society*, London: Sage.

Lewis, G. (ed.) (2002), *Forming Nation, Framing Welfare*, London: Routledge.

Li, T. (2007a), *The Will to Improve: Governmentality, Development and the Practice of Politics*, Durham, NC: Duke University Press.

Li, T. (2007b), 'Practices of assemblage and community forest management', *Economy and Society*, 36, 2: 263–93.

Lister, R. (1997, 2003), *Citizenship: Feminist Perspectives*, Basingstoke: Palgrave.

Lister, R. (2001), 'To Rio via the Third Way: Labour's 'welfare' reform agenda' *Renewal*, 8, 4: 9–20.

Lister, R. (2002), 'Towards a new welfare settlement?', in C. Hay (ed.), *British Politics Today*, Cambridge, Polity.

Lister, R. (2004), 'The Third Way's Social Investment State', in J. Lewis and R. Surender (eds), *Welfare State Change: Towards a Third Way?*, Oxford: Oxford University Press: 157–81.

Lister, R (2006), 'Women and public policy, post-neoliberalism? A UK perspective', Paper prepared for the workshop 'Women and Public Policy, Post Neo- Liberalism? A Study of Continuity and Change?', Canadian Political Association Annual Conference, Toronto, May.

London Edinburgh Weekend Return Group (1979), *In and Against the State*, London: Pluto Press.

London Edinburgh Weekend Return Group (2011) 'In and Against the State', in G. Craig, M. Mayo, K. Popple, M. Shaw and M. Taylor (eds), *The Community Development Reader*, Bristol: Policy Press.

Lovenduski, J. (2002), 'How men deter women from Parliament: Inaugural Lecture of the Anniversary Professor of Politics' Birkbeck, University of London.

Lukes, S. (2007), 'Power and the battle for hearts and minds: on the bluntness of soft power', in F. Berenskoetter and M.J. Williams (eds), *Power in World Politics*, London: Routledge.

Macalpine, M. and Marsh, S. (2005), 'On being white there's nothing I can say; exploring whiteness and power in organisations', *Management Learning*, 36, 4: 453–74.

Mac an Ghiall, M. and Haywood, C. (2007), *Gender, Culture and Society: Contemporary Masculinities and Femininities*, Basingstoke: Palgrave Macmillan.

McCrindle, J. and Rowbotham, S. (eds) (1977), *Dutiful Daughters; Women Talk about Their Lives*, Harmondsworth: Penguin.

McDermont, M. (2010), *Governing Independence and Expertise*, Oxford: Hart.

McDowell, L. (1991), 'Life without father and Ford: the new gender order of post-Fordism', *Transactions, Institute of British Geographers*, 16: 400–19.

McDowell, L. (1997), *Capital Culture: Gender at Work in the City*, Oxford: Blackwell.

McDowell, L. (2009), *Working Bodies: Interactive Service Employment and Workplace Identities*, Oxford: Wiley-Blackwell.

Mackay, F. (2001), *Love and Politics: Women Politicians and the Ethics of Care*, London: Continuum.

Mackay, F. (2010), 'Gendering constitutional change and policy outcomes: substantive representation and domestic violence policy in Scotland', *Policy and Politics*, 38, 3: 369–88.

McLeod, J. and Thompson, R. (2009), *Researching Social Change*, London: Sage.

McRobbie, A. (2009), *The Aftermath of Feminism: Gender, Culture and Social Change*, London: Sage.

Maddock, S. (1999), *Challenging Women: Gender, Culture and Organization*, London: Sage.

Maddock, S. (2010), 'The Big Society: where are the women?', *Transforming Management*, htttp://tm.mbs.ac.uk/comment/the-big-society-where-are-the-women [accessed 12 October 2011].

Mahony, N. (2008), 'Spectacular political experiments', PhD thesis, Faculty of Social Science, Open University.

Mahony, N., Newman, J. and Barnett, C. (eds) (2010), *Rethinking the Public: Innovations in Research, Theory and Politics*, Bristol: Policy Press.

Maitland, S. (ed.) (1988), *Very Heaven: Looking Back at the 1960s*, London: Virago.

Mann, S.A. and Kelley, L.R. (1997), 'Standing at the crossroads of modernist thought: Collins, Smith, and the New Feminist Epistemologies', *Gender and Society*, 11, 4: 391–408.

Mann, S.A. and Huffman, D.J. (2005), 'The decentering of second wave feminism and the rise of the third wave', *Science and Society*, 69, 1: 56–91.

Marsh, S. and Macalpine, M. (2008), 'Choosing the knowledge we carry? Contesting hegemonic managerialism within a neoliberal context', paper presented to the 'European Group of Organisation Studies Conference', Amsterdam.

Marshall, J. (1984), *Women Managers: Travellers in a Male World*, Chichester: Wiley.

Marshall, J. (1995), *Women Managers Moving On: Exploring Career and Life Choices*, London: Routledge.

Maskovsky, J. (2009), 'AIDS activism and the problem of intergenerational knowledge transfer', paper to the 'CASCA/AES Conference', 15 May.

Maskovsky, J. (2011), 'Activist anthropology: problems and perils', paper to the Department of Cultural Anthropology, Duke University, Durham, NC, 14 March.

Massey, D. (1994), *Space, Place and Gender*, Cambridge: Polity.

Massey, D. (2005), *For Space*, London: Sage.

Massey, D. (2010), 'The political struggle ahead', *Soundings*, 45: 6–18.

Massey, D. (2011), 'Economics and ideology in the present moment', *Soundings*, 48: 29–39.

Masson, D. (2009), 'Spaces within the state: funding women's organisations in Quebec', paper presented to the annual meeting of the Canadian Women's Studies Association, Carleton University, Ottawa, ON, 25 May.

Metcalfe, L. and Richards, S. (1990), *Improving Public Management*, London: Sage.

Meyer, D.S. (2002), 'Opportunities and identities: bridge-building in the study of social movements', in D.S. Meyer, N. Whitter and B. Robnett, *Social Movements: Identity, Culture and the State*, New York, Oxford University Press.

Milligan, C. and Conradson, D. (eds) (2006), *Landscapes of Voluntarism*, Bristol: Policy Press.

Mohanty, C.T. (2003), *Feminism Without Borders: De-colonizing Theory, Practicing Solidarity*, Durham, NC: Duke University Press.

Mol, A. (1999), 'Ontological politics: a word and some questions', in J. Law and J. Hassard (eds), *Actor Network Theory and After*, Oxford and Keele: Blackwell and the Sociological Review.

Mol, A. (2002), *The Body Multiple: Ontology in Medical Practice*, Durham, NC: Duke University Press.

Molloy, M. and Larner, W. (2010), 'Who needs cultural intermediaries indeed? Gendered networks in the designer fashion industry', *Journal of Cultural Economy*, 3, 3: 361–77.

Mooney, G. and Neal, S. (2009), 'Community: themes and debates', in G. Mooney and S. Neal, *Community: Welfare, Crime and Society*, Maidenhead: Open University Press.

Morley, D. and Robbins, K. (1995), *Spaces of Identity: Global Media, Electronic Landscapes and Cultural Boundaries*, London: Routledge.

Mulgan, G. (2006), *Social Innovation*, London: Young Foundation.

Mulgan, G. (2007), *Ready or Not? Taking Innovation in the Public Sector Seriously*, London: NESTA.

Mulinari. D. and Räthzel, N. (2007), 'Politicizing biographies: the framing of transnational subjectivities as insiders outside', *Feminist Review*, 86: 89–112.

Narayan, U. and Harding, S. (eds) (2000), *Decentering the Centre: Philosophy for a Multicultural, Postcolonial and Feminist World*, Bloomington, IN: Indiana University Press.

National Audit Office (2006), *Achieving Innovation in Central Government*, London: National Audit Office.

Needham, C. (2011), *Personalising Public Services: Understanding the Personalization Narrative*, Bristol: Policy Press.

Newman, J. (1994), 'The limits of management: gender and the politics of change', in J. Clarke, A. Cochrane and E. McLaughin (eds), *Managing Social Policy*, London: Sage.

Newman, J. (2001), *Modernising Governance; New Labour, Policy and Society*, London: Sage.

Newman, J. (ed.) (2005a), *Remaking Governance: Peoples, Politics and the Public Sphere*, Bristol: Policy Press.

Newman, J. (2005b), 'Regendering governance', in J. Newman (ed.), *Remaking Governance: Peoples, Politics and the Public Sphere*, Bristol: Policy Press.

Newman, J. (2005c), 'Enter the transformational leader: network governance and the micro-politics of modernisation', *Sociology*, 39, 4: 717–34.

Newman, J. (2006), 'Re-mapping the public: public libraries and the public sphere', *Cultural Studies*, 21, 6: 887–909.

Newman, J. (2007), 'Rethinking the public in troubled times: unsettling nation, state and the liberal public sphere', *Public Policy and Administration*, 22, 1: 27–47.

Newman, J. (2009a), 'Working the spaces of governance', paper to the Canadian Anthropological Association Conference, Vancouver, May.

Newman, J. (2009b), 'Emergent publics: what happens next?', Paper to the fourth Economic and Social Research Council seminar in the series 'Emergent Publics', Goodenough College, London, November.

Newman, J. (2010a). 'Towards a pedagogical state? Summoning the "empowered" citizen', *Citizenship Studies*, 14, 6: 711–24.

Newman, J. (2010b), 'Working the spaces of power: feminism and neoliberalism?', paper to the seminar series 'Diagnosing the Contemporary', Birkbeck, London, January.

Newman, J. (2010c), 'Ambiguous spaces of activism in and through "community"', paper to the conference of the Political Studies Association, Edinburgh, April.

Newman, J (2010d), 'Feminisms, activism and social change', paper to the fourth Economic and Social Research Council seminar in the series 'Activism, Volunteering and Citizenship', Newcastle, July.

Newman, J. (2010e), 'Being inside/outside: feminism, transnationalism and the politics of social change', paper to the conference 'Beyond Citizenship: Feminism and the Transformation of Belonging', Birkbeck, London, July.

Newman, J. (2011a), 'Boundary troubles: working the academic/policy interface', *Policy and Politics*, 39, 4.

Newman, J. (2011b), 'Gendered geographies of "irresponsibility"', paper to the RGS/IBG conference, London.

Newman, J. (2011c), 'Public leadership as publicmaking', *Public Money and Management*, 31, 5: 315–22.

Newman, J. (2012a), 'Working the spaces of power: feminism, neoliberalism and gendered labour', *Social Politics*, forthcoming.

Newman, J. (2012b), '"But we didn't mean *that*": feminist projects, governmental appropriation and spaces of politics', in S. Roseneil (ed.), *Beyond Citizenship? Feminism and the Transformation of Belonging*, Basingstoke: Palgrave.

Newman, J. (2012c), 'Landscapes of Antagonism: local governance, neoliberalism and austerity', *Urban Studies*, forthcoming.

Newman, J (2013) 'Governing the present: activism, neoliberalism and the problem of power and consent', *Critical Social Policy*, forthcoming.

Newman, J. and Clarke, J. (2009), *Publics, Politics and Power: Remaking the Public in Public Services*, London: Sage.

Newman, J. and Tonkens, E. (eds) (2011), *Participation, Responsibility and Choice: Summoning the Active Citizen in Western Europe*, Amsterdam, Netherlands: University of Amsterdam Press.

Nutley, S., Walter, I. and Davies, H.T.O. (2007), *Using Evidence: How Research Can Inform Public Services*, Bristol: Policy Press.

Ong, A. (2007), 'Neoliberalism as mobile technology', *Transactions of the Institute of British Geographers*, 32: 3–8.

Orloff, A. (1991), 'Gender in early US social policy', *Journal of Policy History*, 3: 249–81.

Osborne, P. (1996), 'The hitchhiker's guide to innovation: managing innovation in an interagency context', *International Journal of Public Sector Management*, 9, 7: 72–81.

Osborne, P. and Flynn, N. (1997), 'Managing the innovative capacity of voluntary and not for profit organisations in the provision of public services', *Public Money and Management*, 17, 4: n.p.

Patel, P. (2011), *Presentation to 'Big Cuts, Big Society' Roundtable*, Milton Keynes: Centre for Citizenship, Identities and Governance, Open University.

Pearce, J. (2010), 'Learning from Latin America', *Community Development Journal*, 45, 3: 262–75.

Peck, J. (2004), 'Geography and public policy: constructions of neoliberalism', *Progress in Human Geography*, 28, 3: 392–405.

Peck, J. and Tickell, A. (2002), 'Neoliberalising space', in N. Brenner and N. Theodore (eds), *Spaces of Neoliberalism*, Oxford: Blackwell.

Phillips, A. (1995), *The Politics of Presence*, Oxford: Clarendon Press.

Pickerill, J. (2008), 'The surprising sense of hope', *Antipode*, 40, 3: 482–7.

Power, M. (1994), *The Audit Explosion*, London: Demos.

Pratt, M.L. (1992), *Imperial Eyes: Travel Writing and Transculturalism*, London: Routledge.

Putnam, R.D. (2000), *Bowling Alone: The Collapse and Revival of American Community*, New York: Simon and Schuster.

Pykett, J. (2012), 'The new maternal state: the gendered politics of governing through behaviour change', *Antipode*, in press.

Rainbow, P. and Marcus, G. (2008), *Designs for an Anthropology of the Present*, Durham, NC: Duke University Press.

Redfern, C. and Aune, K. (2010), *Reclaiming the F-word*, London: Zed Books.

Rhodes, R.A.W. (1997), *Understanding Governance*, Buckingham: Open University Press.

Richardson, D. (2004), 'Claiming citizenship? Sexuality, citizenship and lesbian/feminist theory', *Sexualities*, 3, 2: 255–72.

Richardson, D. (2005), 'Desiring sameness? The rise of a neoliberal politics of normalisation', in N. Laurie and L. Bondi (eds), *Working the Spaces of Neoliberalism*, Oxford: Blackwell.

Ristock, J. and Taylor, C. (eds) (1998), *Inside the Academy and Out: Lesbian/Gay/Queer Studies and Social Action*, Toronto, Canada: University of Toronto Press.

Roberts, H. (ed.) (1981), *Doing Feminist Research*, London: Routledge.

Robinson, D. (2008), 'Community cohesion and the politics of communitarianism', in J. Flint and D. Robertson, *Community Cohesion in Crisis: New Dimensions of Diversity and Difference*, Bristol: Policy Press.

Rogoff, I. (2003), 'From criticism to critique to criticality', *EIPCP* website, http://eipcp. net/transversal/0806/rogoff1/en [accessed 21 January 2012].

Rose, F. (1999), *Coalitions Across the Class Divide: Lessons from the Labour, Peace and Environmental Movements*, Ithaca, NY: Cornell University Press.

Rose, N. (1993), 'Government, authority and expertise in advanced liberalism', *Economy and Society*, 22, 3: 283–99.

Rose, N. (1999), *Powers of Freedom: Reframing Political Thought*, Cambridge, Cambridge University Press.

Roseneil, S. (1995), *Disarming Patriarchy: Feminism and Political Action at Greenham*, Buckingham: Open University Press.

Roseneil, S. (2000), *Common Women, Uncommon Practices: The Queer Feminisms of Greenham*, London: Cassell.

Roseneil, S. (2008), 'Why we should care about friends: an argument for queering the care imaginary in social policy', in B. Hale, D. Pearl, E. Cooke and D. Monk (eds), *The Family, Law and Society: Cases and Materials*, Cambridge: Cambridge University Press.

Roseneil, S. (2011), 'Taking turns: criticality, not paranoia: a generative register for feminist social research', *Nordic Journal of Feminist and Gender Research*, 19, 2: 124–31.

Roseneil, S. (2012), 'Doing feminist social research after the cultural turn: research with practical intention', in S. Roseneil and S. Frosh (eds), *Social Research after the Cultural Turn*, Basingstoke: Palgrave Macmillan.

Roseneil, S. and Frosh, S. (eds) (2012), *Social Research after the Cultural Turn*, Basingstoke: Palgrave Macmillan.

Rostock, J. and Taylor, C. (eds) (1998), *Inside the Academy and Out: Lesbian/Gay/Queer Studies and Social Action*, Toronto, Canada: University of Toronto Press.

Ross, A. (2009), *Nice Work If You Can Get It: Life and Labour in Precarious Times*, New York: New York University Press.

Roth, S. (2000), 'Developing working-class feminism: a biographical approach to social movement participation', in S. Stryker, T.J. Owens and R.W. White (eds), *Self Identity and Social Movements*, Minneapolis, MN: University of Minnesota Press.

Roth, S. (2003), *Building Movement Bridges: The Coalition of Labor Movement Women*, Greenwood, CT: Praeger.

Rowbotham, S. (2001), *Promise of a Dream: Remembering the Sixties*, London: Verso.

Ryan, M. (1992), 'Gender and public access: women's politics in 19th century America', in C. Calhoun (ed.), *Habermas and the Public Sphere*, Cambridge, MA: MIT Press.

Salskov-Iversen, D., Hansen, H.K. and Bislev, S. (2000), 'Governmentality, globalization and local practice: transformations of a hegemonic discourse', *Alternatives*, 25: 183–222.

Sawer, M. (1990), *Sisters in Suits*, Sydney, Australia: Allen and Unwin.

Scott, J.W. (1991), 'The evidence of experience', *Critical Inquiry*, 17: 773–97.

Scott, M. (2002), 'Women and local government: dialogue, deliberation and diversity', in E. Breitenbach, A. Brown, F. Mackay and J. Webb (eds), *The Changing Politics of Gender Equality in Britain*, Basingstoke, Palgrave Macmillan.

Segal, L. (2007), *Making Trouble: Life and Politics*, London: Profile Books.

Sedgwick, E.K. (2003), 'Paranoid reading and reparative reading, or you're so paranoid, you probably think this essay is about you', in E.K. Sedgwick, *Touching Feeling: Affect, Pedagogy, Performativity*, Durham, NC, and London: Duke University Press.

Sharma, A. (2008), *Logics of Empowerment: Development, Gender and Governance in Neoliberal India*, Minneapolis, MN: University of Minnesota Press.

Siltanen, J. and Doucet, A. (2008), *Gender Relations in Canada: Intersectionality and Beyond*, Toronto, Canada: Oxford University Press.

Simon-Kumar, R. (2011), 'The analytics of 'gendering' the post-neoliberal state', *Social Politics*, 18, 3: 441–68.

Smith, D. (2005), *Institutional Ethnography: A Sociology for People*, Lanham, MD: AltaMara Press.

Smith, M. (2005), 'Resisting and reinforcing neoliberalism: lesbian and gay organizing at the federal and local levels in Canada', *Policy and Politics*, 33, 1: 75–94.

Squires, J. (2005), 'Is mainstreaming transformative? Theorizing mainstreaming in the context of diversity and deliberation', *Social Politics: International Studies in Gender, State and Society*, 12, 3: 366–78.

Squires, J. (2008), 'The constitutive representation of gender: extra-parliamentary re-presentations of gender relations', *Representation*, 44, 2: 187–204

Staeheli, L. (1996), 'Publicity, privacy and women's political action', *Environment and Planning D: Society and Space*, 14: 601–619.

Standing, G. (2011), *The Precariat: The New Dangerous Class*, London: Bloomsbury Academic.

Stanley, L. (1997), *Breaking Out: Feminist Consciousness and Feminist Research*, London: Routledge.

Stone-Mediatore, S. (2000), 'Chandra Mohay and the revaluing of "experience"', in U. Narayan and S. Harding (eds), *Decentering the Centre: Philosophy for a Multicultural, Postcolonial and Feminist World*, Bloomington, IN: Indiana University Press.

Strathern, M. (1991), *Partial Connections*, Savage, MD: Rowman and Littlefield.

Sullivan, H. (2003), 'New forms of accountability: coming to terms with "many hands"', *Policy and Politics*, 31, 3: 353–70.

Sullivan, H. and Skelcher, C. (2002), *Working Across Boundaries*, Basingstoke: Palgrave Macmillan.

Susser, I. (2009), *Aids, Sex and Culture: Global Politics and Survival in Southern Africa*, Chichester: Wiley-Blackwell.

Susser, I. (2012), *Norman Street: Poverty and Politics in an Urban Neighbourhood*, second edition, Oxford: Oxford University Press.

Swindells, J. (1989), 'Liberating the subject? Autobiography and "women's history": a reading of *The Diaries of Hannah Cullwick*', in The Personal Narratives Group (ed.), *Interpreting Women's Lives: Feminist Theory and Personal Narratives*, Bloomington, IN: Indiana University Press

Taylor, M., Howard, J., Harris, V., Lever, J., Mateeva, A., Miller, C., Petrov, R. and Serra, L. (2009), 'Dilemmas of engagement: the experience of non governmental actors in new governance spaces', *Non Governmental Public Action Programme Working Paper 31*, London: London School of Economics.

Walby, S. (ed.) (1999), *New Agendas for Women*, Basingstoke: Macmillan.

Walby, S. (2009), *The Future of Feminism*, Cambridge: Polity.

Ward, D. and England, K. (2007), 'Introduction: reading neoliberalization', in K. England and D. Ward (eds), *Neoliberalization: States, Networks, People*, Oxford: Blackwell.

Watson, S. (1990), *Playing the State: Feminist Interventions*, Sydney, Australia: Allen and Unwin.

Webster, F. (2002), *Theories of the Information Society*, Cambridge: Routledge.

Wedel, J. (2009), *The Shadow Elite*, New York: Basic Books.

Weeks, J. (2007), *The World We Have Won*, London: Routledge.

Wellman, B., Wong, R.Y., Tindall, D. and Nazar, N. (1997), 'A decade of
    network change: turnover, persistence and stability in personal communities', *Social
    Networks*, 19: 27–50.
Wetherell, M. (2011), *Affective Practices*, London: Sage.
Whittier, N (1995), *Feminist Generations: The Persistence of the Radical Women's Movement*,
    Philadelphia, PA: Temple University Press.
Whittier, N. (1997), 'Political generations, micro-cohorts and the transformation of social
    movements', *American Sociological Review*, 62, 5: 760–78.
Williams, R. (1977), *Marxism and Literature*, Oxford: Oxford University Press.
Wills, J. (2011), 'The geography of community and political organization in London today',
    Political Geography, in press.
Women's Budget Group (2010), *The Impact on Women of the Coalition Spending Review*,
    London: Women's Budget Group.
Woodward, J. and Woodward, S. (2009), *Why Feminism Matters: Feminism Lost and Found*,
    Basingstoke: Palgrave Macmillan.
Yeatman, A. (1990), *Bureaucrats, Technocrats, Femocrats*, Sydney, Australia: Allen and Unwin.
Young, I.M. (1990), *Justice and the Politics of Difference*, Princeton, NJ: Princeton University
    Press.

Subject Index